Louis de Chenier

The Present State of the Empire of Morocco

Its animals, products, climate, soil, cities, ports, provinces, coins, weights, and measures. With the language, religion, laws, manners, customs, and character, of the Moors. Vol. 2

Louis de Chenier

The Present State of the Empire of Morocco
*Its animals, products, climate, soil, cities, ports, provinces, coins, weights, and measures.
With the language, religion, laws, manners, customs, and character, of the Moors. Vol. 2*

ISBN/EAN: 9783337087166

Printed in Europe, USA, Canada, Australia, Japan

Cover: Foto ©ninafisch / pixelio.de

More available books at **www.hansebooks.com**

THE
PRESENT STATE
OF THE
EMPIRE OF MOROCCO.

ITS
ANIMALS, PRODUCTS, CLIMATE, SOIL, CITIES, PORTS, PROVINCES, COINS, WEIGHTS, AND MEASURES. WITH THE LANGUAGE, RELIGION, LAWS, MANNERS, CUSTOMS, AND CHARACTER,

OF THE

MOORS;

THE HISTORY OF THE
DYNASTIES SINCE EDRIS;

THE NAVAL FORCE AND COMMERCE OF MOROCCO; AND THE CHARACTER, CONDUCT, AND VIEWS, POLITICAL AND COMMERCIAL,

OF THE

REIGNING EMPEROR.

TRANSLATED FROM THE FRENCH OF
M. CHENIER.

VOL. II.

LONDON:
Printed for G. G. J. and J. ROBINSON,
Paternoster-Row.
M.DCC.LXXXVIII.

THE PRESENT STATE OF THE EMPIRE OF MOROCCO.

BOOK III.

History of the Sovereigns of Fez, Morocco, Suz, and other States—Different Dynasties from the foundation of the kingdom of Fez, to the succession of the Sharifs of the reigning family.

CHAP. I.

Decline of the Empire of the Caliphs. Accession, and reign of Edris. Expulsion and destruction of his family. Various usurpers.

AFTER the Arabs had possessed themselves of Mauritania, and had introduced their religion there, it was for some time governed

governed by the lieutenants of the Caliphs. The distance of the seat of government of these Caliphs, who, extending their conquests, had successively removed their throne from Medina to Damascus, from Damascus to Cufa, and from Cufa to Bagdad, soon changed the order of things, and insensibly enfeebled their authority. The Arab generals in Africa profited by these circumstances in favour of their ambitious projects, excited commotions toward the end of the eighth century, and aspired themselves at sovereignty. The descendants of Mahomet, called, as it were, to the throne by the veneration in which they were held by the vulgar, raised new factions; the Edrissites, who took their name from Edris, son of Abdallah, descendant of Ali, husband to the daughter of Mahomet, were the first. From Herbelot it appears that their dynasty was exterminated by the Fatimites, who pretended they were the descendants of Ali and Fatima, the daughter of Mahomet; this latter dynasty, the founder of which took the name of Mohadi, director of the faithful, had some success in Egypt; but

its

its duration in Mauritania, which was exposed to numerous revolutions, was only momentary. This part of Africa was afterward governed by four principal dynasties, the Morabethoon, the Moahedins, the Benimerins, and the Sharifs of two different branches.

Africa, remaining in the power of the Arabs from the beginning of the eighth century, was governed by the lieutenants of the Caliph Walid, and his succesſors, till the year 739, of the Christian æra. Yezid, lieutenant of the Caliph Omar II., who then governed, being deceased at Cayroan, Abul-Hages, who had been lieutenant of the Caliph Abdelmelek, took advantage of his death to raise an insurrection, and, at the head of the insurgents, reduced the country, proceeded as far as the north of Mauritania, and, defying every effort of Gualid, established himself as the commander of the faithful. It is probable Gualid was the chief of the principal tribe that then inhabited the province of Rif in the lesser Atlas, where still is found the Casile of Beni-Gualid. This Shaik, whom his

his tribe confidered as King, oppofed with all his power the invafion of foreigners, in a country which has ever been ftrongly defended by nature.

We learn, from the Spanifh authors, that the oppreffions of the Arabs in the north of Mauritania, and the contributions they exacted from the Moors, gave birth to many revolts, in which the negroes, who inhabited the deferts to the fouth of Morocco, took part. The Caliph, informed of thefe commotions, fent a confiderable reinforcement of cavalry, which produced not the leaft effect; the Arabs and their horfes having been terrified by that multitude of black men, who, riding almoft naked, had an appearance of great ferocity, and infpired dread.

The example of thefe feditions had a bad effect in Spain, where the Arabs and Moors were equally divided and agitated. Abul-Hages having been flain in the infurrections of Africa, his fon put himfelf at the head of the weftern Africans; nor was the revolt appeafed till the fon alfo fell

fell in battle, combating the army of the governor of Egypt.

At the same period the Caliph Abdallah, competitor of the Caliph Abdelmelek, who had rendered himself master of the Hegias, desirous of ascertaining the Caliphet to his son Mahomet Mahadi, put to death all the kinsmen of Ali at Medina, forgetting only one old man, the descendant of Hassan, son of Ali, son in law of Mahomet, whose posterity a special providence seemed to protect. One of the sons of this old man was beheaded; the other, named Edris, had the good fortune to escape, and fled in 768 into Mauritania, there to avoid the persecuting sword. Edris settled at Tiulit, in the mountain of Zaaron, between Fez and Mequinez, where he behaved with so much prudence that he gained the confidence of the people, who, highly respecting his virtues, were desirous to live under his government, and embrace his religion. The arrival of this Edris, his exemplary conduct, and the lessons he gave, first scattered the seeds of Mahometanism in these countries, where that religion, having great analogy with the manners of the Moors, was well calculated to make a rapid progress.

Edris, profiting by his afcendant over the minds of men, fent troops into Spain to fuccour the Mahometans; and this zeal for the propagation of his religion ftill increafed the affection of the Moors. Edris dying left a pofthumous fon, who was alfo named Edris, and whom, out of refpect for the father's memory, the people acknowledged as Sovereign: it even appears that, during the minority of this prince, the Moorifh armies gained fome victories.

In 793 Edris II. founded the city of Fez, capital of the kingdom fo called. This was the firft monarchy eftablifhed in Africa after Mahomet; and the Mahometans long called it the court, or kingdom of the weft. Edris interefted himfelf much in favour of the Arab Moors in Spain; and having profited by the war, and by the œconomy he had eftablifhed, he continued building the city of Fez in 840,

840, and erected the mosque called after his name, in which his memory and his tomb are still held in reverence.

The ardour with which this prince inspired the Mahometan Africans induced them to build in the same city the famous mosque called Carubin, for which the city was indebted, perhaps, to the devotion and liberalities of the people of Cayroan, who, having retired to Fez that they might not be exposed to the commotions which then disturbed the eastern part of Africa, may have contributed to the foundation of that magnificent mosque.

We are not acquainted with the race of the kings of Mauritania, the descendants of Sidi-Edris, but we know that family continued to reign, and that Edris bestowed the government of cities on ten of his sons. From Marmol we learn that the house of Edris and the house of Mequineci reigned in Mauritania in 914, and that Mahomet Motaras, Lord of Ceuta, passed over into Spain, with troops, at the solicitation of Abdelrahaman, king of Cordova.

He afterwards sent new reinforcements from Mauritania into Spain in 920 and 925.

The divisions which were in the kingdom of Fez, during the tenth century, were but the presage of those by which that empire has so long been convulsed; and the family of Edris, that had reigned about a hundred and fifty years, was disturbed by a croud of usurpers. The tribe of Zenetes, called Mequineci, seized about that time on several provinces, and founded the city of Mequinez, nearly ten leagues from Fez. A Marabout of that tribe, profiting about the same time by the fluctuating state and credulity of the people, seduced their minds by fanatic predictions, and brought much discredit on the successors of Edris. Having formed a considerable party in the province of Temsena, he marched against the king of Fez, declared war against him; and the latter, wearied of that he sustained against the Zenetes, rather chose to conclude a peace, and yield him the crown, than to behold

an

an increase of enemies, or expose himself to the fickleness of his subjects.

The progress these missionaries made in Mauritania, among an ignorant people flocking after innovators, raised up one who proclaimed himself El-Mohadi, the director, or pontif, of the Mussulmen, a descendant of Ali and Fatima, and whose origin, according to Herbelot, was doubtful: this man declaimed against the house of Edris, which he accused of heresy, and of following the sect of Ali, a sectary unknown to the Moors. Having made himself master of various cities, he deposed the sons of Edris from their governments before the succours they had intreated from the king of Cordova were arrived. El-Mohadi cut off the descendants of Edris, after having seized on their governments*, declared himself Caliph, and marched toward Mount Atlas to extend his domains.

---

* One of these princes, named Sharif El-Edriffi, author of the work, entitled *Geographia Nubiensis*, fled at this time into Sicily to the court of King Roger, to whom he dedicated his book.

Arrived

Arrived at Sugulmeſſa, the governor had him ſeized as an impoſtor; but, fearing to irritate the people, and reſpecting his origin, he calling himſelf the deſcendant of Fatima, the daughter of Mahomet, the governor gave him his liberty.

El-Mohadi was in the ſouth, when one of the generals of the king of Cordova arrived with an army to aid the houſe of Edris: this general, named Al-Habid El-Monſor, conquered a part of the kingdom of Fez, fortified Arzilla near Tangiers, left a garriſon there, and that city for ſome time remained under the government of the kings of Cordova.

By this revolution El-Mohadi could not preſerve the kingdom of Fez to himſelf. This prince going to viſit the governor of Sugulmeſſa, that he might gratify the reſentment he had conceived againſt him, aſſaſſinated him, excited new troubles, and thus became odious to the people who had followed his ſtandard. The uſurper, whoſe reign was momentary in Mauritania, was obliged to paſs into the eaſtern

part

part of Africa, where he met with new obstacles from another bigot, who, in turn, had brought him into discredit, in the opinion of the people whom he had deceived by an affectation of humility. This latter chief was, in derision, called the Knight of the Ass, because one part of his pretended humbleness consisted in always riding on an ass, with his face covered like the Molathemins. Molathemins is a name given in Africa to a tribe who, going to battle with another more powerful, obliged the women to take arms; and, that they might not be distinguished, the men, like them, artfully veiled their faces.

All Africa at this time was torn by divisions, on a tradition that, three hundred years after Mahomet, another director of the faithful, or Mohadi, should come from the west; and various impostors profiting by this tradition imposed on the vulgar credulity, that they might seize the government. Obeidallah, founder of the dynasty of the Fatimites, left Sugulmessa, and, penetrating as far as Egypt, he there vanquished the troops of the Caliph. The wars

wars he sustained in Egypt, Syria, and the eastern parts of Africa, changed the situation of affairs in the west, where a succession of innovators, profiting by these divisions to the furtherance of their projects, reciprocally snatched the sceptre from the power of their predecessors.

CHAP.

CHAP. II.

Of the Dynasty of Morabethoon.

ABU-Teſſifin Marabout, nephew of Abu-Beker Ben-Omar, of the tribe of Lumthunes*, and chief of the Morabethoon, profited by the commotions which had drawn the arms of the Arabs toward Egypt to produce an inſurrection; he ſent Marabouts to preach, and excite the people to revolt, under the pretext of defending their liberties. The Moors, weary of the arbitrary government of theſe Arab foreigners, willingly followed the ſtandard of

---

* The country which the Marabouts inhabited, lying between Mount Atlas and the deſert, was called Lamtha; whence the tribe had the name of Lamthoonah, or Lumthunes.

Herbelot, Bib. Orien.

Teſſifin,

Teſſifin, who preſently found himſelf at the head of a numerous army.

The tribe of this chief was ſurnamed Morabethoon, becauſe of the rigidity with which religion was by them obſerved; the word Marabout ſignifying a monk, or a man engaged to the performance of his vow. This tribe firſt took birth in the neighbourhood of Tunis, but was obliged to leave that country for the weſtern part of Africa, that it might eſcape the perſecution of ſects more voluptuous, whoſe intereſt it was to extirpate this riſing tribe.

Abu-Teſſifin, at the head of his followers, traverſed Mount Atlas in 1051, and conquered the city of Agmet and its environs: here he fixed his reſidence, at the foot of Mount Atlas, extended thence his conqueſts northward, and proclaimed himſelf Emir El-Mumenin, or chief of the faithful. He is one of the firſt ſovereigns known of the race of Morabethoon, or more commonly called Morabites; his armies were conſtantly victorious, and, after various battles,

battles, he remained sovereign of Mauritania.

Abu-Teffifin died in 1086, and was succeeded by his son Joseph, whose subjects proclaimed him King *. This prince not being pleased with the situation of the city of Agmet, at the foot of the mountains, built or finished that of Marakesch, or Morocco, which had been begun by his father, and there established his seat of empire.

During his reign the province of Temsena afforded an asylum to a multitude of Zenetes, who preached new errors. Joseph was very industrious to prevent these innovations among his subjects, and sent them Morabite preachers to reconvert them to their former religion; but the people, fond of novelty, were so far from listening to the remonstrances of the reformers,

---

* The Arab authors of Spain call this prince Abul-Ia Ibrahim-Ben-Joseph-Ben-Teffifin. It was the custom of these people to call their children by the names of their ancestors.

whom Joseph had sent them, that they put them to death at Anafai, where they were assembled.

Irritated by a conduct so insolent, Joseph passed the Morbeya with a powerful army. At the news of his march the Zenetes, with their chief, thought proper to retreat, and proceeded toward Fez, where they demanded aid of the king; but this prince, instead of granting succour to these public disturbers, went in search of them with his forces, and, having come up with them on the banks of the Buregreb, where they were harrassed with famine and fatigue, he fell upon them, and cut them in pieces.

Joseph, after having ravaged the lands of Temsena, and destroyed all its habitations, returned victorious to Morocco. Ambitious and desirous of extending his power, he some time after marched with his army and made war on the king of Fez, whom he vanquished; taking advantage of the inconstancy of the people, he seized on his kingdom, which was thus, for the first time, united to that of Morocco.

Encou-

Encouraged by the succefs of his arms, Joseph advanced as far as Tremecen, thence he proceeded to Bugia, and having obliged the Moors of that part of Africa, and even those of Tunis, to become his vassals, he once more returned triumphant to Morocco, where he was again proclaimed, with this increase of power, commander of the faithful. He afterward made war upon the Brebes, who had retired among the mountains, and over whom he gained several advantages.

The victories of Joseph Ben-Teffifin had acquired him reputation so great that, in 1097, the Mahometan kings of Spain sought his alliance, and even offered him the supreme sovereignty, hoping, by his assistance, they should be enabled once more to establish and extend their empire. On this invitation Joseph passed over into Andalusia, and, joining his forces to those of the Mahometans of Spain, conquered the city of Seville and its environs; whence, after projecting further victories, he returned into Africa to make the necessary preparations.

In Africa, Joseph proclaimed the Gazia, or war, of religion. Having assembled numerous troops, drawn together by fanaticism, and the hope of plunder, he marched, embarked at Ceuta, and proceeded to Malaga. This campaign, and those which followed, were highly glorious to the king of Morocco, since, in 1102, he was master of all Andalusia, Grenada, and Murcia, and in the same year returned into Africa loaded with laurels.

The following years this prince again passed over into Spain to continue his conquests, penetrated as far as Cordova, and gained several battles, particularly that fought on the twenty-ninth of May, 1107, against the army of Don Alphonso VI. whose son, Don Sancho, the commander, with six other of the first nobility, lost their lives. This is the battle which the Spaniards have called the battle of the seven Counts. After this victory Joseph returned to Morocco, where he died, in 1110, and was succeeded by his son Ali.

Ali,

Ali, the son of Joseph, third king of Morocco, of the race of Morabethoon, built the grand mosque at Morocco, continued to succour the Mahometans of Spain, and made his power respected there by the armies which he personally headed, between the years 1112 and 1115. Some authors say he was killed at the battle of Moriella, where his army was attacked by that of king Alphonso; that his son, Tessifin-Ben-Ali, continued in Spain with some troops, and that the remainder were transported into Africa.

Brahem, the son of Ali, and the last king of Morocco, of the same dynasty, who was proclaimed after the death of his father, confirmed the princes who governed the oriental provinces dependent on him in their possessions, and was declared commander of the faithful. Africa, under the reign of this prince, was torn by intestine divisions, which were fatal to the dynasty of the Morabites, and which did not permit Brahem to go himself into Spain, nor to maintain that sovereignty there which the Arab Moors had offered to his ancestors; and which they had so well deserved by their valour.

The governors of the principal places of Andalusia profited by this momentary weakness to erect the cities and provinces, over which they presided, into small principalities: the king of Morocco was at this time too much employed in opposing the insurgents of his own states to prevent these their usurpations. Brahem was beside an indolent prince, and addicted to pleasure; to the gratification of which he sacrificed affairs the most important. His subjects, at length, loaded with taxes, and oppressed, refused to acknowledge him as their master.

The relaxed state of the government, and the discontent of the people, favoured a revolt, which was at this time incited toward Mount Atlas by another innovator, who, assuming the imposing title of Mohadi, director of the faithful, entered Mauritania, and drew the people to his party, who were easy to seduce, by projects of reformation.

This

This preacher, whofe name was Mahomet Abdallah, calling himfelf a defcendant of Ali, met, according to Herbelot, near Melilla, another doctor, named Abdulmomen, who faid he was the Mohadi, or prophet, expected at the end of ages. Thefe two men, united, approaching Morocco, preached there publicly, drew over profelytes to their belief, and Abdallah was acknowledged king.

Brahem, abforbed in pleafure, had defpifed this revolution, but was at length obliged to head his army, and give the Reformer battle, who was now become ftrong in confequence of difcontent and enthufiafm. Brahem was defeated, and forced to fly. Purfued from one place of refuge to another, he at length came to Oran, where the Moors, not daring to expofe themfelves to the refentment of Abdulmomen, who was following to take Brahem, refufed him an afylum. Brahem, feeing himfelf thus hunted, unable to furvive his grief, threw himfelf, according to fome hiftorians, headlong from a rock; others affirm he perifhed in a caftle, which

was

was fired by Abdulmomen, and the death of this prince ended the dynasty of Morabethoon.

Abdulmomen, general of Abdallah, having subjected all the provinces of Mauritania to the power of his master, during this expedition, and bearing with him hostages to insure their submission, returned to Morocco. Here he found Mahomet Abdallah dead in his camp. The chiefs, being assembled, acknowledged Abdulmomen, who also affirmed himself one of the descendants of Mahomet and Ali, their sovereign, and commander of the faithful.

CHAP. III.

Dynasty of the Moahedins.

ABDULMOMEN* was the first king of the race of the Moahedins, whom the Spaniards have called Almohades; he was chosen king of Morocco in 1148: after his election he destroyed the city of Morocco, into which the inhabitants refused him entrance, and which they would have preserved for Isac son of Brahem. Abdulmomen was so enraged at this that he made a vow the city should pass through a sieve.

After carrying Morocco by assault, he, with his own hands, strangled the young

---

* Herbelot calls him Mohamet Abdulmomen Ben-Tomrut; according to Marmol, his name was Abulmomen Ben-Abdallah Ben-Ali.

Isac, son of Brahem, who had there been acknowledged king, and who was the last of the house of Teſſifin, the founders of Morocco, as well as of the empire. Abdulmomen, that he might perform his vow, reduced a part of that capital to duſt, and paſſed its aſhes through a ſieve; and that he might leave no veſtige of the grandeur of its kings, and bury their name in oblivion, he deſtroyed their palaces and moſques.

This prince afterward rebuilt the city, and gave orders that all the Morabethoon found throughout his empire ſhould be put to death, that he might have nothing to fear from their vengeance. The animoſity that was maintained, between theſe two ſects, occaſioned a ſucceſſion of revolutions in Africa, while they mutually enfeebled each other, and gave the eaſtern provinces the power of ſhaking off the yoke of the kings of Morocco, and electing independent chiefs for themſelves.

Abdulmomen, however, remained maſter of all Mauritania, and preſerved the

two

two kingdoms of Fez and Morocco, which had been united under Joseph Teffifin. He was also able, in 1149, to send aid to the Mahometans of Spain, and to permit them to recruit among the mountains of Gomera, between Tetuan and Tremecen. In 1151, the power of this prince being still more firmly established, the Mahometans of Grenada and of Jaen, who stood in need of his support, offered him homage and submission; he accordingly sent thirty thousand men to their succour.

This army having been vanquished, Abdulmomen sent more considerable reinforcements, by which the Mahometans of Spain were empowered to prolong the war with some success. This prince had an intention of going himself into Spain with a mighty army, but he died in 1155 during these his preparations. The castle of Bulahuan, in the province of Duquella, is said to have been built by Abdulmomen; it has since been augmented and embellished by a Sharif of the reigning family.

After the death of Abdulmomen, his son Joseph was unanimously acknowledged king of Morocco. Joseph, out of deference to the memory of his father, and also to merit the love of his subjects, testified his aversion to the Christians, and passed over into Spain, in 1158, with a powerful army. On his arrival, the Mahometan kings of Andalusia, as well from respect to his power, as to acknowledge the services they received, swore fidelity to him, and proclaimed him sovereign. The kings of Murcia and Valencia, who were more distant, were the sole who did not think proper to submit. Having united his army with that of the Arab Moors in Spain, Joseph seized on some places in despite of the efforts of Don Sancho III. The nobility who commanded the army of the latter, consulting their valour only, followed Joseph to Seville, and gained a victory over him under the walls of that city. Profiting by the divisions of the Spaniards, Joseph, the next campaign, obliged the kings of Valencia and Murcia to become his vassals.

Joseph

Joseph remained at Seville till the year 1168 employed in making incursions upon the territories of the Christians, or in repelling those which the Christians made on his domains. Receiving information at this time that some tribes of the Zenetes had taken advantage of his absence to raise commotions in his African states, he returned thither; and, after having quelled the insurgents, again came to Spain in 1171 with a powerful army.

Joseph now obliged all the Mahometan kings to acknowledge him sovereign, nor was there one who did not pay him homage: he continued to keep up his armies in Spain, where his son long commanded during his absence; he once more returned thither in 1184, and took the city of Sanctaren by assault. He was attacked before this place by the armies of the kings of Portugal and Leon, and, falling from his horse, was killed by the accident; this occasioned the loss of the battle, and most of the Moors who composed his army returned into Africa.

No sooner was the death of Joseph known in Africa than several divisions arose among the Moors; but Abu-Jacob, his son, surnamed Almonsor, the invincible, and who had already distinguished himself at the head of armies, having taken upon him the government of the empire, subdued these commotions, and was proclaimed Emperor.

The kings of Tunis and Tremecen, who had been feudatory dependents on his ancestors, and who were desirous to shake off this dependency, endeavoured to incite rebellion among the distant tribes that they might embarrass Jacob. This prince marched with his forces, and, after having restored tranquillity, he transported those tribes, among whom commotions had been incited, to the centre of his empire, and dispersed them, through the different provinces of his states, so distant from each other that they might be unable to reunite. This is a political system which all the kings of Morocco have observed with respect to powerful tribes; and, thus divided, by the prudence or caprice of the sovereigns,

reigns, thefe tribes have infenfibly loft all memory of their origin.

The conduct, courage, and activity, of Jacob, foon eftablifhed his fupremacy over the African coafts as far as Tunis, and at the fame time preferved that which had been acquired over the Arab Moors of Spain. Of all the fovereigns who have reigned in Africa after the Caliphs, he was, beyond difpute, the moft powerful; thence happened it that he acquired the furname of Almonfor, the invincible, to which might likewife be added the magnificent.

Almonfor built the caftle of Manfooria, at the entrance of the province of Temfena, eight leagues from Sallee, of which fome ruins ftill remain; the city of Alcaffar-Quiber, three leagues from Laracha; that of Alcaffar-Seguar, fituated on the ftraits of Gibraltar, between Tangiers and Ceuta; and the city of Rabat, facing Sallee. After erecting a caftle toward the fea for the defence of this laft place, he built in a vaft enclofure, ruins of which ftill exift, magnificent palaces, that time,

time, infurrections, and the caprices of men, have laid wafte. During fummer this prince refided in that beautiful cincture called Guadel, where tafte and fplendor were alike difplayed. He alfo employed Rabat as a place of arms, whence he might with facility invade Spain with his forces.

After adding the furname of invincible to that of commander of the faithful, Jacob Almonfor paffed over into Spain with a powerful army; but the ficklenefs of the Moors being incited by his abfence throughout the vaft ftates he poffeffed in Africa, he was obliged to return without performing any memorable act. Marmol fays, he left a part of his army under the command of Don Ferdinand Ruis de Caftro, lieutenant general, who, although a Chriftian, had entered into his fervice from motives of difcontent.

No fooner had Jacob Almonfor again reduced his fubjects to fubordination than he publifhed the Gazia, or war againft the infidels, fimilar to the crufades

of

of the Christians; the Moors flocked in multitudes to his standard, and he embarked for Spain with a powerful army, where, being landed, he marched toward Toledo. Alphonso III. coming to oppose him was not terrified by the numbers of the Moors, but most valorously attacked the army of Jacob, which defended itself with intrepidity, and which gained a complete victory over the Christians, in sight of the town of Alarcos, July the eighteenth, 1195. This victorious army had a continuation of success till the year 1197, when Almonsor, having signed a truce with the king of Castile, returned into Africa, where new commotions rendered his presence necessary.

The governor of Morocco, profiting by the absence of Jacob Almonsor to incite the neighbouring people to revolt, the latter, on his return, found them all in arms. The intimidated rebels, not daring to wait this valiant prince in the open field, shut themselves up in that capital, which he was obliged to besiege. Almonsor, having passed a tedious year under the walls of the place,

place, determined to scale the city; and, animatedly addressing his soldiers, shewed them t at, independent of the glory they would acquire in taking Morocco, there was still a more legitimate and more honourable motive, that of recovering their wives and children, who were then in the power of the usurpers.

Enflamed by his discourse, the besiegers assaulted the city, which was unable to resist their impetuosity; and, falling furiously upon the inhabitants, put all to death they met. Almonsor, that he might chastise the rebels, even after their death, refused them the rites of burial *; and, when he was reminded of the effects which might result from putrefaction, said, "Nothing smells so well as the body of a dead enemy, and especially of a traitor."

---

* The Moors believe that the souls of bodies, deprived of the rites of burial, are driven from the abodes of the blessed. In fabulous ages it was further believed that the souls of such bodies wandered on the banks of Cocytus, and were refused admittance into the Elisian fields

After Almonſor had taken Morocco, the governor, having ſhut himſelf up in the caſtle with ſome ſoldiers, mediated his peace by the good offices of a Marabout, whoſe ſanctity was held in veneration; but Almonſor, although he had granted this man pardon, put him to death the moment he had him in his power, and, by the violation of his promiſe, tarniſhed his glory. The Marabout reproached him with his ill faith. I am not, anſwered the prince, obliged to keep my word with thoſe who have forfeited theirs.

According to the Arab hiſtorians, the ſovereign, full of regret for not having obſerved his promiſe, diſappeared, and wandered over the world. The probability is that this prince performed the pilgrimage to Mecca, as a private perſon, in expiation of his crime. His brother, Brahem, governed during his abſence; but, he not returning in the ſpace of a year, his ſon, Mahomet Ben-Naſſer, called alſo Naſſer-Al-Melek Ben-Manſoor, was proclaimed king by the people.

Mahomet Ben-Naſſer, having ſucceeded his father in 1210, confirmed the princes of Africa in the poſſeſſion of their ſtates, and broke the truce which Almonſor had concluded with Alphonſo of Caſtile. This prince being deſirous of extending his conqueſts in Spain, went thither with a powerful army, conquered ſome towns, ravaged their territories, and returned to repoſe under the walls of Cordova. Thither Alphonſo, having received conſiderable reinforcements from the Chriſtian princes, marched to give the king of Morocco battle. The two armies met on the ſixteenth of July, 1212, in the plains of Toloſo, and the Moors ſuffered a total rout. This defeat, beſide humbling the Mahometans, infinitely decreaſed that conſideration in which Mahomet Ben-Naſſer had been held.

After this action Mahomet returned to Africa, and left the command of his army to his brother Abeu Saad, living himſelf in a kind of retirement; and, deſpiſed by his ſubjects, who, prejudiced as they were, attributed

tributed the loss of the battle to his ill conduct and cowardice.

Preyed upon by chagrin, Mahomet Ben-Nasser died a short time after, and left his empire to Said Barrax, one of his grandsons, against whom the governors of the eastern provinces of Tremecen and Tunis revolted. Said raised an army in support of his authority, but, having been assassinated by a traitor, the spirit of discord renewed its progress.

After the death of Said, the principal persons of the Moahedins elected his uncle, Abdel Cader, in his stead; but, this prince not having gained the confidence of the people, and finding that, in these times of trouble, his party was not sufficiently powerful, he fled toward Morocco, and the governors of the principal places profited by this momentary weakness to divide the empire.

CHAP. IV.

Dynasty of the Benimerins.

ABDALLAH, governor of Fez, of the race of the Benimerins, was the first of that dynasty who possessed himself of the sovereign authority. Jacob, his brother, having assembled troops, took the cities of Rabat and Anafa, and defeated an army of Moahedins between Fez and Mequinez; his successes awed the people, and supported the authority of his family in that part of Africa.

After the death of Abdallah, who, from governor of Fez, had become the sovereign, his son, still young, was his successor, under the regency of Ben-Joseph, his uncle; who also, in his turn, was sovereign, his nephew being first dead.

Similar

Similar revolutions took place at the fame time in the provinces of Morocco: that of Tedla, with thofe of the mountains in its neighbourhood, headed by Mahomet-Budobus, joined with the king of Fez, to aid him againſt Abdel Cader, of the race of the Moahedins. Abdel Cader, informed of this treaty, eſcaped from Morocco at the approach of the rebels; but, having been overtaken in his flight, he was murdered at Sugulmeſſa.

Budobus, now become maſter of thoſe provinces that lay near the capital, thought proper to renounce the alliance he had made with Ben-Joſeph, and further declared war againſt him, in expectation of conquering the kingdom of Fez. A quick termination was put to this war by the death of Budobus, and the defeat of his army. Ben-Joſeph not only preferved the kingdom of Fez but alfo conquered that of Morocco; and, by this revolution, the Moahedins were wholly deprived of fovereign power.

The kingdom of Morocco, by this change of its monarchs, which long held the minds of the people in fuspence, loft the fovereignty of Spain. Thofe who governed the provinces of Seville, Cordova, Jaen, and others, in the abfence of the king of Morocco, erected themfelves into fovereign princes; and, feconded by the African troops, that had remained in Andalufia, were thus enabled to maintain thofe divifions, and that diverfity of opinions and interefts, which were inceffantly renewed.

Ben-Jofeph, now mafter of Mauritania, eftablifhed his authority there the more folidly by not occupying himfelf with foreign conquefts, or government. The affairs of Spain felt fome relaxation by the truces which were renewed between Caftile and the Mahometan kings, till the acceffion of Don Ferdinand, to the throne of Caftile. War again broke out in 1240, with an obftinate zeal, and the Mahometans loft, almoft in an inftant, the kingdoms of Cordova and Seville, and the greateft part of Andalufia.

The

The kings of Grenada and Murcia then called loudly for affiftance of Ben-Jofeph, fovereign of Fez and Morocco. Alphonfo X., the fucceffor of Ferdinand, fent a fleet, by way of diverfion, to befiege Sallee in 1261, and the place was taken, but was afterward abandoned on the approach of the king of Fez.

Don Alphonfo being folely occupied by his political interefts in Europe, the king of Grenada took advantage of the truce to make a new alliance with the king of Morocco, to whom he even offered the fovereignty of his ftates with the towns of Tariffa and Algefira, as a fecurity that he would perform his promife, and alfo as places for the debarkment of the troops.

Thus invited, Ben-Jofeph took fhipping for Spain in 1275, with his army, poffeffed himfelf of the two above-named places, committed ravages in the territories of Andalufia, and then returned into Africa. He fent his brother, Ottman, the next year with troops, who again brought new havoc. Ben-Jofeph returned himfelf the following campaign, and his army, united to that of Grenada, gained very decided advantages over that of the Christians. After vanquishing the Castilian fleet, Ben-Joseph raised the siege of Algesira in 1278, and rebuilt that town in the place where it at present stands. This prince afterward made a truce with Don Alphonso, and generously granted him aid against his son, Don Sancho, who, with the consent of the people, had seized on the sovereign authority.

After the death of Ben-Joseph he was succeeded by his son Abu-Said, who, like his father, made several expeditions into Spain; all of which were unsuccesful. Having lost Tariffa, which had been taken by Don Sancho III., he made fruitless efforts to recover that place; but, perceiving that his attempts to regain the sovereignty of Spain exhausted his revenues, he renounced them in future, and in 1294 restored the town of Algesira to the king of Grenada. The empire of Morocco was, during a time, delivered from wars and revolutions. Abu-Said, occupied solely by the

the administration of his African states, reigned in tranquillity to the year 1303. At his death he was succeeded by Abu-Artab-Ben-Said; but neither did he take any part whatever in the Mahometan wars of Spain: his successor, indeed, Joseph-Ben-Jacob, in 1318, appears to have sent succours to the king of Grenada, who ceded some places to him, of which his troops took possession.

After the death of Joseph-Ben-Jacob, king of Fez and Morocco, his two sons, Abul-Hassen and Said, made war on each other for the succession. Said, having been vanquished, withdrew to the king of Grenada, and his brother, Abul-Hassen, was proclaimed. The latter took offence at the asylum given by the king of Grenada to Said, and shewed tokens of his resentment; on which the king of Grenada determined to pass over into Barbary, in 1330, that he might come to an explanation with this prince.

This voyage had the most fortunate success, for the king of Grenada, after having removed

removed all the suspicions of Abul-Hassen, obtained from him a considerable body of troops, commanded by his son Abdelmelek, who went in 1333, landed at Algesira, took possession of that place, and was there acknowledged sovereign. This army, protected by a fleet, afterward seized on Gibraltar, which the Spaniards, in vain, attempted to retake.

The war, which some years after broke out between the king of Tremecen and Abul-Hassen, obliged the latter to recall his his son Abdelmelek, with his troops. To these were likewise added a detachment, sent by the king of Grenada, who had made a truce with Castile. This war was unfortunate to the king of Tremecen, who, with his kingdom, lost all he possessed toward Sugulmessa. The king of Fez, profiting by his victory, pursued his conquests as far as Algiers and Tunis, which he again brought under the subjection of the kings of Fez and Morocco.

Inflated with success, Abul-Hassen resolved to recommence the Moorish expeditions.

ditions into Spain, hoping there to recover the dominion his predeceffors had enjoyed; for 'this purpofe he fent troops, ftores, arms, and ammunition, under the conduct of his fon Abdelmelek. Abdelmelek committed many ravages on the territories of Andalufia, but the Chriftians were able to repulfe his attacks; and, after feveral campaigns, in which the advantages were nearly equal, his army was attacked and routed by the Caftilians. Abdelmelek, having found an opportunity to fly on foot, perceiving the approach of Chriftians, counterfeited death, and the latter coming up gave him two wounds with their lances, of which he died in reality. The body of this prince was tranfported into Barbary, and inhumed at Shella, near Rabat, where his tomb is ftill to be feen.

The death of Abdelmelek afflicted the king of Fez fo deeply that he determined to go and take perfonal vengeance on the Spaniards. For this purpofe he fitted out more than two hundred veffels at Ceuta, in 1340, which, in defpite of the efforts of the king of Caftile, being favoured by

circum-

circumstances, met no obstacle in the short passage from the coast of Africa to the coast of Spain. Beside his troops, he took with him many Moorish families, who were to people some towns round Malaga. The Moorish fleet, being in the bay of Gibralter, was attacked by the fleet of Castile, but which, being by no means so powerful, was totally defeated.

The kings of Fez and Grenada, at the head of a mighty army, first laid siege to Tariffa; but the kings of Castile and Protugal, with their combined forces, marched to the relief of that place, and attacked and defeated the Mahometan army near Rio-Salado; which afterward retreated to Algesira. The king of Fez, fearing he should be there besieged, immediately embarked for Ceuta.

That he might revenge the Mohometan defeat at the battle of Rio-Salado, Abul-Hassen again made great preparations of troops and stores to return into Spain. His fleet, united with that of his allies, was attacked in port, and he lost about twelve

twelve vessels; but this check did not prevent the remainder of the fleet from setting sail: this, however, being once more attacked in the Strait by the combined fleet of the Christians, was entirely defeated; the invasion of the Mahometans was thus prevented, and, notwithstanding every effort of the king of Fez and Morocco, Algesira was taken, in March 1344, and a ten years truce concluded.

The expences which had been incurred by Abul-Hassen to support these his attempts in Spain, and the ill success that followed, occasioned his subjects to murmur, as is the custom of nations, that judge only from appearances. Abdalharaman, one of the king's sons, seized this moment of discontent to revolt, and drew over several tribes to his side. Don Alphonso, in the mean time, broke the truce in Spain, where he attacked the Mahometans. Abul-Hassen, although he had stifled the rebellion, found his own states in too critical a situation to admit of his going in person to assist the Mahometans of Spain. He sent his son, Abu-Ali, thither, with a body of troops, to aid

aid Gibraltar, which the king of Castile besieged in 1349; the troops of Morocco, however, could effect nothing, but were obliged to repass the strait, a rebellion having been once more raised by Abu-Hennon, another of the sons of Abul-Hassen. The king was unfortunate in this civil war, and was obliged to retire into the province of Sugulmessa, his son having seized on his kingdom.

Abu-Hennon was an ambitious prince, and desirous of establishing his fame with his subjects; for which purpose he prepared formidable armaments for the invading of Spain. His father took advantage of these preparations to attempt recovering his domains, and, assembling some troops round Sugulmessa, assaulted and subjected various cities of the kingdom of Fez. The projects of Abu-Hennon were suspended by this diversion; but, having overcome his father in 1354, near the mountains of Fez, he remained in peaceable possession of his states, and preserved his supremacy over the small kingdoms of the coast from Tremecen to Tunis. This prince

prince entered into a negotiation with Peter the cruel, who had ascended the throne of Castile, and who, from political motives, was disposed to favour the rebellion of Abu-Hennon. The latter, at length, in full enjoyment of peace, embellished the city of Fez with some edifices, and built a college there, which still bears his name.

Abu-Hennon died in 1409, and his son, Abu-Said, was his successor. Addicted to pleasure and debauchery, this prince occupied himself too little with the care of his own estates to think of succouring the Mahometans of Spain; he even neglected to fortify, or send aid, to Ceuta, which was besieged and taken in 1415 by Don John, king of Portugal; the neighbouring Moors united to recover the place, but their attempts were unsuccessful, as well from their ignorance, in the art of besieging towns, as from the skill with which they were repulsed by Don Henry, son to the king of Portugal.

The cities of Spain, which had been under the government of Abu-Said, seeing they

they were to expect no affiftance whatever from him, were reunited to the Mahometan kingdom of Grenada; Gibralter alone remaining in the poffeffion of the king of Fez. Hither Abu-Said fent his brother Said with fome troops, as well to preferve that place, and to recover others that had been loft, as to remove Said, whofe valour and eminent qualities made him remarked by the people, and who foon or late might become a dangerous rival.

This expedition was unfuccefsful, the king of Grenada having befieged Gibralter, Said, in vain, demanded fuccours from his brother, who faw, with fecret pleafure, the difficulties in which he was involved. Said notwithftanding defended himfelf with the utmoft fortitude; but, having been conquered, he was taken prifoner to Grenada, where his brother wifhed he might be put to death. The king of Grenada, more politic, preferved the life of this prince, as well out of refpect to his birth as in the hope of being able to make him a party in thofe infurrections which fo often divided the Moors of Africa.

Future

Future events juſtified the foreſight of the king of Grenada: the Moors of Fez, offended at the conduct of their ſovereign, rebelled againſt him, and he was ſtabbed by his Vizier, who, at the ſame time, aſſaſſinated his children. The kingdom of Fez fell into the greateſt diſorder in conſequence of the death of this prince; the people lived ſome time totally independant, each province and each tribe governing itſelf according to its will. The king of Grenada profited by this ſtate of anarchy to ſend over Said into Barbary with troops, and thus to inſure his friendſhip and alliance; but this Prince had many difficulties to encounter, having a competitor in Jacob, one of his brothers, whoſe ſtandard had been followed by the principal tribes, which occaſioned open war between theſe two princes.

The kingdom of Fez, troubled by theſe civil broils, remained eight years without a ſovereign, when, in 1423, a ſon of Abu-Said appeared, named Abdallah, with whom his mother had fled to Tunis. Abdallah was received with the greater joy becauſe

because that the people, divided in their choice of a prince, thought it their duty to reunite in favour of one whom Providence seemed miraculously to have preserved, that their calamities might find a period. The uncles of Abdallah Said and Jacob approved the nation's choice, and relinquished the throne.

Abdallah reigned with justice for some years; but, at length, he imposed so many vexatious and tyrannical oppressions, on his people, that they were incited to revolt. In the midst of the civil commotions which ensued, an inhabitant of Fez, who was a Sharif, and who bore the name, slew the king Abdallah, who was the last of the family of the Benimerins, and was proclaimed in his stead.

All the grandees attached to the Dynasty of the Benimerins rose against the usurper, and an obstinate war ensued. Muley Shaik, one of the generals who was at the head of this party, and who commanded toward Arzilla, presented himself before Fez to besiege the city; but, having

ing been vanquished by the Sharif, he retired into his government. The Sharif then sent an army into Temsena to subject that province; and Muley Shaik, while the Sharif was thus weakened, made a second attempt upon Fez, in which he besieged the Sharif.

Don Alphonso, of Portugal, desirous of profiting by the intestine distractions of the empire, appeared before Arzilla with his fleet, and took it in 1471. Muley Shaik, being informed of this, departed from the blockade of Fez to go and succour Arzilla, which, as well as Tangiers, he found taken on his arrival. The Moorish prince then determined to make a truce with the king of Portugal, that he might once more undertake the siege of Fez; and he accordingly obliged the Sharif to abandon that city.

Muley Shaik, now become master of the capital and the appending monarchy, was the first of the kings of the race called Merini, the descendants of a branch of the Benimerins. The dominion of the Merini only extended over the kingdom of Fez, becaufe, in thefe difcordant times, the provinces of Morocco, Suz, Sugulmeffa, and others, were fubjected to other fovereigns, who found themfelves capable of maintaining their independence.

CHAP.

CHAP. V.

Sharifs of the Merini — Troubles that happened under their reign.

THE family of Merini, which is also called Beni-Aotas, was so lightly esteemed that it was not able to render its authority respectable in the kingdom of Fez. Independent of those provinces which had shaken off obedience, there were cities that were governed within themselves, or by the authority of chiefs which they had elected. The Portuguese, who already had got footing on the coast, profiting by the weakness of these small governments and their internal divisions, possessed themselves of various places, and insensibly extended their conquests. Several tribes of Moors, from animosity, or provoked by the ambition of their chiefs, rather chose to become

become the allies of the Portuguese, than to remain dependant on numerous masters, who reciprocally deposed each other.

The kingdoms of Fez and Morocco continued in this kind of anarchy till the beginning of the sixteenth century; and the race of Merini, whose power was feeble, reigned only over the city of Fez and the neighbouring provinces. At this time a Moor, of the province of Dara, whose name was Mahomet-Ben-Achmet, calling himself a Sharif and descendant of the Prophet, perceiving that the contentions which existed in the provinces might favour a revolution; and knowing, also, the ascendant which religion has over the minds of the vulgar, thought proper to employ these means to accomplish his projects of ambition.

This Sharif sent his three sons, Abdel-Quiber, Achmet, and Mohamet, in 1508, on pilgrimage to Mecca, that they might thereby acquire the greater consideration. These young men, on their return, affecting all the exterior of religion, were most respectfully

respectfully received by the Moors, who flocked after them in crouds, contested who first should touch their garments, and venerated them as saints, who were come to console them amid their afflictions.

The superstition and enthusiasm of the people raised their fame so high that, when they returned into their province, the father, without hesitation, sent the two youngest to Fez to make themselves known in that metropolis, famous for its science and religion. The eldest of these two became the head of the first college, and the king confided the education of his children to the younger.

When the reputation of these Sharifs was well established, their father, who slowly pursued projects which had been deeply laid, engaged them to represent to the king of Fez the calamities which resulted from the divisions among the Moors, and those which were in future to be dreaded in consequence of their alliance with the Portuguese, who, soon or late, would

would seize on their wealth, and reduce their persons to slavery.

They artfully insinuated to this prince how glorious it would be to himself, and how conducive to the prosperity of religion, could he unite all the Mahometans to repel, and drive these foreigners from the states. This enterprize might be crowned with success, according to their flattering representations, would he permit them to traverse the provinces with a drum and a standard, awaken the spirit of religion among the people, instruct them in their true interests, and incite them to rise in arms against the Christians. Acknowledging this prince as their legitimate sovereign, they requested he would bestow on them some mark of authority which might give credit to, and make their mission respectable in the southern provinces, where the Portuguese were so powerful.

The king of Fez, who had no authority in these southern provinces, and who had no suspicion that the intentions of the Sharifs were inimical to himself, granted their

their requeſt, in contradiction to the repreſentations made to him by his brother, Muley Naſſer, who, better informed than he was concerning former revolutions, affected by the Morabethoon and the Moahedins, under the veil of religion, prophefied evil from this project of the Sharifs, and foreſaw in it more of ambition than of zeal. Neglecting this advice, the king of Fez granted them a drum, ſome ſoldiers to protect them, and royal mandates diſplaying the object of their miſſion. The two Sharifs entered the province of Duquella, and paſſed through the others till they came to that of Suz, in every place exciting the enthuſiaſm of the people againſt the Portugueſe, whoſe ambition they failed not to exaggerate.

Politically conſidered, this miſſion was neceſſary, ſince, on one ſide of the coaſt, the Portugueſe, in 1508, were maſters of Saffi, and had made alliance with the moſt powerful of the neighbouring tribes, while, on the other, the Duke of Braganza, in 1513, had lately taken Azamora, inſomuch that, from thence to Santa Cruz, the coaſt

coaſt for more than a hundred leagues was in their power toward the ſouth, independent of the towns of Arzilla, Tangiers, and Ceuta, which they poſſeſſed to the north. In this critical ſituation, the empire being enfeebled and divided as it then was, they might moſt eaſily have conquered the whole coaſt; all which perfectly juſtified thoſe alarms which the Sharifs ſpread, although their perſonal motives had a very different tendency.

The miſſion of the Sharifs had every effect which might reaſonably be expected, and, under the pretence of the defence of religion, a number of tribes, that were then governed by themſelves, eagerly joined their ſtandard. Money being neceſſary to the Sharifs for the maintenance of theſe armies, the tribes granted them the tenth, as ordained by the Koran, which gave them a ſemblance of ſovereign power.

The city of Tarudant, which had been ravaged by the wandering tribes, acknowledged the old Sharif for its chief, and ena-

bled

bled him also to maintain some troops. Thus aided, Mahomet-Ben-Achmet fortified himself in Tarudant, pretending thereby to free himself from the dominion of the Portuguese, and impede their incursions. Succoured by the Moors of Suz and Dara, he was presently able to make war on the tribes near Cape Aguer, or Santa-Cruz, and also to enter the provinces of Hea, Duquella, and Temsena, where the people, as much moved by his sermons as terrified by his arms, acknowledged him their sovereign, under the modest title of Prince of Hea.

The Portuguese, and Moors of the environs of Saffi, their allies, made incursions at the same time into the province of Duquella, and spread terror to the very walls of Morocco: the old Sharif alone opposed their progress; but, dying during the time he was warring with them, he left the accomplishment of his projects to the care of his sons.

These princes, having by their arts obtained the people's veneration, and who were

were as exact in paying their tenths as they were prompt at obedience, gradually extended their power. They remained with their forces between Saffi and Morocco to oppofe the incurfions of the Portuguefe, whom, in various actions, they repulfed; but their advantages were, in fome fort, balanced by the death of Abdel-Quiber, the eldeft of the three brothers, who fell in battle.

The Sharifs, having formed the defign of feizing on Morocco, made an alliance with Naffer Bufhentuf, who commanded in that city, and held the neighbouring tribes in dependence. This governor, having made himfelf fovereign, received the Sharifs in Morocco, refpecting their piety, and in the hope that he himfelf might find his advantage in their alliance. This confidence became fatal to Naffer Bufhentuf, for his death quickly followed, which happened on returning from a hunting party with one of the Sharifs, who has been accufed of having given him a poifoned bifcuit. Achmet, the eldeft of thefe princes, who had remained in Morocco,

rocco, profited so well by his death, that, aided by the principal men of the city, whose friendship he had gained, he was proclaimed king.

Muley Achmet, now king of Morocco, sent information of his election to the king of Fez, and, in gratitude for the services he had received from the latter, affirmed, he only intended to govern under his authority, and paying him feudal homage. This quieted the fears of the king, and gave Muley Achmet time to establish his power.

Morocco and its environs being thus subjected to the Sharifs, they, by artifices, endeavoured to possess themselves of other provinces, and with such adroitness did they foment factions that, when the different parties made war on each other, each of them depended on the assistance of the Sharifs, should either need their aid. These princes, however, who had only raised dissentions that they might enfeeble the tribes, put their troops in motion, fell upon them, totally defeated them, plundered

dered their Douhars, and returned to Morocco victorious, and enriched with fpoils. Their victories fpread terror among the people, and the province of Duquella and its environs were thus fubjected.

Become more powerful, the Sharifs now freed themfelves from that acknowledgement of fuperiority which they had voluntarily paid to the king of Fez, only fending him fome fmall prefents as they pleafed, which were lefs to be confidered as tributes than as tokens of friendfhip. The king of Fez complained of their inattention, but his death foon after happened, and his fon, who had been the difciple of the Sharif Mohamet, diffembled, and confirmed the ufurpers in their principalities, on condition of fome fmall acknowledgement.

After the death of the king of Fez the ambition of the Sharifs increafed with their power; they artfully allied themfelves with the chiefs of tribes in the environs of that city, that they might fow divifion; and, not only refufed to fubmit to the

the least homage, but, sent to inform the new king, their benefactor and sovereign, that, being descendants of Mahomet, they had a more incontestible right than any person whatever to the Mahometan throne.

The two brothers at the same time divided their conquests; the eldest, Muley Achmet, retained Morocco; Muley Mohamet took up his residence at Tarudant, by which they could mutually succour each other against the Portuguese and their allies, who were masters of most of the western coast, from the cape of Aguer to the province of Duquella inclusive.

The king of Fez, who had too long connived at the perfidious conduct of the Sharifs, resolved, though somewhat late, to make them repent of their ingratitude, and, with two pieces of cannon, went in person to besiege Morocco. His army, not being sufficiently numerous to invest the city, could not prevent Muley Mohamet from throwing in succours, which he brought from Tarudant. This same Sharif

rif made a fally, a few days after, with his troops, and fell on the camp of the king of Fez with fo much intrepidity that he forced his army to retreat, leaving the field of battle covered with the flain.

After this check the king of Fez was obliged to raife the fiege, as much for want of fufficient force as to go and re-eftablifh order in his own kingdom, where his brother, Muley Meffaoot, profiting by his abfence and ill fortune, had raifed an infurrection. He was followed in his retreat by the Sharifs, who attacked his rear-guard, which they came up with in the province of Efcura; after which, paffing into that of Tedla, and coafting the mountains, they obliged the people, fubjects to the king of Fez, to pay them contributions.

Having appeafed the revolt, incited by Muley Meffaoot, the king of Fez, more than ever enraged againft the Sharifs, marched once again to befiege Morocco. The Sharifs likewife marched to meet him, though with an inferior army, and waited for him on the banks of the river of negroes

to

to dispute his passage. The king of Fez, arriving at the opposite shore, encamped likewise, and the two armies observed each other for some days; at length, the king determined to attempt the passage; he divided his army into three corps, gave the command of the first to Abu-Abdallah, king of Grenada, who, having lost his own kingdom, had taken refuge with the king of Fez, the second to his brother-in-law, and headed the third himself.

The king of Grenada, having with him the son of the king of Fez, passed first; and, as he proceeded to the middle of the ford, and his van-guard began to ascend the banks of the river, where the land was high, the king of Suz attacked this van-guard with so much valour that it was defeated: the son of the king of Fez was killed, as also was the king of Grenada. This prince, who never had exposed his life in defence of his own kingdom, lost it on this occasion in defence of another; the confusion among the soldiers was fo great that the van-guard of the king of Fez, forced back in the river, overwhelmed thofe who were coming to their affiftance, and they thus mutually drowned each other. The king of Fez, not having yet begun the paffage with his detachment, feeing the diforder irretrievable, retired with fo much hafte that he abandoned his wives, baggage and artillery, took the road to Tedla, and returned to Fez.

This victory, which highly influenced the vulgar opinion, was fo favourable to the Sharifs, that they were emboldened to greater undertakings, and determined the following year to pafs mount Atlas with numerous forces, where they feized on the kingdom of Tafilet. On their return they raifed contributions on the provinces of Fez, left troops in them, and forced thofe of the king of Fez to retire. After this fuccefs, Muley Mohamet left his brother at Morocco, and returned to Tarudant. In 1536, this prince came before Aguadier, or Santa Cruz, then in the power of the Portuguefe; the fiege of this place was somewhat

somewhat long, but it was obliged at last to capitulate. The power of the Sharifs was still farther extended after this conquest, because that the Moors, who had been allies of the Portuguese, unable longer to receive aid from them, determined to pay homage to these princes.

This increase of dominion, which every where embroils nations, became at length a subject of discord between the Sharifs. Muley Achmet the eldest, who possessed the kingdom of Morocco, had ceded that of Suz to his brother Muley Mohamet, on condition of some tribute being paid; but the latter, whose valour, and other qualities, had rendered him the most popular, felt how easy it would be for him to rid himself of this dependence; and, instead of remitting his brother the fifth of the spoils he had made during the last campaign, thought proper to send a smaller part. This offended the king of Morocco, who imagined he had a right to prescribe such homage as he pleased. Muley Mohamet refused compliance, and explanations

tions enfued between the brothers, which did but incite new aggravation, and each of them began to commit hoftilities on the domains of the other till war became almoft inevitable.

To prevent the confequent calamities, a Moor, who was held in veneration, perfuaded the two brothers to an interview, which gave occafion to an irreconcileable hatred. Muley Achmet treacheroufly endeavoured to ftrangle his brother as they embraced, but the latter, more adroit, efcaped the danger; and, now become open enemies, they prepared for war.

Muley Achmet immediately fent his fon, Muley Sidan, with troops into the province of Dara, which appertained to the kingdom of Suz, there to levy contributions. Muley Mohamet, on his part, oppofed thefe hoftilities, and different actions enfued between the armies of the two princes, in which fortune generally was in favour of the king of Morocco. The loffes of Muley Mohamet did not, however, difhearten him, but rather ferved farther

ther to raise his courage. Having assembled the governors of provinces, and the chiefs of tribes, he rehearsed to them his brother's acts of injustice, and so effectually inspired them with a dread of his tyranny that they all swore eternal fidelity to Muley Mohamet. After receiving their protestations, the sovereign gave them assurance, holding by his beard in token of a vow *, that, if they would be as faithful as they promised, he would vanquish his brother, and lead him prisoner to Tarudant.

The two armies soon took the field, each endeavouring to profit by every kind of stratagem to surprize the other. Having, at length, met at the entrance of a valley, that of the king of Suz, which was upon the height, assaulted the army of the king of Morocco with such impetuosity that it was obliged to give ground, and the

* When the Moors hold by their beards, while they swear, it gives strength to the oath, which, after this formality, they rarely violate.

cavalry, being so confined as to be unable either to form itself or act, the soldiers were obliged to alight from their horses, that they might escape with greater facility.

During the rout the king of Morocco, and his son Muley Boeza, were made prisoners, and conducted to Tarudant; but his eldest son, Muley Sidan, after collecting the remains of the army, retreated to Morocco. In this extremity the inhabitants of this city thought the best means were to negociate, and, after council held, Muley Sidan sent his wife to the king of Suz, his uncle, to effect an accommodation, and implore his clemency. The princess pleaded so effectually that Muley Mohamet granted his brother freedom, on condition that they should divide their conquests. There were many other clauses in their treaty, but, it was so little observed, that, to recite them, would be superfluous.

The king of Morocco, once again returned to his states, protested against the validity of the treaty, affirmed that, it having

having been made while he was a prisoner, it could neither injure his rights nor those of his descendants, who, by their birth, had a legitimate claim over his domains, which it was not in his power, by any renunciation, to take from them. After such a protestation the two brothers, equally irritated, again made dispositions for war, and the king of Suz passed Mount Atlas, by hasty marches, to invade the territories of Morocco.

The two armies met, seven leagues from that capital, on the nineteenth of August, 1544; and Muley Mohamet attacked his brother with so much valour that he totally defeated his army, and pursued it to the very gates of Morocco.

Here he summoned the inhabitants to deliver up the city, if they would not expose themselves to all the rigours of war; and the governor, having received no tidings of his master, supposing he might have been taken or slain, and not daring to defend the place, represented to the inhabitants

habitants that, Suz and Morocco being governed by princes of the fame blood, it was but juft that he fhould open the gates. Muley Mohamet, on his entrance, was faluted by the people as their fovereign.

After having vifited the fortrefs, and placed guards in every part, the prince entered the palace of his brother, where all was in confufion; the treafury was pillaging; the wives and daughters of Muley Achmet were folely occupied, during the tumult, to conceal what they poffeffed moft precious; but the prince foon quieted their fears, and took care at the fame time to fecure the treafury.

Muley Achmet, who had loft himfelf during the night, arrived while thefe things paffed, with few followers, at the private gate of the palace, where he knocked aloud. He was anfwered from the top of the walls, and advifed to fly, for that his brother was mafter of the city. Accordingly this prince retired immediately to the fanctuary of Sidi-Abdallah-Ben-Ceffi, as to an inviolable afylum.

From

from this place Muley Sidan and Muley Boeza went to Fez, to intreat affiftance from the king, who beheld, with fecret fatisfaction, the divifions of thofe Sharifs, whofe perfidy he himfelf had proved, and therefore promifed aid to the moft feeble, hoping by this means he fhould be enabled to deftroy the moft mighty.

The confecrated perfons appertaining to the fanctuary where Muley Achmet had fled for refuge, were bufied in their endeavours to procure an interview between the two brothers, which accordingly, in a few days, took place. Muley Mohamet, who, on fimilar occafions, had made proof of the ill faith of his brother, took his precautions, and received him in his tent, as well as his children, with his fabre in his hand; thefe faluted their uncle, and proftrated themfelves before him to embrace his knees. Muley Achmet approached the laft, and his brother went to receive him at the entrance of his tent, where they embraced, wept, and remained for fometime filent.

Muley

Muley Mohamet, at length, reproached his brother concerning the little faith with which he had obferved the treaty concluded at Tarudant, adding that, to this his breach of faith, more criminal in kings than even in other men, he muſt attribute his misfortunes; that Providence had defpoiled him of his ſtates but to revenge his having broken a promiſe, pledged; that, being his elder brother, he had ever treated him as his ſuperior and ſovereign, and that, ungrateful as his conduct had been, he ſhould ſtill continue ſo to do; but that, having given his word to the inhabitants of Morocco not to ſuffer him any more to enter the city, he could not break it, leſt he ſhould thereby incur ſimilar reproaches; it therefore appeared moſt proper that he ſhould, for a time, retire to Tafilet with his ſons, and there await a better deſtiny; that they ought to regard the conqueſts they had already made, with the aid of the Almighty, as harbingers of ſtill greater ſucceſs. Muley Achmet made ſome reply, in his own juſtification, and, confiding in the generoſity of his brother, took the way to Tafilet.

Muley

Muley Mohamet, thus become master of the south of the empire, put himself in a condition to make Muley Oatas Merini, king of Fez, repent the kind reception he had granted his nephews. Seeking a quarrel with him, he demanded the province of Tedla as appertaining to the kingdom of Morocco, and at the same time sent his second son, Muley Abdel Cader, with troops to levy contributions, and besiege a castle, which was in that province. This castle, which was well defended, was vigorously attacked by the young prince, who yet was unable to take it, the king of Fez having come to its relief.

Hearing this, Muley Mohamet assembled all the cavalry of Suz and Morocco, marched in person toward Tedla, and joined the troops that were under his son's command. The army of the king of Fez was superior to that of the king of Morocco; but, being composed, in part, of the inhabitants of Fez, who were fickle of temper, not inured to war, but rather accustomed to effeminacy and pleasures, this army was daily weakened by desertion.
Muley

Muley Mohamet, well acquainted with the levity of the people of Fez, eluded action as long as he thought convenient, till, at length, determined to give battle, he harangued his troops, and declared, that, defiring only to fight with men who were determined on victory, he gave liberty to all thofe to retire who felt they wanted this refolution; that, perfuaded as he was, men, bred in the city of Fez, though fuperior in numbers, were unable to ftand before foldiers fo courageous as thofe he commanded, he intended to give battle, confiding in their valour, and not doubting but that the victory would render him the greateft fovereign of Africa.

Animated by this difcourfe, the foldiers called aloud to be led to the enemy, and, on the next morning, the army advanced in order of battle. This order was in the form of a crefcent, according to the cuftom of the Moors; the two extremities of which were commanded, the one by Muley Meflaoot, the king's fon, and the other by the Alcade Mumen, fon of a Genoefe renegado; the king was in the centre with his

his other children, having the Arquebufiers in his front, and the artillery drawn by peasants, or carried by mules.

The two armies remained facing each other without beginning the attack; the Sharif had commanded that no motion should be made till the signal had been given; the heat of the day was excessive, and the prince artfully waited till the sun was on the decline; and at the moment when, being behind his army, it shone in the face of his enemies, the firing of a cannon was the signal of attack, and this was made with such impetuosity, and success, that the army of the king of Fez was immediately put to rout. As this prince was riding to pass the river of Derna, and rally his flying forces, his horse fell, and he and his son, Muley Buker, were made prisoners. All the troops of Fez, that composed the main body of the army, retired in disorder. Muley Buhafon, Prince and Lord of Gomera, in the province of Rif, who commanded a detachment, was the only Moor who fought courageously, and retired in good order.

A de-

A detachment of Turks, commanded by a refolute Perfian, intrenched behind a battery, likewife prevented the victorious Moors from furrounding them. The Sharif, aftonifhed at the valour of thefe foreigners, offered to take them into his fervice on the fame conditions they had enjoyed under the king of Fez. The Perfian general accepted the propofal for himfelf, and fuch of his detachment as thought proper to follow him, provided the king of Morocco would pledge his word for their fafety. Muley Mohamet fent his ring by one of his fons, and the Perfian general entered into his fervice with thofe of his foldiers who were not married at Fez; the reft laid down their arms and retreated.

After he had reftored order in the camp, Muley Mohamet fent for Muley Oatas, king of Fez, and confoled him in his misfortunes, which, he faid, muft be attributed to the fins that were openly committed at Fez without reprehenfion. The king of Fez, enfeebled as he was by his wounds, affumed ftrength enough to reply, that it

was

was not always in the power of the sovereign to extirpate habitual and rooted vices, and that, be the irregularity in his adminiftration what it might, it did not thence refult that he had a right to make war upon him, and feize upon his ftates, more efpecially when the benefits were remembered which he had received from his father. An agreement was afterward made between the Sharif and the king of Fez, that the latter and his fon fhould be reftored to liberty, for which he fhould yield up the city of Mequinez.

The Sharif took the road to Fez to enforce this agreement, but Muley Buhafon, who had entered Fez with the remains of the army, beholding the confufion there was in the city, while it remained without a monarch, had Muley Caffari, a young fon of the king, proclaimed, on condition that he fhould reftore the crown to his father fo foon as he fhould recover his liberty. The king of Morocco mean while came and encamped, with his army, four leagues from Fez, whence he difpatched letters from the king, his prifoner, to his mother and

the

the principal men of the city, that they should put Mequinez into his power; but Buhafon, who directed in Fez, occasioned the answer to be delayed, that he might shut up the Sharif, between the army of Fez and another which was raising at Mequinez. Being informed of this, the the king of Morocco decamped before the passes were seized, taking with him his prisoners.

Muley Mohamet, having gained intelligence of the dissensions among the Moors in the environs of Fez, profited by these, in 1548, to send troops thither, the command of which he bestowed on his two eldest sons, Muley Haram and Muley Abdel Cader, who committed some ravages round Alcassar and Mequinez. This diversion, and the want of concord throughout the government of the north, further shook the wavering faith of the towns, and tribes of the kingdom of Fez, who were half in commotion, and who were with difficulty restrained from rebellion. In this juncture the Moors, who were by profession saints, interfered, as usual, to pacify the people;

people; and it was at length agreed that the city of Mequinez fhould be given to Muley Mohamet, on condition that the king of Fez fhould be reftored to liberty, which was accordingly performed; but the Sharif exacted a promife from the king, before his departure, that, whenever he fhould make the demand, he would alfo yield him the city of Fez.

The king being come to Fez, his fon reftored him the government; but Muley Mohamet, who would not give him time to re-eftablifh his authority, appeared before the metropolis about two months afterward, of which he demanded the poffeffion. The king of Fez anfwered that his fon, and the inhabitants, would not fuffer this, and therefore it was not in his power to comply. The Sharif was fo enraged, by this meffage, that he caufed the ambaffador who brought it to be beheaded, and fent a detachment of cavalry to the very gates of the city to commit hoftilities; but this detachment was beaten, and forced to retreat.

Muley Mohamet then repaired to Mequinez, whence he fent for two of his fons to join him with what troops they could affemble in Morocco, and the fouthern provinces; after which he marched to meet this reinforcement, and encamped near the river Seboo. The different actions that happened between the troops of the king of Fez, and thofe of the king of Morocco, were to the advantage of the latter, who marched toward Fez and blockaded the city. Some fallies were made by the king of Fez, which made but little impreffion, while the inhabitants, in want of provifions, went by hundreds to the Sharif, who received them with open arms, and further ftraitened his lines to cut off all communication. After a long fiege, the inhabitants gave up the place to the Sharif, who, for form fake, beat down a part of the walls, and entered the city unknown to the king, who was then in New Fez

The news being brought him, this prince flew to recover his capital; the two parties fought from ftreet to ftreet with equal rage, and he would even have recovered

vered Fez, had not the people, according to their usual inconstancy, declared themselves for the Sharif, and forced his troops to retire. Without subjects, and without soldiers, the king rather chose to submit to the clemency of the conqueror than to abandon his crown, his wives, and children. The king of Morocco, however, took possession of the city and castle of Fez, married one of the king's daughters, and sent him and his children to Morocco and Tarudant, where he caused them to be assassinated. Such was the tragical end of the house of Merini, and such the ingratitude and perfidy it received from those Sharifs which itself had raised, and who, having stripped it of its possessions, and exterminated its race, soon themselves felt the vicissitudes of fortune.

CHAP. VI.

The Revolutions of the Sharifs.

AFTER having seized on the kingdom of Fez, Muley Mohamet sent his brother, Muley Achmet, into the desert, with a part of his family, that he might have nothing to fear from his ambition. The change of government in Fez, however, soon raised troubles in the northern provinces, which obeyed with repugnance a prince who had deposed their rightful sovereign. Muley Mohamet therefore determined to send troops into the provinces, as well to make his authority respected as to keep the soldiers occupied, and prevent the effects of their inconstancy. He sent his three sons, Muley Haram, Muley Abdel Cader, and Muley Abdallah, against the city of Tremecen, of which they possessed themselves without

without the least resistance. Haram advanced toward Oran, but could not conquer it; and, having returned to Fez, he there fell sick and died. The Algerine Turks, having heard of the reduction of Tremecen, marched with an army to effect its recovery. The king of Morocco sent three of his sons, with various detachments, to its relief; but the want of concord between these brothers, who, born of different mothers, had little affection for each other, and acted as if they had opposite interests, occasioned the loss of the place, and of a battle, in which one of them was killed, and another wounded.

At the same time, Salah Reis, governor of Algiers, who had acquired the reputation of valour, informed by Muley Buhafon, prince of Gomera, of the perfidious conduct of the Sharifs, to the king of Fez, offered his alliance to dethrone Muley Mohamet. Buhafon accepted the proposal, and also assured him he would allow a thousand pistoles, daily, for the maintenance of his troops, and abandon to him all the silver, gold, and jewels, which might be taken from the Sharif. Salah Reis accordingly departed, in 1553, with his artillery, and 4000 men, who were joined during their progress by a multitude of volunteers, that continually increased.

The Sharif, then engaged in subjecting the mountaineers of the environs of Morocco, having heard of this march, went to the relief of Fez, and sent all the cavalry he could collect to encamp in its neighbourhood. Salah Reis, as he advanced toward this city, had an engagement with Muley Abdallah, son of the king of Morocco, who commanded the rear-guard of his army, in which the young prince lost the baggage and stores, which obliged the Sharif to hasten his march and enter Fez. Salah Reis, a few days after, having encamped near the city, the king of Morocco determined to sally out, because the inhabitants enjoy the privilege of capitulating, if the enemy approach the city within half a league.

The

The king of Morocco, after having held council, marched to difpute the paffage of the Seboo with the enemy. His pofition was nearly the fame as it had formerly been when oppofed to the king of Fez, with this difference, that Salah Reis was a more able general, had a more formidable artillery, and better gunners. Salah Reis, intending to pafs the river, cannonaded the army of the Sharif to prevent its acting, while his cavalry effected a paffage; each horfeman carried an Arquebufier behind him, who, as faft as they gained the fhore, entrenched themfelves behind palifadoes, which they brought with them, while protected by their cavalry, whom the Moors were unable to drive from their pofts. By this fkilful conduct Salah Reis gained the oppofite fhore, encamped, and lay all night under arms.

The next morning the Sharif difpofed his army in order of battle. Salah Reis did the fame; and, notwithftanding the fuperiority of the Moors, whofe numbers were

were more than five to one, by his good generalship, taking advantage of his enemy's mistakes, and opposing art to strength, Salah Reis obliged Muley Mohamet, whose troops began to give ground, to sound a retreat, and retire into New Fez. Salah Reis and Buhason then advanced toward Old Fez, where they found some resistance from one of the sons of the Sharif; but Buhason, having advanced with five hundred resolute Turks, burst the gates and entered the city, which was easily taken, Muley Abdallah, while he attacked the one gate, retiring through the other to join his father in New Fez. Muley Mohamet, perceiving the enemy master of Old Fez, thought only of flight, bade his wives carry every thing they had most precious with them, and follow him; but he, being in haste to secure himself, could not wait for them, and several of them fell into the conqueror's power. Before he left the city he opened his treasury, and suffered it to be pillaged by his own people, to prevent its falling into the hands of his enemies, whose booty consequently was small.

After

After Salah Reis had taken Fez, there was some altercation concerning the election of a king; he consented, however, at length, that Muly Buhafon should be proclaimed, according to stipulation; and, having been paid, agreeable to treaty, he returned to Algiers with his troops, loaded with plunder. Yet was not Salah Reis contented with Buhafon; he therefore informed the king of Morocco of his departure, and assured him he would grant his enemy no farther assistance, should he undertake the recovery of Fez. Muley Mohamet, however, who had hastily marched for Morocco, did not confide in this intelligence, but even wrote to Muley Abdallah, his son, to abandon Mequinez, which thus fell likewise into the power of the conqueror.

Muley Achmet, who had abandoned Tafilet by the order of his brother Muley Mohamet, and retired to the desert, learning that he had lost Fez, profited by this momentary weakness to seize upon Tafilet, in which there were no troops. He sent informa-

information of his intentions to Muley Buhafon, and intreated his aid.

Muley Mohamet diffembled his knowledge of thefe proceedings, till he was well certified of the return of Salah Reis, and his forces, to Algiers; he then affembled two armies, at Morocco, the one of which he led toward Tafilet, and gave the command of the other to his fon, Muley Abdallah, for the recovery of Fez. The latter approaching this city, Muley Buhafon fent his two fons, Nacer and Mohamet, to oppofe him with an army; but the two princes, difunited in opinion, did not concert their operations together. The latter, defirous of obtaining all the honour of victory, advanced with his detachment, attacked the army of Muley Abdallah, was totally defeated, and obliged to fly.

Irritated at this defeat, Buhafon affembled his forces, and marched himfelf to attack Muley Abdallah, who now, being himfelf routed, was obliged to return to Morocco.

Muley

Muley Mohamet, who had blockaded Tafilet, being informed of the defeat of his son, carefully spread a contrary report, by which the courage of Muley Achmet was so sunken that he imagined there was no resource, except in his brother's clemency; to intreat which he sent his sons. By this artifice Muley Mohamet retook Tafilet, sent his brother to a sanctuary near Morocco, and detained his two sons, whom he shortly after caused to be massacred.

He then departed from Tafilet toward Fez, to make another attempt on that city, and revenge the defeat of his son Abdallah. Muley Buhason marched to meet and give him battle; victory was disputed by both with the greatest obstinacy; but Muley Buhason, having been killed by a lance, his troops took to flight; the Sharif remained master of the field, and victoriously re-entered Fez.

In his wrath against the inhabitants, whose fickleness and cowardice he had proved, he treated them with the utmost [severity,

severity, exacted the repayment of his lost treasury, and an indemnification of his expences, for the defence and recovery of the city. In vain did the people remonstrate on the impossibility of paying a sum so exorbitant, especially after the losses to which they had been exposed. They agreed, however, to pay him the amount of three millions of livres, or one hundred and twenty-five thousand pounds, to relieve themselves from persecution. The king afterward seized on the possessions of wealthy individuals, and cut off many that he might obtain their riches. To avoid witnessing the hatred of the inhabitants, he made Morocco his place of residence, and left his son Abdallah at Fez, in quality of Viceroy.

Returned to Morocco, Muley Mohamet brought his brother thither, and put him under a guard. In 1556, he made dispositions to subject the Brebes of the mountains, who had given signs of commotion, and left his son, Muley Abdulmomen, at Morocco, with Ali-Ben-Buker, as governor. He passed Mount Atlas with his army,

army, but nothing remarkable happened during the campaign, except the death of this king, who was killed by a Turk, that had entered into his service with that express intention. Thus, as he rose to empire by treachery, he himself perished by the hand of a traitor.

After the death of this prince, while waiting for the arrival of Muley Abdallah, who was at Fez, Ali-Ben-Buker, governor of Morocco, fearing the people might elect Muley Achmet, had him murdered in his prison; and thus both these Sharifs, who had perfidiously made religion and good faith a pretext to despoil their masters and benefactors of sovereignty, whom, between them, they caused to perish, fell themselves, as did most of their posterity, by the hands of murderers, the merited reward of their crimes.

Muley Abdallah, hearing at Fez of the death of his father, left the government of this city to his brother, Muley Abdulmomen, and departed, in 1557, for Morocco, where

where he was joyfully received. Having affembled the chiefs of the army, and the principal men of the city, he was proclaimed king of Fez, Morocco, and other towns and provinces, under the dominion of the Sharif. In the beginning of his reign this prince gave tokens of generous fentiments, by which he acquired the affection of his people; but it was not long before he began to act the tyrant. Uneafy at perceiving the popularity of his brothers, on whom he had beftowed governments, he determined to recal them, intending to rid himfelf of them and his fears.

Muley Ottman, who was at Tarudant, repaired to court, as did his two nephews, who were governors, the one of Dara, and the other of Mequinez; but his brother, Muley Abdulmomen, excufed himfelf on a pretext of bufinefs. Muley Abdallah put the three others to death, and, that he might varnifh his tyranny, accufed them of not having fulfilled the duties of their office, and of failure in their adminiftration of juftice. This cruel act rendered

Abdal-

Abdallah odious to his subjects, and insupportable to himself, which occasioned a fit of sickness that almost brought him to the grave.

After his recovery, Muley Abdallah once more sent to his brother, Abdulmomen, to concert with him a meditated enterprize against Mazagan; but the latter, knowing what had happened to Ottman and his nephews, replied, he would be at Morocco as soon as possible, and, under the pretext of departing for this city, having collected his riches, he took the road to Tremecen, in 1559, that he might pass thence to Algiers. He was received with distinction at Algiers by Hassen, son of Barbarossa, Dey of that city; and, after acquiring reputation by his good conduct and bravery, Hassen bestowed one of his daughters on him, and confided to him the government of Tremecen.

Muley Abdallah heard, with displeasure, of the reception his brother had met from the Dey of Algiers, dreading lest their union should affect the good intelligence

telligence he had held with that regency, the power of which he had proved; he confoled himfelf, however, with reflecting that, being rid thus of his brothers and nephews, he had no competitors now to dread. The principal governments in his kingdoms he beftowed on his fons, and, in 1562, determined to lay fiege to Mazagan, which he had for fome time meditated; but his enterprize was unfuccefsful, and he was conftrained to retreat, after fuffering great loffes.

Muley Abdulmomen remained in peaceable enjoyment of his government of Tremecen, when the fon of Muley Abdallah, then governor of Fez, refolved to have him affaffinated. He concerted the means with one of his faithful fervants, who, pretending he had quarrelled with his mafter, fled from him, and took refuge at Tremecen. This Moor acted his part fo well that Abdulmomen gave him a moft gracious reception, and granted him unlimited confidence. The favourable moment being come, the traitor, having made every preparation for flight, killed the

prince

prince, while at prayers, with his crossbow, and had time to mount his horse and return to Fez, where he was generoufly rewarded by his mafter. Another kind of reward, however, followed, and fuch as his crime deferved; for the inhabitants of Morocco, who loved Abdulmomen, their former governor, having accufed the king, Muley Abdallah, of the murder of this prince, he, to juftify himfelf, fent to Fez for the guilty Moor, whom he dragged through the ftreets without hearing him, that he might neither betray himfelf nor his fon.

The conduct of Muley Abdallah toward his brothers and nephews difgraced him the more with his fubjects, becaufe he had alienated their affections by his mode of life. He wanted courage, and addicted himfelf to drunkennefs and pleafures, regardlefs of all decorum; he had, neverthelefs, fome good qualities, employed his revenues to ufeful purpofes, built palaces, added colleges to the mofques, and, in 1572, erected the caftle of Cape Aguer, having received information that Don Sebaſtian, king of Portugal, was equipping a fleet at Liſbon, that he might again poſſeſs himſelf of Santa Cruz and its road. Notwithſtanding the diſlike of his ſubjects, this prince, who had removed his brothers that he might indulge himſelf more licentiouſly in his pleaſures, reigned ſeventeen years without ſuffering any revolution, and, dying in 1574, left his eldeſt ſon, Muley Mohamet, his ſucceſſor.

Muley Mohamet, ſurnamed the negro, becauſe he was the ſon of a negroeſs, had ſcarcely aſcended the throne before, imitating the inhuman policy of his father, he diſpatched two of his brothers, and impriſoned the third, that he might enjoy his power in tranquillity. This cruelty rendered him alſo odious to his ſubjects, and Muley Abdelmeleck, or Moluc, one of his uncles, profiting by this diſpoſition, incited them to revolt, and dethroned him without difficulty.

Muley Mohamet, availing himself of the intelligence there was at that time between the Moors and the Portuguese, repaired to Lisbon to supplicate assistance from Don Sebastian, who was then assembling an army to invade Africa. In this army Muley Mohamet served, and convinced the king of Portugal that his presence was of great utility to his projects. The expedition of Don Sebastian, however, was unsuccesful; he was defeated and slain in the plains of Alcassar, and Muley Mohamet, who was then in his army, was drowned in crossing a river. Muley Abdelmeleck, who had usurped the crown, and was ill before the battle began, expired in his litter, in the very moment of victory; and thus do vast projects vanish in an instant.

Muley Achmet, brother of Abdelmeleck, after having won the battle, was proclaimed king of Fez by the army, and the governors of provinces and cities. His brothers were obliged by him to swear fidelity to his son, Muley Shek, and insure to him the succession. In 1594 this prince made

made preparations for extending his dominions, when he was informed of the arrival of Muley Nacer, who had long remained in Spain, and who, depending on promifed aid from Philip II., endeavoured to incite a revolt in his own favour. Muley Achmet fent one of his fons with a body of troops againſt this uſurper, who, after having been wounded in the battle, was obliged to abandon his camp and baggage, and renounce his hopes.

Muley Achmet, beloved and refpected by his people, was the laſt defcendant of the Sharifs, whoſe reign was troubled by no revolution. He died in 1603, and left his ſtates diſtracted by factions, which greatly increaſed the regret felt for his death.

The hiſtory of Spain informs us that Philip II. maintained a friendly corefpondence with him, and even fent an ambaſſador to his court, by whoſe intervention thoſe Lords, who had been taken at the battle of Alcaſſar, were recovered from ſlavery. Muley Achmet alſo fent the

body

body of the king, Don Sebaſtian, to Philip. From other Spaniſh writers we learn that Philip II. ſent painters to the king of Morocco, who generouſly rewarded them for their works *. Hence we may conclude that moſt of the paintings, to be found in the palaces of the Mooriſh kings, are probably the performances of Chriſtians.

After the death of Muley Achmet, Muley Sidan, the youngeſt of his ſons, being preſent with his father, was proclaimed ſucceſſor; but this proclamation did not prevent his three brothers from forming parties to maintain their claims, and, in leſs than two months, all the four were alternately maſters of the empire. In the different actions occaſioned by theſe revolutions, victory always declared for Muley Sidan: this prince having, at length, ſubjected Sallee, which, from its ſituation, gave a balance in favour of its poſſeſſor

* Viage d'Eſpana, de Don Ant. Pons. Tom. I. Lett. II.

throughout thefe difputes, remained victorious over his rivals.

His eldeft brother, Muley Shek, had recourfe to the king of Spain, Philip III., to obtain a fupply of money, and, in November 1610, put into the hands of this fovereign the city of Laracha, of which he was poffeffed, as a fecurity, both for his friendfhip and the fum received. This aid, however, did not prevent Muley Sidan from ftill remaining fovereign of the empire.

The repofe of the monarch was difturbed by the Brebes, or inhabitants of the mountains, near Morocco, who obliged him to quit his capital, that he might free himfelf from their inroads. Having found means to divide thefe tribes, and fubject them either by his arms or his negotiations, he peacefully paffed the remainder of his reign, and died at Morocco in 1630, leaving princes, as his fucceffors, who were little qualified to govern. It appears that, in 1622, this fovereign received an ambaffador from Holland, who was accompanied by by Golius, the disciple of Erpenius, and professor of the Arabic language. Muley Sidan was astonished at the learning of Golius, who wrote Arabic perfectly, but who could not speak it with facility *.

Muley Abdelmeleck, eldest son of Muley Sidan, succeeded his father, and was the first king of Morocco, who, beholding several small kingdoms united under his government, assumed the title of Emperor. At the commencement of his reign this prince affected to be religious, but, afterward, yielding to his character, he rendered himself so hateful to the people, by his drunkenness, cruelty, and a multitude of other vices, that the citizens of Fez called his brother, Muley Achmet, to the throne. The latter, having manifested similar propensities, was not less disagreeable to his subjects, who perceived they were not bettered by the change.

The public discontent incited new factions, and Muley El-Valid and Muley

* Bayle Dic. Hist. & Crit. mot Golius.

Semen both disputed for empire with their brother. But, neither of them inspiring sufficient confidence to raise up a powerful party, they were obliged to desist from their enterprize. After reigning four years, Muley Abdelmeleck, in 1635, was assassinated in his tent by a discontented slave, who, finding him in a state of intoxication, shot him with a pistol.

Muley Abdelmeleck being dead, Muley El-Valid, his brother, ascended the throne; this came the more unexpectedly because he had been imprisoned by order of his deceased brother, whose intention it was to have put out his eyes as a punishment for the rebellion he had raised. Such are the sports of fortune. The reign of this prince was distinguished by his mildness and affability, which obtained him the esteem and affection of his subjects, restless as they had been when suffering under the cruelty of his predecessors. El-Valid likewise gave proofs of a generous and great mind, by pardoning and releasing state prisoners, and by augmenting the pay of his troops.

His

His reign, however, was troubled by an infurrection, which his brother Semen, a reftlefs and ambitious man, had incited, and which was promoted by an Alcaid, whom Muley El-Valid had releafed from prifon. The fedition, however, was foon quelled by the defeat of the troops of Semen, who, together with the Alcaid, was taken; the latter was beheaded in reward for his ingratitude, and Muley Semen ftrangled; a rigorous judgment for Muley El-Valid, who, in the beginning of his reign, had fhewn fo much humanity and clemency. This feverity, perhaps, contributed to over awe the turbulent, for his reign was no more troubled by rebellion, and he died a natural death, in 1647, after having reigned twelve years. M. Sanfon, ambaffador from France, who had met fo many obftacles under the reign of Muley Abdelmeleck, obtained from Muley El-Valid the ranfom of various Frenchmen, who had been held in captivity in the ftates of Morocco.

Muley Achmet Shek, the laft of the fons of Muley Sidan, was elected Emperor,

peror, after the death of his brother, Muley El-Valid. An enemy to labour, addicted to pleasures, and ever immured with his wives, this prince wholly neglected the government of his kingdom, commiting it to the care of covetous ministers, who abused their influence and authority.

The indolence and effeminacy in which this monarch lived, and the oppressions of the governors of provinces, and cities, excited murmurs among the people, and, at length, universal discontent. The mountaineers, more restless and more resolute than his other subjects, consulting their ferocity only, and profiting by the weak state of the empire, besieged and took Morocco. After subjecting the inhabitants to all the calamities of war, they put Muley Achmet to death, and proclaimed one of their chiefs, named Crom-El-Hadgy; who had no right of birth to the crown, and who reigned some years without the love of his people.

This prince inhumanly massacred all the descendants of the Sharifs, who might any

any way have disturbed his reign, and, by his cruelty, revenged the blood and the rights of the house of Merini, whose monarchs these same Sharifs had destroyed, after having stripped them of wealth and sovereignty.

Raised to the throne by a factious multitude, Crom-El-Hadgy was ever considered as a usurper. Having never been proclaimed by the people, his power was limited to the metropolis, and extended not to the remainder of the empire. His surname of Hadgy, which leads us to suppose he had been at Mecca, was, perhaps, the only circumstance that produced his election, because of the veneration in which the Moors hold those who have performed this pilgrimage. Crowned by the caprice of fortune, this sovereign, having no ideas of government, despised the Moors so much that he confided all his authority to a Jew, as also the collecting of his revenues. This Jew, that he might avenge those humiliations his nation so often had suffered, sometimes abused his power; his will was law, and, without his

his confent, nothing could be tranfacted. The conduct of Crom-El-Hadgy, and his mifplaced confidence, fo offenfive to the prejudices of the Mahometans, made him the contempt of his fubjects; and, after having reigned about feven years, his end was tragical.

Having fallen in love with the daughter of Muley Labes, whofe brother he had murdered, he determined to make her his wife, notwithftanding the fecret averfion in which fhe held him; and this princefs, like another Judith, facrificed him to the public hatred, and her own refentment. After confenting to efpoufe him, fhe gave him wine to drink on the bridal day, in which was a foporific infufion, took this occafion to poniard him, and avenged, by the murder, the blood of her family, which had ftained the throne of the ufurper.

It appears probable that this princefs had a paffion for Muley Shek, the fon of Crom-El-Hadgy, fince fhe fent him intelligence of his father's death, and afterward

ward married him, which, at leaft, highly diminifhed a her pretenfions to generofity, or noblenefs of mind. Muley Shek did not long enjoy royalty, to which he had not the leaft claim; he was dethroned by a new revolution, that placed the reigning family on the throne of Morocco, as we fhall fee in the following book.

BOOK.

BOOK IV.

Sharifs of the reigning family to the accession of Sidy Mahomet — Reign of Muley Sharif, the founder of this Dynasty — Reign of Muley Mahomet — Reign of Muley Arshid — Reign of Muley Ishmael — Reign of Muley Achmet Daiby — Reign of Muley Abdallah.

CHAP. I.

Muley Ali brought from Mecca; held in veneration, and called, by distinction, Muley Sharif. Reigns peaceably.

WHEN we attentively consider the present situation of Africa, and all the changes that have happened on its northern boundaries for a succession of ages, we are led to imagine it was destined by Providence ever to remain the theatre of great revolutions; and those which have ravaged the empire of Morocco, since the introduction of Mahometanism, seem to have been still more fermented by this religion.

After

After the Arabs had subdued the northern coast of Africa, we beheld Edris, the descendant of Mahomet, fly from Medina to its western boundaries, as to the further end of the world, to escape tyranny and persecution. The Moors, who inhabited the mountains where he fixed his abode, edified by his virtues, eagerly embraced his religion; and, respecting his birth, they still further claimed him as their sovereign. By some inexplicable contradiction, Edris, a humane and just prince, the enemy of wars and devastations, became the founder of an empire ever in commotion; and the first acts of a rustic, restless, and ferocious people, were homages paid to virtue.

Mahometanism, which, by the nature of its customs and institutions, must ever be most successful in hot climates, made such a rapid progress, in Africa, that it there invariably stamped the character of despotism, which was the basis on which it first rose, and which, prodigally bestowing on the sovereign unbounded authority, inspires only fear and despondency in the subject.
The

The Moors, more susceptible of fanaticism than any other people, because they are more ignorant, and because the heat of the climate more suddenly inflames their imagination, presently saw those different sects sprout up, that pride and superstition have multiplied, and that, sometimes under the veil of excessive austerity, at others assuming the mask of indulgence and reformation, seduce the mind, over which they alternately domineer. Then is religion the cloak of ambitious conquerors, who impose upon an ever fickle, turbulent, ignorant, and fanatical multitude. Thus has the northern part of Africa, the prey of credulity, oppression, and despotism, successively groaned under an army of usurpers, and changed the master almost with the moment.

The Empire of Morocco, which, in the thirteenth century, under Jacob Almonsor, had acquired an extent of power scarcely credible, lost this power with equal rapidity, because that those passions, which actuate kings, and raise insurrections among the people, neceſſarily bring on the fall of empires, that only proſper under the protection of certain and fixed laws, and want baſis and ſupport where the government is arbitrary.

Having taken a retroſpect of this empire, overturned by a ſucceſſion of crimes, originating in the ambition of uſurpers and the reſtleſſneſs of the people, we ſhall now ſee it, under the reigning houſe, acquire a kind of conſiſtency by the aid of devaſtation and ferocity, which ſtill are much more proper to overthrow than to raiſe up empires; yet have not theſe violent concuſſions ſhaken the throne of Morocco; nay, its foundation ſeems to have been further ſecured, in proportion as it has been cemented by blood. Equally the inſtruments and the victims of tyranny, ever divided by prejudice and hatred, the Moors know not how to make one ſtep toward liberty. Confirmed in their belief of irrevocable fate, which impoſes upon and over-awes their minds, they only behold, in the will and caprice of a never-ſatisfied deſpot, the eternal decrees of that Divinity whoſe

whose image and oracle he is supposed. Thus, by prejudice consecrated to slavery, these people never can change their condition, whatever may be the example of revolution, the progress of reason, or the power of time. Reason, indeed, can make no progress in an arbitrary and ever absolute government, where tyranny and violence present incessant barriers. Their government resembles the brambles of their deserts, which stifle, in their first growth, those genial plants that only flourish by care and culture.

After the extinction of the family of the Sharifs, who had dethroned the house of Merini, and who afterward fell themselves the victims of their own ambition and perfidy, there were several years of dearth at Tafilet, and these countries underwent all the horrors of famine. The Moors of that province, who then made a pilgrimage to Mecca, brought back a Sharif, named Muley Ali, a descendant of Mahomet, born at the town of Yambo, near Medina, whom the people treated with the utmost respect

respect. According to Moorish tradition, the palm trees bore no fruit before the arrival of the Sharif. Seasons having returned to their former course, the harvests became so abundant that the simple and superstitious people of the country attributed a change so miraculous to the presence and religion of the Sharif. All the Moors of the Morocco states, discouraged as they had been by the devastations which had afflicted the empire, and wondering at so happy a return of plenty, easily believed Providence had sent them Muley Ali, to bring their calamities to a period, and this prince, on whom they had bestowed the name of Muley Sharif, as a title of distinction, was proclaimed king of Tafilet. The remaining provinces of the empire proclaimed him also, except Morocco, and its environs, which were then in the power of Crom-El-Hadgy.

The last of the sons of Muley Sidan having been destroyed by that usurper, the princes of the ancient families, who had governed the empire, were all extinct.

Muley

Muley Sharif, therefore, king of Tafilet, was, by the rights of birth, of religion, and the public wish, the legitimate sovereign.

The Dynasty acquired the surname of Fileli, derived from Tafilet, from this prince, whose posterity was so numerous that he is said to have had eighty-four sons, and a still greater number of daughters; those of his male children, who have been most known to history, are Muley Mohamet, Muley-Quiber, Muley-Haran, Muley-Meheres, Muley-Arshid, and Muley-Ishmael-Semein. The first and the two last have reigned in succession; the latter, sons of a Negroefs, distinguished their reign by some warlike actions, but much more by a continuation of tyranny and cruelty that degrade humanity.

The veneration in which the people held Muley Sharif was the most certain pledge of their fidelity, and he had no need of the aid of armies to make his power respected; he therefore remained at Tafilet,

filet, without shewing himself throughout his empire; and the provinces, exhausted by the divisions with which they had been scourged during the preceding reigns, were governed with equity, by those rulers to whom they were assigned by the monarch.

We perceive, notwithstanding, that most of the Shaiks of 'the tribes, distributed among the mountains, silently profited by the troubles which divided the empire, the advantages of situation, the propensity of the People, the distance of the Court, and the indolence of the Emperor, to extend their own authority. This authority would, at length, have become acknowledged, and hereditary in their families, had not the ambition and barbarous policy of Muley Arshid stopped its progress.

Muley Sharif reigned some years, undisturbed by the wavering temper of his subjects, to make whom happy he had dedicated his life. His death was highly regretted,

gretted, and Muley Mohamet, his eldeſt ſon, who gave hopes of virtues equal to his father's, aſcended the throne, and was unanimouſly proclaimed.

CHAP. II.

Accession of Muley Mohamet. Rebellions and stratagems of Muley Arshid.

MULEY Mohamet peaceably reigned at Tafilet, after his father's example, when a rebellion was raised by his brother Muley Arshid. This prince, intelligent, but ambitious and bloody, knowing the inconstancy of the Moors, projected a division of the empire, and again exposed it to revolutions similar to those by which it had been so long distracted. Retiring toward Dara, he presently found himself at the head of a numerous party; but Muley Mohamet expeditiously followed him with a body of cavalry, seized and threw him into prison, and inflicted exemplary punishment on the rebels.

Muley Arſhid having eſcaped, and been retaken, he was guarded with greater precaution; but, by the aid of a negro ſlave, appropriated to ſerve him, and who alone had the liberty of ſeeing him, he effected a breach through the tower, in which he was ſhut up, and, during night, was delivered from his dungeon. The faithful ſlave, after procuring liberty for his maſter, and having prepared horſes for flight, while ſtooping to put on the ſpurs of Muley Arſhid, was cloven down by the inhuman monſter who thought only of his own ſafety.

This black ingratitude, the reward of the labours and fidelity of a ſlave, was alſo the ſignal of new calamities, by which the empire was afflicted. Muley Arſhid haſtily fled to the mountains of Shavoya, eaſt of Temſena, and, without diſcovering himſelf, went and offered his ſervices to Sidi-Mahomet Ben-Buker, who there was abſolute, and held in veneration for his holineſs. Arſhid, diſſembling his birth and projects, ſerved as a common ſoldier, and

and gained his master's confidence by his zeal and fidelity.

Some Moors of Tafilet having discovered this prince in the market, the sons of Ben-Buker took offence, and Muley Arshid thought proper to fly, went to Quiviana, in the mountains of Rif, and offered his services to Ali-Soliman. This prince, who reigned as sovereign, remarking his abilities, soon confided to him the administration of his domains. Arshid behaved with so much art, and dissimulation, that he obtained the unlimited confidence, both of prince and people. Going to visit the states dependent on Ali-Soliman, Arshid, under the pretence of restoring order, raised contributions there, took possession of some castles, cut off the governors, whom he accused of malversation, and distributed the wealth he had acquired among his soldiers.

He next proceeded into a district, called the mountain of the Jew, because a Jew governed there, and because the Brebes, whom he had subjected to his laws, respected

spected him as their sovereign. After spreading terror through the country, he massacred the Jew as unworthy of commanding Mahometans, seized on his wealth, and rewarded his troops.

Muley Arshid, having gained the confidence of his soldiers, whose numbers were augmented by his courage, generosity, and ambition, he declared to them whom he was, no longer concealed the plan he had formed, but promised to subdue the country, and give it a new Lord, if they would second his endeavours, and partake his fortune and fate. The proposition was accepted by all the chiefs of the mountains, who, induced by his valour and generosity, swore fidelity, and acknowledged him their master.

The Shaik, Ali-Soliman, informed of the perfidious conduct of Arshid, marched to give him battle, before his party was further strengthened. The daring Arshid waited his approach, and so artfully spread the rumour of his liberality that most of the soldiers of the Shaik abandoned him, and

and deserted to Muley Arshid. Soliman was himself delivered up to this prince, who brought him prisoner to Quiviana, that he might get possession of his treasures, menacing him with death if he did not discover them with the utmost exactitude. Abandoned by his troops, and beholding himself in the power of a perfidious and furious man, Ali-Soliman did not hesitate to give up all his concealed riches; but Muley Arshid, regardless of his promise, put him to death, thus to confirm his own authority.

The conqueror then called his soldiers, and said to them: " However precious " these metals may be, a prince, who " buries them in the earth, deserves not to " reign. Come, my friends, and divide " with me what you have merited by " your activity and affection." The gold he kept, that it might be of after service; but he gave all the silver to the officers, that they might distribute it among the soldiers.

The fame of Muley Arſhid was extended by this conduct, and was an irreſiſtible recommendation among the Mooriſh tribes. Covetous, poor, and rendered vile by oppreſſion, they forgot the perfidy of a traitor, who had robbed his benefactor of dominion, and afterward of life, remembering thoſe proofs of generoſity by which their avarice was provoked. Muley Mohamet, king of Tafilet, alarmed at this propenſity of the people, in his brother's favour, endeavoured to ſtop his progreſs, and marched with an intent to meet and give him battle. Their armies approached each other among the mountains; and that of Muley Mohamet, twice thrown in diſorder, was at laſt obliged to fly. Muley Arſhid continued the purſuit as far as Tafilet, where Muley Mohamet had ſhut himſelf up, and to which place the former laid ſiege. The king, intimidated by his brother's courage, and ſtill more by his ferocity, fell ill, and died, a few days after, in 1664.

CHAP.

CHAP. III.

Reign of Muley Arſhid; his politic liberality; conqueſts; barbarities and accidental death.

THE city of Tafilet was ſoon taken, after the death of Muley Mohamet; the face of the whole empire was changed, and Muley Arſhid made the neceſſary difpoſitions to maintain his fovereignty. He entered the province of Rif, which he poſſeſſed himſelf of, as likewiſe of the city of Teza, where he paſſed the winter. In the ſpring of 1665 he marched for Fez, which city, having taken by ſurprize, and ſending for the governor, after having obliged him by torments to declare where his wealth was concealed, put him to death. He attempted the ſame practice with the governor of New Fez, who, acquainted with his

his perfidy, chose rather to expire in torments than to discover where his treasures were concealed, haughtily telling him, he hoped they would become the instruments of destruction to him, and all his posterity.

All the Shaiks of the neighbouring districts, and the governors of cities, who, during the relaxation of government, had erected themselves into petty sovereigns, terrified by the rapid and bloody progress of Muley Arshid, hastened to render him homage, and offer him presents. The Alcaid Looeti, one of the number, had a beautiful daughter, whom Muley Arshid espoused; and the power she obtained over him gave her father, also, an ascendency over this prince, by which Looeti moderated the severity of his decrees.

Desiring to subdue the province of El-Garb, which extends along the western coast, from the mouth of the Strait to Mamora, the king, before he departed, sent for the richest tradesmen of Fez, and commanded each of them to build a house in

the

the new city, in which to lodge his soldiers at his return.

His army now amounted to forty thousand men, and he subdued the people who inhabited the eastern part of the province he had undertaken to conquer. The Alcaid Gailand, a courageous man, who governed in this country, made fruitless efforts to oppose the victor; abandoned by his forces, he was constrained to take refuge in Arzilla, whence he fled by sea to Algiers, that he might escape the wild fury of this prince. The conquest of El-Garb induced the inhabitants of Sallee to make their submission; and, from this city, Muley Arshid sent presents to those Shaiks, of the Shavoya mountains, by whom he was known, that he might there obtain new allies, insomuch that, in two campaigns, Muley Arshid was master of all the north of the empire. He soon departed for the mountains of Shavoya, subduing on his route the Shaiks of different tribes, and seizing on their riches, which he divided among his soldiers. He next invaded the territories of Ben-Buker, under whom he had

had ferved as a common foldier, and who waited for him with an army of mountaineers, intending to give him battle; but this Shaik, abandoned by his troops, was delivered up to Muley Arſhid, who poſſeſſed himſelf of his treaſures, and put him to death.

After thus having cruſhed theſe ſmall riſing principalities, Muley Arſhid paſſed the winter among the mountains, where he reinforced his army by a number of volunteers; he then began to march toward Morocco, in 1667, intending to dethrone Crom-El-Hadgy, who, about this time, had been poniarded by his wife, and had left his ſon, Muley Shaik, the heir of his uſurped domains. The latter, intoxicated by his pleaſures, troubled himſelf little concerning Muley Arſhid, and did not think of defence till the conqueror was at the gates of his city; he then ſallied out with ſome troops, little inured and ill diſpoſed to war, and that, far from fighting in his defence, were each more eager than the other to deſert to Muley Arſhid, and acknowledge him their ſovereign.

Thus abandoned by his troops, Muley Shaik endeavoured to fly into the neighbouring mountains, but was taken and brought to Muley Arſhid, who had him dragged into the city on the fortieth day of his reign, tied to the tail of a mule. The city of Morocco was glad to ſubmit itſelf to Muley Arſhid, having for ſome time been under the government of uſurpers, without name, birth, or abilities; they even requeſted the body of Crom-El-Hadgy might be taken from the ſepulchre of their kings, which was granted; and this corpſe, with that of the Jew, who had commanded under him, and all his family, then living, were burnt, to ſtrike terror into the Jewiſh nation, and teach it no more to interfere in the principal adminiſtration of government.

No ſooner was Muley Arſhid maſter of Morocco, than this monarch, whom I ſhall hereafter call Emperor, his predeceſſors having aſſumed that title, received homage in the metropolis from all the neighbouring tribes. He afterward departed for the eaſtern ſide of Mount Atlas, the frontiers of Tafilet, to fubjugate the inhabitants of that country. Terrified by the rapid fuccefs of his arms, thefe tribes eagerly haftened to pay him fubmiffion. He next marched toward Tarudant, where the people were equally ready to implore his clemency, and fwear fidelity.

Mafter of all the provinces of the empire, this monarch now returned to Morocco, where he made preparations for two new expeditions. The firft of thefe, intended againft Fez, he was himfelf to command, and the other to be fent againft the Shabanets, or Chabanets, who inhabited various vallies near Mount Atlas, his nephew, Muley Achmet, was to conduct.

It would be difficult at prefent to afcertain the origin of this tribe. From the moft ancient accounts, it appears they were the pofterity of more than forty thoufand flaves, male and female, who, during the reign of Jacob Almonfor, and before his time, had been tranfported from Spain to Africa, who had built the extenfive walls of Rabat, and had been employed in various works. To recompence the labour and fidelity of these slaves, Jacob Almonsor determined to grant them their liberty. The principal people of his court remonstrated concerning the danger there would be in setting free so great a number of foreigners, who, having made a conquest of part of the country, might easily return, and vanquish the whole.

Jacob Almonsor had pledged his word for their freedom, and was determined to keep it; he therefore offered them the choice of the province they most would prefer for their abode; and this choice fell on a district among the mountains, which the Brebes were obliged to abandon. This emigration took place during the moon called Shaban; and, according to Moorish tradition, the people were for that reason called Shabanets.

For some generations the descendants of these slaves professed the Christian religion, which they gradually changed for Islamism, having no place of public worship,

ship, and because that most of the men married Mahometan wives. This cast long preserved the reputation of valour, but, confounded with the neighbouring tribes, it has forgotten all remembrance of its origin, which, indeed, would be but a poor recommendation among the Moors, who are much more proud than is imagined of the antiquity and purity of their descent.

Muley Arshid, arriving at Fez in the spring with four thousand horse, summoned, on his arrival, the tradesmen, whom he had commanded to build houses, or barracks, for his soldiers. This order they had neglecting to execute, trusting to the incertitude of human events, and not so suddenly expecting the return of their tyrant. He, enraged, commanded them to be tied to orange trees, and began to massacre them himself with his sabre, when the Alcaid Looeti, his father-in-law, interceded in their behalf, obtained their pardon, and prevailed on the Emperor to be satisfied with a fine of thirty quintals of silver, or upward of eight thousand pounds.

The widows of the tradesmen, who had been killed, refusing to pay a part of this contribution, Muley Arshid obliged them by torture, himself presiding, a spectator of their torments*; he would even have had them drowned in the river, after having received their money, had not the Alcaid Looeti obtained a revocation of this order. What are kings, if monsters so execrable are worthy of the title!

During the time that Muley Arshid was thus employed at Fez, Muley Achmet, his nephew, marched to subject the Shabanets, who, at first, obtained some trifling victories; but the prince, having, at length, been entirely succesful, he compelled them to render homage to Muley Arshid.

---

* He had the detestable barbarity to put the breasts of these women between the lid of a coffer, and to get upon it himself, to oblige them to give up their money.

No sooner did the Emperor hear of the resistance these mountaineers made to his troops, than he departed from Fez to encounter them himself; and, although he learnt on his arrival at Morocco that they where subjugated, he determined to proceed. To prove that he applauded their valour, he offered to entertain and treat those among them well who would serve in his armies. This tribe, abounding with valiant men, beheld, with pleasure, the arrival of Muley Arshid, whose warlike deeds they respected: the chiefs among them again paid homage to him personally, and a body of six thousand men followed his fortunes.

Inflated with prosperity, and projecting the conquest of Africa, Muley Arshid entered with his army into the province of Hea; the inhabitants of which, animated by the first efforts of the Shabanets, had resolved to dispute his passage. Discouraged, however, by the defeat and submission of these mountaineers, they went to meet him with rich presents, and brought him

him their young virgins, as vaffals bring up to their lord their firft fruits.

Muley Arfhid received the deputation favourably, and, without abufing his power, fent the maidens back to their parents with prefents.

He then marched toward the Cape of Aguer, or Santa Cruz, where the inhabitants, difperfed among the mountains, determined to take up arms. The Emperor had then about feventy-five thoufand men under his command, all valiant, armed with fabres, maffy-clubs, and arrows. Irritated by the refiftance he found, he gave no quarter to thefe tribes, but feized on all their riches. His feverity fpread terror fo much, throughout the country, that the town of Santa Cruz made its fubmiffion, previous even to his arrival.

Ambition, and the fuccefs of his arms, determined Muley Arfhid to proceed to Illec, the capital town of the principality of Suz, at that time governed by Sidi Ali, a Maa Marabout, held in great veneration throughout thofe diftricts. The Emperor laid fiege to the town, which was unable to refift for want of provifions. Sidy Ali, preffed by the inhabitants, whofe inconftancy he dreaded, faw the town muft be taken; but, defirous of efcaping the cruelty of the conqueror, he and his whole family fled, by night, through a door in his garden, and efcaped, into the province of Sudan, lying to the north of Senegal, where he claimed an afylum, and the protection of the king.

After the departure of Sidy Ali, Illec having opened its gates to Muley Arfhid, he, covetous of glory, and emulous of furmounting difficulties, refolved to pafs into Sudan, and collected the neceffary provifions for the traverfing of the deferts, which feparated thefe countries.

When he came to the frontiers of the fouth with his cavalry, harraffed by fatigue, he found more than a hundred thoufand negroes in arms to difpute his paffage. Unwilling to rifk the chance of
a battle

a battle in a country so barren, and where he had no place of retreat, he sent some Alcaids to the king, to inform him he was not come to make war, but to request he would deliver into his hands the prince of Suz.

The king of Sudan replied, Sidy Ali had fled to him for refuge and protection, consequently he could not deliver him up without violating the laws of hospitality, a crime impossible for him to commit; that, having already been deprived of his states, it was but just to preserve his life; and that he further desired, he, Muley Arshid, would declare, whether he came as as a friend, or an enemy.

Remembering the hazard and peril of his present situation, Muley Arshid dissembled his anger; and, after having assured the king of Sudan his intentions were friendly, marched back toward his own country. On this occasion he prevailed on many negroes to follow him, to whom, treating them with generosity, he confided the guard of the palace.

Having

Having extended his empire from the Straits of Gibraltar to Cape Non, Muley Arſhid beheld himſelf the moſt puiſſant monarch of Africa; he was equally deſirous of being the moſt wealthy, and beſtowed all his attention on the amaſſing of riches. Detachments were ſent throughout the provinces to levy extraordinary contributions, with orders to pillage on the leaſt refuſal.

A Cafile, compoſed of ſeveral tribes, made ſome reſiſtance, and this emperor ſent a detachment thither, with a command to bring him the heads of the rebels. The news of this expedition having occaſioned the greateſt number to fly among the mountains, the old men, women, and children, only remained, who fell the miſerable victims of this abject, this abhorrent decree. Their heads ſent to Fez, and, expoſed round the walls of the city, ſpread terror throughout the empire.

To maſk his barbarity, under a pretence of paying ſome attention to juſtice, for deſpots, as well in Morocco as elſewhere,
think

think it neceſſary thus to colour their capricious cruelties, this Emperor commanded that thoſe who robbed travellers, or granted any aſylum to thieves, ſhould be ſought out, and their families exterminated; further ordering, that each province, and each Douhar, ſhould become reſponſible for the crimes committed within their diſtrict, that, by their watchfulneſs, crimes might be prevented. This ordinance gave the people impréſſions ſomewhat more favourable concerning their ferocious tyrant, and was in itſelf good and uſeful; the roads became ſafe, and the country people could go and come, without danger, to their markets, where they might barter their mutual products.

The law was favourable to the poor, who were much the moſt numerous; but it alſo ſerved to cloak the avidity of the monarch, who, devoured by the thirſt of accumulating gold and ſilver, employed every means his avarice could ſuggeſt to ſtrip the rich and great of their wealth, and thus deprive them of the deſire, or the means, of inſurrection. This maxim,

ſo

so proper in itself to exterminate nations, appears to have become a state system in Morocco, and the devastation of that empire demonstrates what are its wretched consequences.

No longer occupied by projected conquests, Muley Arshid commanded various castles to be built in the provinces of his empire, thereby to give his power stability, and prevent the effects of inconstancy among the people. The small square fort, which stands alone at Rabat, was built for this intent.

The tyrant had now begun to indulge himself in ease, when the sons of his brother Mahomet, king of Tafilet, who had taken refuge among the mountains, entered into a conspiracy there to revenge the death of their father, and to seize on the empire themselves. They had gained over the governor of Old Fez, who had enjoyed their father's confidence, and him they informed by letter of the place where he was to meet and join their forces. This letter they confided to a renegado, recommending him to kill the bearer, that they might be certain of not being difcovered.

The renegado had fome fufpicions, and, inftead of taking the letter to the governor, went and prefented it to the Emperor, who generoufly rewarded his fidelity. The Emperor immediately went to the place appointed, that he might himfelf furprize his nephews; but, underftanding they were betrayed, they took to flight, and efcaped, though fired after by their purfuers; they, however, were overtaken and brought to their uncle, who fent them prifoners to the caftle of Teza, where he commanded them to be put to death.

Having gone into the province of Rif, in the begining of the year 1672, to amufe himfelf with hunting, Muley Arfhid was there informed, that his nephew, Muley Meheres, whom he had left viceroy at Morocco, profiting by his abfence, had taken up arms. The young prince had confided in the Alcaid Abd-Elhafis Araze, whom the Emperor had appointed to watch over his conduct.

conduct. This governor betrayed him, and, that he might do so the more effectually, promised to second his projects.

Muley Meheres proposed that he should go and seize on Saffi, whither he might transport his treasure, and take precautions for safety, in case of ill-success. Abd-Elhafis acquiesced in all the wishes of the prince, and departed sooner than was intended, under the pretext of furthering his designs, which, however, he took the best means to circumvent. After having required the Alcaids of Saffi, and the neighbouring towns, to be watchful for their safety, he repaired with all diligence to the Emperor, and informed him of what had passed.

Little suspicious of this, Muley Meheres departed, during night, for Saffi, where he expected he should meet the Alcaid Abd-Elhafis. Finding, on his arrival, that the town persisted in refusing to grant him admittance, the prince, seeing himself betrayed, took the road for Mazagan, to demand refuge from the Portuguese; but,

being

being informed that the governor of Azamore was in arms to prevent his paſſage, he fled toward Sallee that he might eſcape to Mamora, which was under the dominion of Spain. As he was croſſing the river of Sallee he perceived he was known; he, therefore, took the road toward Fez, that he might avoid raiſing any fuſpicion. He ſoon, however, ſaw he was followed by the horſe of the Alcaid of Sallee, who had orders not to loſe ſight of him; eſcape was now become impoſſible, for, at three quarters of a league from the river, and at the entrance of the foreſt, he encountered the army of the Emperor, who was returning from Rif, and marching in all haſte toword Saffi. Here, therefore, Muley Meheres was arreſted, and gave up his arms. The Emperor, having his nephew in his power, immediately marched to Morocco, that he might prevent any inſurrection in favour of this adventurous prince, who was exceedingly beloved there by the people; but the city having teſtified no inclination to revolt, Muley Arſhid, to recompence the fidelity of the officers, confirmed

firmed them in the places which had been bestowed on them by Muley Meheres.

The Emperor then commanded his nephew to come before him, reproached him for his disloyalty, but, attributing this to his youth and want of proper reflection, ordered him to repair to Tafilet, there to employ himself in the study of the Coran, and in gaining a more perfect knowledge of his duties, as well as in the means of rendering the enterprizes he should in future undertake more succefsful. The feast of sacrifices approached, and, that it might be celebrated with the greater magnificence, Muley Arshid sent for the governors of provinces and cities to be present, according to the custom of that court. On this occasion the Emperor, having drank excessively of wine, in company with some of his confidential friends, a custom to which he was much addicted, took the fancy of mounting his horse, to amuse himself after the manner of the Moors. After prancing about in the allies of his garden, he spurred him forward, as may be well supposed,

suppoſed, with too much ardour, and the horſe ran with him into an alley of orange trees, where he fractured his ſkull, and died three days after, on the twenty ſeventh of March, 1672, in the forty-firſt year of his age.

Of all the Emperors who had governed Morocco, Muley Arſhid was the firſt who had demonſtrated a character natively ferocious; his reign was ſhort, but marked by a ſucceſſion of cruelties, the remembrance of which will not eaſily be loſt: he had ſo far contracted cruelty, by habit, that it was even become one of his amuſements.

An Alcaid, returning from a journey, vaunted of the ſafety of the high roads throughout the empire, which was ſo great that he had ſeen a ſack of walnuts which nobody had taken away. "And " how didſt thou know they were wal- " nuts?" ſaid the Emperor. " I touched " the ſack with my foot," replied the Alcaid. " Sever that foot from his body," continued Muley Arſhid, " as a puniſh- " ment for his curioſity."

I confine

I confine myself to this anecdote, unwilling to afflict the feelings of the humane, by here relating the extravagant and mad actions of a monster. The relation of such events as influence the fate of nations, or the manners of men, are alone absolutely necessary to history.

CHAP. IV.

Muley Ishmael, equal in policy, and cruelty to, and more avaricious than, his predecessors: embassies, rebellions, and sieges, during his reign.

AFTER the death of Muley Arshid, his brother, Muley Haran, in all diligence, began his journey toward Fez, that he might seize upon the public treasury as a certain means of securing empire to himself and soldiers for the defence of his power. Muley Ishmael, however, who was at Teza, and to whom the news was brought by a messenger on a dromedary *,

was

---

* A domedary can travel sixty leagues in a day; his motion is so rapid that the rider is obliged to be girthed to the saddle, and to have a handkerchief before his mouth to break the current of the wind *.

* Reckoning the league at two miles and a half, and the day at twenty-four hours, this is still extraordinary travelling;

was already at Fez, and even proclaimed Emperor before the arrival of his brother. The latter, not daring to enter Fez, went to Tafilet, there to aid his nephew, Muley Achmet, with his advice, that he might make himself master of that part of Morocco where he was beloved. Muley Haran, having formed a party in Tafilet, was acknowledged king; and this was the first division of the empire, after it had been united under Muley Arshid, in consequence of an unnatural mixture of valour, prudence, and blood-thirsty cruelties.

Muley Ishmael, who possessed the same qualities, and still greater vices, than his brother, Muley Arshid, was publicly acknowledged Emperor in the city of Fez. The Alcaid Carra, governor of the city of

---

ling; yet M. Saint Olon, ambassador from Louis XIV. to Muley Ishmael, says, the Moors assured him the Emperor's uncle had travelled a hundred leagues in one day upon a drodary; which account, however, he held to be exaggerated. Perhaps it was upon this occasion that the uncle of Muley Ishmael made such extraordinary haste. T.

St. Olon. Relation de l'Emp. de Mar. p. 24.

Morocco, devoted to Muley Achmet, caufed the gates of the palace, of which he was mafter, to be fhut, and proclaimed Achmet, king of Morocco, at the head of the troops that were under his command. He fent intelligence of his proceedings to the prince, preffing him to come and fecure his election by his prefence.

Muley Achmet immediately departed for Morocco, where he was received moft favourably; he was perfonally beloved, and had alfo married the daughter of Muley Labes, who was born in that city, and who therefore had a claim to the affection of its inhabitants.

Informed of what had happened at Morocco, Muley Ifhmael marched thither with his army in the fpring of 1673, before his nephew had had fufficient time to provide for his fecurity. After paffing the river of the negroes, Muley Ifhmael pitched his camp near the green mountain, to the eaft of the province of Duquella, where he learned that his nephew was encamped within a league

league of the capital. Receiving advice of this, Muley Ishmael struck his tents, and marched within a small distance of his nephew, posting himself in a vast plain, where he immediately made preparation for battle.

The two armies did not long remain idle spectators of each other; fortune, for a time, seemed indecisive; but victory, at length, declared itself in favour of Muley Ishmael, who had the best troops. Little accustomed to gunpowder, the inhabitants of Morocco had retired toward their ramparts, there to wait the event of the battle. A profusion of dust, also in the plain, had occasioned so much confusion that numerous soldiers perished in the canals, dug in the earth, of which they were not aware.

Muley Achmet discovered much courage in this action, and was desirous of defying his uncle to single combat; but, having been wounded by a ball in the thigh, and in danger of being taken, he retired, for momentary respite, to the palace of his brother, Muley Talbe; and, after there having his wound dreſſed, he fled from the city to gain the mountain before the concluſion of the battle.

After Muley Iſhmael had made victory ſure, he entered the caſtle, where he imagined he ſhould have found his nephew: the governor, Carra, informed him, he was fled; and this Emperor, with one ſtroke of his ſabre, ſevered the head of Carra from his body.

Some horſemen, who had gone in purſuit of Muley Achmet, took him, he being betrayed by the ſon of a Shaik, to whom he had fled for aſylum. Aſhamed of his perfidy, the father purſued the horſemen with a detachment, and once more recovered the young prince, who immediately fled to Tafilet.

We behold with veneration, that, in climates like theſe, deſtined to ſlavery, there are mountains which ſerve as barriers to independency, and people, though ferocious and uncultivated, whoſe fidelity is unſhaken toward the wretched fugitives whom they protect.

Muley

Muley Ishmael remained sometime at Morocco to receive homage from the neighbouring tribes and provinces, and then made preparations to march into the north of his empire. Not treating his soldiers with the same generosity as Muley Arshid had done, they at first discovered marks of discontent with the monarch's conduct. The city of Fez, informed of the secret disposition of the soldiers, entered into a conspiracy, the members of which sent a deputation to Tafilet, to desire Muley Achmet would come and put himself at their head.

The city of Teza submitted to this prince, and the troops, that had partook the dangers and difficulties of Muley Ishmael, retired, and deserted from his standard in open day. All the provinces were eager to receive Muley Achmet wherever he approached. The Alcaid Gayland, who had fled from Arzilla under Muley Arshid, informed of these changes and troubles, solicited and obtained aid from the Algerines to recover his property and his government,

vernment, in which he was prefently reinftated at the head of an army.

The old and new cities of Fez, divided in their inclinations and interefts, daily combated each other, the old in behalf of Muley Achmet, the new for Muley Ifhmael; but, as the latter had the beft general, it had alfo the moft influence among the neighbouring tribes.

To prevent the mifchiefs that muft refult from the defection of the provinces, Muley Ifhmael, who had come before Teza, thought proper to raife the fiege, and march with twelve thoufand men, the whole of his remaining forces, to give battle to the Alcaid Gayland, who had encamped near Alcaffar. The Emperor attacked this brave general with fo much intrepidity that he put his forces to flight. Gayland, notwithftanding the rout of his army, fought like a man in defpair; he had four horfes killed under him, and, having received a ball in his body, he fell, at length, the victim of numbers, and his head,

head, carried at the end of a lance, was the most important trophy of victory.

The defeat of this general intimidated the insurgents, who thought proper to submit, beholding fortune declare itself so decidedly for Muley Ishmael. The conqueror pardoned the city of Alcassar; and, after establishing peace in the province of Garb, he marched toward Old Fez, endeavouring, by promises, threats, and every means which policy could suggest, to gain over the inhabitants. Embarrassed and undecided how to act, the citizens assembled in the mosque, where, following the counsel, and assisted by the good offices of Sidi Abdelcader Fessi, a person held in veneration, and whom they supposed could penetrate the secrets of futurity, they resolved to implore the clemency of Muley Ishmael. Neither, however, confiding in the faith of this Emperor, nor in all the promises he gave, they demanded that he should solemnly make oath on the body of his brother, which had been transported from Morocco to Fez, there to be entombed.

Muley

Muley Ifhmael having concurred with every requifition of the citizens, the deputies repaired to his palace, where, proftrating themfelves to the earth, they fupplicated pardon for the paft. The Emperor raifed, embraced them all, and, after hearing every thing Sidi Abdelcader Fefli had to fay, he took him by the hand, proceeded with him to the fepulchre of his brother, and there folemnly fwore peace, according to the conditions demanded by the deputies: the joyful people again returned to caft themfelves at the feet of the monarch, and thanked him anew; after which, each man went quietly back to his houfe.

Muley Ifhmael took advantage of this momentary fecurity, cunningly, and without tumult, to fend foldiers into the houfes of the city, and feize on the arms of the inhabitants. This was done with fo much fecrefy, and dexterity, that no individual fufpected what had happened to his next-door neighbour. The Emperor remained two months longer at Fez, where he diftributed money among the troops, and thus gained their affection.

In the beginning of 1674 Muley Ishmael went to encounter his nephew, Muley Achmet, who was encamped at no great distance from Fez. Being come in sight of each other, the armies were obliged to remain inactive for some time, because of the rains that fell; each party likewise hoped to vanquish the other by stratagem. This suspence was favourable to Muley Ishmael, who beheld a part of his nephew's troops, discouraged by the ill-fortune of the latter, desert to his army. Muley Achmet, at length, retreated, and took refuge in the province of Dara, there to wait a more fovourable opportunity of once more appearing in arms.

Muley Ishmael, having returned to Fez, distributed money among his soldiers, and marched toward the southern provinces, there to re-establish tranquillity, and relieve the city of Morocco, which was all but besieged by the mountaineers. The latter, informed of the approach of the Emperor, retired to their mountains, and the monarch continued his march to Morocco,

rocco, where he was received with demonstrations of joy.

After a temporary repose, Muley Ishmael proceeded to the province of Hea, where he levied heavy contributions. He next turned his march toward Mount Atlas, subjected the Shabanets, and put numbers of them to death by torture. He thence departed into the province of Shavoya, where the people obstinately refused to pay tribute. These mountaineers, intrenched in their vallies, and behind trees that they had felled, rendered all the efforts of Muley Ishmael for a time fruitless; at length, one of his generals marching round the mountain with four thousand horse to put them between two fires, they, seeing themselves thus surrounded, took to flight, and abandoned their wives and children, who were put to the sword; the plunder, which was very considerable, was distributed among the soldiers.

After this expedition, which, in its circumstances, greatly resembled those of Muley Arshid, Muley Ishmael returned to Fez,

Fez, where he exacted a contribution from the inhabitants of fifty quintals of silver, which he, as a favour, reduced to thirty-three, amounting to two hundred thousand livres (between eight and nine thousand pounds.)

The custom of paying contributions by a determinate weight of silver is very ancient, as we read in Sallust. When Jugurtha, king of Numidia, intreated clemency from Rome, Metellus, who commanded in Africa, first provisionally exacted that he should pay the Romans two hundred thousand pounds weight of silver. The quintal of silver in Morocco, as now understood, is a stated sum of a thousand ducats, amounting to six thousand six hundred livres, although a quintal of coined silver is equal to more than ten thousand livres.

In 1675 an ambassador arrived at the court of Muley Ishmael, from England, who came to demand peace, and who, among his presents, had brought some Moors who had been enslaved. The Emperor,

peror, agreeably to the usual mode and expressions of the court of Morocco, answered, he would act according to his request, and that he should return with satisfaction. At the very moment when the treaty was to be concluded, a Marabout, all in rags, but one of those who are saints by trade, approached the king, and told him, that the Prophet had appeared to him the night before, and had commanded him to inform the Emperor, Mahomet would aid him to vanquish his enemies, if he would not make peace with the English.

The king, pretending to venerate these reveries, kissed the dirty head of the Moor, and informed the ambassador, he was exceedingly sorry he could not make peace with him, for that he durst not incur the wrath of the Prophet. This anecdote perfectly depicts the conduct and instability of the court of Morocco, where the despot never wants a specious pretext to act according to his will, or an excuse for neglecting what he ought to perform, and that which he may have most solemnly promised.

In

In the same year the seeds of insurrection again began to sprout in the southern part of the empire. Muley Achmet, for whom the people still had some predilection, had a momentary hope of ascending the throne. The Moors of Tarudant, and some tribes of mountaineers, sent him their deputies, swore obedience, and offered to combat under him as their leader.

Confiding in this return of prosperity, the prince expedited a courier to the princess, his wife, who was at Morocco, to inform her of what had passed, and induce her to procure him partisans in the capital. This princess, by her artful and kind behaviour to those women who visited her, so well disposed the minds of the citizens, in her husband's favour, that they promised to receive him into the city, and proclaim him Emperor. Muley Achmet, pre-informed of these events, presented, himself before Morocco; the great were all in his interest, and the common people, impatient under the oppressions of their then governor, were still more desirous of this change

change. To prevent any tumult which might refult from public proclamation, the night prayer was called on the towers of the mofques, and heaven invoked for the prefervation of Muley Achmet; this occafioned it to be fuppofed that the prince was already in the city, and all infurrection was thereby impeded. Muley Achmet entered in reality, followed by a numerous train; and the Alcaid, who governed in the name of Muley Ifhmael, was obliged to retire.

Muley Ifhmael was at this time proceeding toward Sallee, when he heard of the admiffion of Muley Achmet into Morocco. He fent his general, Meffaoot Gerari, with four thoufand horfe and five hundred foot, whom he had felected at Sallee, to threaten the deftruction of their families if they failed in their duty, and waited himfelf for the remainder of his army from Fez. Meffaoot Gerari paffed the river of the negroes with little refiftance. Muley Achmet, who had only collected a few troops to oppofe him on his paffage, had, with the remainder, lain in ambufcade,

and

and fell fo opportunely on the van of the forces of Meffaoot that he totally defeated the general, and obliged him to repafs the river in diforder. Muley Achmet gave a favourable reception to the vanquifhed, and prevailed on many of them to enter into his fervice.

Hearing of the defeat of his general, the Emperor began his march, to come in perfon and attack his nephew. By the treachery of one of his generals, Muley Achmet was perfuaded to return to Morocco, and not march and give battle; it was urged this would but expofe him to the hazard of a defeat, in combating an army which would deftroy itfelf. The army of Muley Ifhmael, in effect, fuffered greatly for want of fubfiftence, the provinces having been laid defolate, and almoft rendered defert by the late fucceffion of civil wars. The Emperor approached but flowly toward Morocco, having been informed by the general, who was in his intereft, that his army was inferior to that of his nephew.

Nor was this incertitude the only difficulty Muley Ishmael had to encounter during the campaign. The comparison which his troops drew, between the character of himself and that of his nephew, was so highly to the favour of the latter, that a conspiracy was formed in his camp; from the consequences of which the Emperor escaped almost by miracle. The principal Alcaids, secretly inclined to favour Muley Achmet, entered into a plot to assassinate the monarch, who even was slightly wounded in the arm by the ball of a musket, which one of the conspirators fired. The guilty, however, were seized, put to death, and their effects confiscated by the Emperor. A few of them only escaped, who entered into the service of Muley Achmet.

The treachery of the general of Muley Achmet having been at this time discovered, by the intelligence the fugitives brought, and various intercepted messages, he was put to death, and his body, after being dragged through the city, was denied the rites of sepulture.

Muley Ishmael, unable to meet his nephew with equal forces, determined to march beside Mount Atlas, and there endeavoured to gain over some tribes to his party. He passed thence toward Santa Cruz, which place had put itself under the government of Muley Achmet. Not daring to entangle himself among the mountains, he could only send letters, hoping, by gentleness and promises, to regain the city.

The inhabitants of Santa Cruz, who were capable of self-defence, and who abhorred Muley Ishmael for his various cruelties, returned his letters unanswered, and even commanded the messengers to inform him of the imprecations they uttered on his head. Obliged to dissemble his resentment, the Emperor retreated, again marching beside the mountains, to wait some fit opportunity of surprizing the enemy.

His march was attended with unexpected success; his nephew, having supposed him at the distance of seven days journey from Morocco, had sent a part of his forces,

forces, confisting of husbandmen, to gather in the harvest, and remained only with a few soldiers. Muley Ishmael, informed of this, suddenly advanced, and came and pitched his camp within a day's march of Morocco. Muley Achmet hastily assembled the husbandmen of the environs, and, finding himself at the head of twenty-eight thousand men, pitched his camp without the walls of the city.

Muley Ishmael approached the camp of his nephew, where he two days remained, observing the enemy's motions, hoping that the soldiers of Muley Achmet would desert, as the intelligence of some fugitives had led him to suppose. Desirous of coming to action, Muley Achmet made a motion with his army, and Muley Ishmael then began the attack. The nephew, who had made this manœuvre purposely to bring on a battle, fought with so much valour that he routed the forces of Muley Ishmael, who lost more than three thousand men.

Muley

Muley Achmet, now master of the field of battle, had not the prudence to profit by victory; instead of pursuing the retreating enemy, his army was employed in rejoicings, which gave Muley Ishmael time to rally his troops, and come to a second action, in which victory declared in his favour. The forces of his nephew, who little expected again to be attacked so suddenly, were entirely routed, and the prince, obliged to re-enter Morocco, precipitately abandoned a part of his army, which miserably perished.

Muley Ishmael then thought proper to blockade the capital, but the sallies which Muley Achmet occasionally made obliged him not to approach too near; a greater misfortune for him still was that, his army not being sufficiently numerous totally to circumvent the city, it received supplies with facility, while Muley Ishmael was himself in want, because of the detestation in which he was held by the neighbouring people.

Wearied by the length of the fiege, Muley Ifhmael made propofitions of peace to his nephew, offering him the vice royalty of Morocco in perpetuity; but the youthful prince, full of courage, proud of paſt fuccefs, and ſtill prouder of the fidelity of his foldiers, haughtily anfwered, that he who thrice had been a king never ſhould confent to become a fubject, and that it would be his glory to defend fovereignty by feats of arms.

Muley Ifhmael next propofed an interview with him in a neighbouring fanctuary, whither each of them was to repair, accompanied by ten perfons. Muley Achmet confented, and was the firſt at the appointed hofpitium. Muley Ifhmael came, but with perfidious intents; he had commanded a detachment of cavalry to come to his aid, and carry off his nephew.

The interview began by mutual compliments. Muley Ifhmael purpofely endeavoured to lengthen the conference, that he might obtain time for the arrival of his horfe;

horse; but one of the attendants of Muley Achmet, who was upon the watch, perceiving a cloud of dust at a distance, related his suspicions to his master, and the young prince accordingly mounted his horse, and reproached his uncle with cowardice and treachery. Less irritated by this just obloquy than by the failure of the plot he had contrived, Muley Ishmael returned to his camp, where he vented his wrath against the soldiers; a great number of whom forsook him, and went over to Muley Achmet.

Muley Ishmael attempted once more to cut short this protracted siege, by keeping spies in the city of Morocco, and making preparations to scale the city walls with a small detachment, which was to render itself master of one of the gates. The project, however, failed; some of the most determined assailants arrived safely on the walls; but, having been there encountered by the customary patrole, and unable to descend, because that the scaling ladders were taken away, they were cut in pieces.

Muley

Muley Achmet profited by this lesson, and resolved to employ none but those soldiers of whose fidelity he was well assured, in guarding the out-works. He also forbade the inhabitants to assemble, and cut off a number of the Sharifs who were in the city, and who had acted as spies for Muley Ishmael.

The besieged continued to make some sallies, which equally enfeebled both parties. Muley Achmet would himself have been taken by the generals of his uncle, had they not been most fortunately killed by the cannon of the city, at the very moment when it was impossible he should have escaped. Muley Ishmael lost on this occasion his general, Messaoot Gerari, and a confidential Alcaid.

To the length of this siege, and the incertitude of success, was added a still greater cause of vexation; the Emperor had no means of gratifying his troops, that, for sometime past, had received no pay. To extricate himself from this difficulty, in 1677, he invited the Shaik Sidi Semagh, Alcaid of the mountains of Tedla, to come and pay him a visit; the monarch made him eat with himself, flattered, caressed him, gave him hopes of a still better government, and intreated he would lend him a sum to pay his forces.

Vain of the distinguished manner in which he was treated, and the benevolent intentions of the Emperor, the Shaik sent to his government, and ordered a present of six hundred negroes, of both sexes, eight hundred horses, a thousand camels, four hundred mules and twenty-five quintals of silver, amounting to a hundred and sixty thousand livres *, (or upward of six thousand six hundred pounds), which he intreated the monarch would accept. Muley Ishmael was astonished at the magnificence of the gift; it led him to suppose that this Shaik was still possessed of greater wealth, and, listening

---

* Twenty-five quintals of silver, according to the former and following estimates of the author, are but a hundred thousand livres; the sum of sixty thousand livres, therefore, is either appropriated to the remainder of the present to which it is apparently inadequate, or there is an error of the press. T.

only to his avidity, he arrested him, under the pretence that he intended to revolt, and six months after had him beheaded, having first seized on all his possessions, which, indeed, was the only crime of which he could be accused.

Other Shaiks, coming likewise to visit Muley Ishmael with very considerable presents, met a like favourable reception; but, terrified by the capricious conduct of the Emperor toward the Shaik of Tedla, they knew not how to interpret all the politeness he testified; a thousand times they reiterated their protestations of fidelity, which served but to discover the secret dread by which they were tormented. Artful and treacherous in his nature, Muley Ishmael turned this embarrassment, which the Shaiks, by their conduct, made visible, to his own profit, and exacted from them a hundred and fifty quintals of silver, or a million of livres (upward of forty-one thousand pounds), a number of sheep, oxen, horses, camels, and a thousand negroes, of both sexes. The governors did not fail to raise

this

this contribution, and esteemed themselves happy in having escaped so well.

Similar extortions, and certain homages, which were voluntarily paid, by some tribes, to the Emperor, enabled him to maintain his army before Morocco, without, however, empowering him to take the city. Muley Achmet, on the contrary, blockaded as he was, found himself exposed to the want of succour, when a happy incident relieved them both from their perplexity.

Muley Haran, king of Tafilet, the brother of Muley Ishmael, uncle and father-in-law to Muley Achmet, beheld with regret these two princes at war with each other, and determined to repair to Morocco, in the hope of being able once more to establish concord. This Sharif was exceedingly well received by Muley Ishmael, whom he promised, a few days after, to enter the city of Morocco, which he accordingly did, and where Muley Achmet received him with all kindness.

Muley

Muley Haran took infinite trouble to pacify his brother and nephew, and, by his repeated efforts with them individually, he, at length, accomplished his wished-for purpose; a treaty was concluded, in which it was stipulated that Muley Achmet should preserve the title of king, but retire to Dara, the sovereignty of which he should possess, that the soldiers attached to this prince should be permitted to leave Morocco, and follow him with arms and baggage, and that Muley Ishmael should pardon the city of Morocco, with each and all of its inhabitants, without entering into any enquiries concerning the origin of, or persons concerned in, this war; to which were added, other articles of reciprocal security.

Muley Achmet, not having consulted the citizens of Morocco concerning this treaty, left the place by night, with all his effects and equipage, and accompanied by the most faithful of his troops, under the pretence of going on some secret expedition.

Informed

Informed on the morrow of the peace concluded between Muley Ifhmael and his nephew, the inhabitants of Morocco were in the utmoſt alarm; the Talbes were deputed by the city, followed by all the children, and preceded by white flags, to implore mercy from the Emperor, who apparently granted them pardon.

The Emperor entered the city, in company with his brother Muley Haran; after which he viſited the caſtle, and there, perceiving that the magazine ſcarcely contained proviſions ſufficient for a week, he tore his beard up by the roots in his rage, accuſed Muley Haran, his brother, of treachery, cauſed him to be ſeized in his camp, and ſent one of his generals with a large detachment to deprive him of his kingdom of Tafilet. He afterward ſuffered his troops to enter the city, permitted them to pillage, and commit all kinds of licentiouſneſs, and perſonally practiſed every violence, which his own barbarity could inſpire, againſt the principal inhabitants, without reſpect to his word, his treaty, or the faith

of

of that capitulation, on which the city had been yielded.

The actions of Muley Ifhmael can only be recollected with horror; his art, his cunning, his falfehood, his contradictions, and all the defpicable means he employed to accomplifh his defires, betokened a mean foul, incapable of elevation, and by nature ignoble.

Scarcely had he reduced Morocco before he received advice of an infurrection, which had fuddenly broken out in the province of Shavoya, and the neighbourhood of Mequinez. The arrival of Mahomet El-Hadgy-Ben-Abdallah, one of the fons of the Alcaid Ben-Buker, who governed this country during the reign of Muley Arfhid, gave occafion to this revolt. The Shaik, after making a long abode at Mecca, had journied to Conftantinople, there to folicit protection from the Grand Signior, who, accordingly, had commanded the divan of Algiers to grant him fuccours.

Mahomet

Mahomet El-Hadgy was received in his domains with tranſports of joy; ſo great was the degree of reſpect that he acquired, among the tribes ſcattered over the mountains, that Muley Iſhmael, conceiving the danger to be conſiderable, ſent various detachments, firſt, and afterward marched himſelf, with the remainder of his army. Mahomet El-Hadgy, having more than ſixty thouſand men under his command, little, it is true, inured to war, made the neceſſary diſpoſitions to encounter Muley Iſhmael, who was marching to give him battle.

Arrived at the foot of the mountain with ſome artillery, the Emperor ſo diſpoſed his cavalry that it might attack the enemy when retreating. His troops received the diſcharge of muſketry, arrows, and ſlings, of this ill-diſciplined army; to which Muley Iſhmael replied by an exploſion from a battery of ten cannon, loaded with balls, which made the inſurgents give ground; the cavalry had time to eſcape, but the infantry, being ſurrounded, was moſt of it put to the ſword;

sword; the Emperor pursued the cavalry with a detachment for three days, and put all to death who fell into his power.

On his return to the camp, he fell sword in hand upon the women and children, and sent ten thousand heads to Fez and Morocco to be fixed upon the walls of those cities, thereby to announce his victory, and spread terror throughout the whole empire.

Having thus terminated, by events as fortunate as they were inhuman and detestable, a war, which had endured three years, Muley Ishmael repaired to Mequinez, there to enjoy repose. During his absence, the vast palace he had begun had been finished, in which he displayed the utmost magnificence. On his entrance into this palace, he received visits from all the grandees of his kingdom, who eagerly came to make him rich presents.

In full enjoyment, at length, of all the sweets of ease, and voluptuousness of vice, the Emperor indulged himself in the native affections of his temperament, and the impulse

pulse of his character. That he might add to the variety of his pleasures, he daily augmented the number of his concubines; he kept a nursery of slaves, ever agitated by fear, and whom he ill-treated, or cut off, on the slightest pretext. The domestics of his palace, and those Christian slaves whom the fate of arms delivered over to the power of his Corsairs, underwent a similar treatment.

Wholly regardless of the lives of men, this Emperor made it his pastime to assassinate them with his own hand. The days set apart for prayer were generally dedicated by him to these massacres, and thus did he estimate his sacrilegious devotion by the number of his murders.

Turn we our eyes from acts so horrid, at which nature shudders; the relation of them is to be found in so many books that it would be superfluous, here, to add new testimonies of the barbarities of tyranny and despotism.

Afflicted as it had been by a succession of devastations, the empire of Morocco, in 1678, had still new to encounter; the plague, which had been introduced by the communication between Algiers and Tetuan, made dreadful ravages; there are narratives that say this contagion swept away more than four million of people from the empire, which, to me, appears, indeed, very extraordinary. This dreadful scourge of man, the sacrifices which Muley Arshid and Muley Ishmael made to their ambition, their avarice, and wild ferocity; the revolutions which succeeded under Muley Abdallah, and the various other calamities which, beneath a government so arbitrary, continue to destroy the human race, are so many physical and moral causes that account for the present depopulation of the empire.

Notwithstanding the progress of the contagion, which spread still more fatally in the northern parts, the Alcaids of the environs of Tangiers made various attempts on that town, which, at that time, was under the dominion of England. The Alcaid of Alcassar, Amar-Hadoo, in the month of March,

March, made himself master of two small advanced forts, in which he surprized twenty soldiers, and seized a single brass cannon, on which was the arms of Portugal.

Conducted to Mequinez with much pomp, and displayed as a trophy, Muley Ishmael himself left the city, attended by a numerous train, to go and receive this cannon. Thrice he prostrated himself to earth, thanking God for the first victory he had gained over the Christians. The Alcaid, Amar Hadoo, was made viceroy of the province of Garb.

This same year the Emperor determined to leave Mequinez; the plague committed its ravages in the environs of the city, and he himself was inwardly devoured by that spirit of inquietude which was irreconcilable to so long a repose. He went to pass the hot season among the mountains, in the neighbourhood of Atlas, on the banks of the Mulluvia, whence he sent to demand contributions from the neighbouring Brebes. These mountaineers, favoured as they were by by situation, refused to obey the commands of the Emperor; and he, finding himself unable to subject them by force of arms, dissembled his resentment, and thought proper to rest satisfied with such tribute as they should think proper to pay.

About this time there was an insurrection at Tafilet, which was raised by Muley Haran, the brother of the Emperor, whom he had stripped of sovereign power. Muley Ishmael, having repaired thither, routed the insurgents, and restored tranquillity to that part of his empire. Toward the end of the year, leaving Tafilet, he marched beside Mount Atlas to exact contributions from the Brebes, who were dispersed among the mountains. The tribes that were unable to oppose him by force of arms submitted, and paid what he required; but those that, by their situation, were able to resist him, opposed his will with so much resolution that the Emperor was, not only obliged to renounce his enterprize, but, endeavour to make them his friends, promising to leave them in tranquillity.

This solemn promise was guaranteed by the sacrifice of a camel, slain at the foot of the mountain, as a pledge of the faith of Muley Ishmael. Thus secured, the chiefs left their mountains to salute the Emperor, and offer him their presents; and they, also, in turn, received presents on his part. These people hold such kind of sacrifices in so much reverence that it is the attestation of mutual confidence, which is employed as a means to calm the anger of the monarch; or make peace, when any cause of rancour exists among themselves.

Although it is customary among the Moors to offer up sacrifices to God, in gratitude for favours bestowed, and afterward to distribute the animals thus sacrificed among the poor, I do not think such oblations ought to be confounded with the sacrifice performed on this occasion by Muley Ishmael, and which often are offered up by the different Moorish tribes to calm or dispel their intestine quarrels. Such sacrifices should, I apprehend, be considered as solemn vows, which are not to be violated: this is a custom made sacred by ages, known in times

times more remote than the birth of Mahometanism, and, perhaps, peculiar to the nations of Africa. From Livy we learn that Hannibal, on the eve of giving battle to Scipio, on the banks of the Po, after making many promises to the soldiers of his army, to encourage them to fight valorously, took a lamb, and intreated Jupiter and the heavenly deities, that, should he break his promise, he might himself perish, as that lamb was about to perish. The soldiers, adds the historian, received the promised hope, as if it had been sent from the Gods themselves *.

The valour with which these mountaineers had first resisted Muley Ishmael inspired all the people of the neighbourhood with courage, which, however, could not make him desist. Impelled by the hope of booty, he rashly entered among the mountains, without sufficiently foreseeing all the dangers of the enterprize. Endeavouring to terrify these Brebes, who lived in brutal

* Liv. lib. XXI.

ignorance, he threatened he would give them to the Chriſtians to eat alive, of whom they had formed fanciful and monſtrous pictures; but this terror had little effect, when they beheld, as they themſelves ſaid, that a Chriſtian had the head, the body, the arms, and the legs, of a man.

The army of the Emperor was detained among the mountains by ſnow, which had cloſed up the roads, and might have expoſed it to periſh with famine. However, he opened himſelf paſſages among theſe precipices, and abandoned his camp to a detachment, which, that it might not miſerably periſh with cold and hunger, afterward abandoned it alſo. In this campaign, Muley Iſhmael loſt about three thouſand tents, the wealth that he had amaſſed, and a part of his army, the rear guard of which was harraſſed by the mountaineers, who took the baggage.

Having gained the plain of Morocco, the Emperor there was joined by the Baſhaw Seroni, who waited for him at the head of the troops of that province. This reinforcement

ment so far recruited his army that he was enabled to grant repose to the soldiers, who had escaped this unfortunate expedition.

Humbled by his imprudence, Muley Ishmael slowly returned toward Mequinez, and put to death his Visir, Abdaraman Fileli. Abusing the power committed to him by the monarch, this minister had indulged himself, during the absence of Ishmael, in every kind of prevarication, violating the most sacred rights, without respecting even the wives of the principal Moors, who accused him publicly in person. After breaking the arm of this man with a pistol shot, Muley Ishmael commanded him to be dragged through his camp, sewed up in the hide of an ox.

All the persons in the train of this visir were put to death, as accomplices of his extortions, and the abuse of his authority, during the absence of the Emperor. This severity, which presents a picture of the violence of arbitrary government, was, perhaps, equally criminal on the part of the prince

prince with the guilty acts his vifir had committed.

Here it is proper to obferve that the monarchs of Morocco, defirous to imitate the Ottoman court, have fometimes had vifirs; but fuch eminent fituations, in this empire, have neither the fame fplendor nor the fame power as thofe at Conftantinople. Authority cannot be delegated, except when it is founded on rational principles, which it is not in a government truely and abfolutely defpotic, where each act depends on the arbitrary will of one man. A vifir, of Morocco, is called by the fame title occafionally there as in Turkey; but equal puiffance he never can enjoy.

Muley Ifhmael arrived at Mequinez at the feaft of facrifices, whither he had convoked all the grandees, who haftened to bring him prefents; for, at that court, the vifit and the prefent are not only paid together, but, it is, in fome meafure, admiffible to delay the vifit, provided care is taken only to fend the prefent.

The

The ambitious projects of Muley Ishmael, and the various difficulties he had to encounter in the beginning of his reign, made him suppose the necessity of maintaining a body of confidential troops; he therefore conceived the project of forming a corps of negro soldiers, that should immediately be under his command. To accomplish this the more quickly, exclusive of the negroes that Muley Arshid already had collected, he purchased himself a great number of blacks, male and female, and accustomed his grandees to send them as presents.

After marrying and setting apart territories for their habitations, he gave a degree of stability to this generation of slaves, educated them in the Mahometan religion, accustomed them to the use of arms, and made soldiers of them, who became formidable to the natives. A monarch so absolute, and so capricious, as was Muley Ishmael, had good reason to fear the fickleness and discontent of his enslaved subjects, whom his violent conduct must continually render liable to revolt, and who could not be kept

peaceable

peaceable but by overawing them with troops, whose interest should also be the interest of the despot.

In this precise situation were the negroes. They were despised by the Moors, as well because of the prejudice entertained concerning their colour, which the white men have every where consigned to slavery, as because of the idolatrous worship they maintained*. They also were foreigners. While fighting for the glory of their master, they fulfilled their military duty, and at the same time took vengeance for the hatred in which they were held by the Moors. By this artful policy, and the rivalship which Muley Ishmael knew how to raise between his soldiers and his subjects, this monarch found the means of holding in subjection, during a long reign, all the provinces of an empire accustomed to a change of masters, and which otherwise

---

* The negroes adore the Sun, and even mingle this adoration with Mahometanism; although this, of all errors, is the most pardonable, the Moors do not the less regard it as idolatrous.

the barbarity of the prince muft foon or late have obliged to rebel.

After having exercifed his negroes in military dicipline, the Emperor, that he might add to the ftrength of men the power of fuperftition, confecrated them, with ceremony, to the profperity of religion. Following the example of the Sultan Amurath, who, when he formed the corps of Janizaries, fent them to Hadgy Bectafch *, that he might beftow his benediction on them, Muley Ifhmael appointed his negroes as a patron, and the fignal of rallying, Sidi Boccari, one of the commentators of the Koran, on which book he made them take the oath of allegiance. This book, from that time, was, and is ftill, carried refpectfully in the army. It is depofited in a diftinguifhed tent, placed in the centre of the camp, as the image of their worfhip, and the pledge of their fidelity.

* Hadgi Bectafch, a Saint, in eftimation among the Turks, and the founder of the Dervifes, cut the fleeve from a felt robe which he wore, that it might ferve as a model for the bonnet of the Janiffaries.

Herbelot Bib. Orien.

Ali

All the troops act under the same auspices, but none, except the blacks, the Ludaya, or other tribes, destined personally to guard the Emperor, obtain the surname of El-Boccari, which is thus meant to signify those soldiers who are immediately in the service of the prince; that is to say, who constitute the standing army. This negro corps, from that time, became the individual guard of Muley Ishmael, nor did he ever find guards more faithful. His successors, though they have made some reforms, have nearly followed the same plan.

After the monarch had quieted those troubles, by which his empire had been distracted, he was seized with a passion for building, and the embellishment of his palace became his amusement. Indulging his own instability of temper, and having in the beginning no fixed plan, what he built one day he would pull down the next, giving himself the plans of the works he would have executed. In dedicating himself to this employment, the barbarian found

more

more frequent occasions of indulging his cruelties; these, indeed, he made his sport.

Christian slaves, or other workmen, employed in executing his commands, often fell the victims of his blood-thirsty caprices. If the bricks they made were found too small, they were broken upon the head of the brickmaker. The workmen all were punished, either by pecuniary mulcts, or by chastisements analogous to their profession. Still further to diversify his amusements, and render his idleness more supportable, he sent for various lions, which he ordered to be enclosed in a park; and to these he occasionally delivered the poor wretches he selected, finding an inhuman pleasure in being a spectator of the combat.

In the beginning of April, 1680, Muley Ishmael, ever the enemy of tranquillity, sent forces, under the Alcaid Amar-Hadoo, to lay siege to Tangiers. This general made himself master of a small fort, garrisoned by forty men, who, finding it impossible they should receive succour from
the

the town, rather chofe to capitulate than to expofe themfelves to perifh, by defending their poſt.

The governor of fort Charles, alfo, perceiving he could not long defend himfelf for want of provifions, determined to abandon this fort, and, with his troops, to reinforce the garrifon of the caftle. Having concerted his retreat with the commander of the caftle, he cut his way through the intrenchments of the Moors. Of feventy men who had garrifoned fort Charles, and had made this defperate fally, about forty were faved, and attained the caftle; the reſt were either taken, or killed. The commander had undermined fort Charles, and blew it up. The Moors took eighteen cannon, which had been fpiked, and were therefore rendered ufelefs. Muley Ifhmael made great rejoicings for this fuccefs.

In the fame year, the Chevalier de Chateau Renaud, the commander of a French fleet, appeared in the road of Sallee with ten fhips of war. His intent was to block up this port, and endeavour to make an advantageous peace. The Alcaid Amar-Hadoo, viceroy of Garb, whose duty it was to negotiate with him in the absence of the Emperor, had several conferences with the persons sent by the French commander. These negotiations, however, were all fruitless, and tended to no other purpose than that of multiplying presents, and increasing expences, according to the custom of the court of Morocco, where they will promise any thing, but where no affairs can be brought to a conclusion.

The Emperor, at this time, had marched toward Tremecen, there to chastise the mountaineers who had granted an asylum to his fugitive brothers. He received homage from the tribes inhabiting the lesser Atlas: they made their excuses for having granted the refuge, by which he was offended, and, without difficulty, paid the contributions he thought proper to impose.

As the Moors of Tremecen had often demanded assistance from Muley Ishmael against

against the Turks of Algiers, who were in possession of that city, he wished himself to examine the condition in which it was; but he found it so well guarded, and in so good a state of defence, that he saw no hope of a succesful enterprise. The Divan of Algiers penetrated his intentions, and wrote to him that, if he thought the limits by which they were separated somewhat too confined, he must impose it as a duty on himself, to extend them (i. e. remove himself) far even as from the Ocean to the Desert. Muley Ishmael received this letter, struck his tents, and returned no other answer than that of marching back toward Mequinez.

Having re-entered his capital, the pleasure he took in building again revived, and, under the pretence of enlarging and aggrandizing his palace, he alternately built up and pulled down; partly to indulge the inconstancy of his temper, and partly to occupy those about his person. He remarked, with great acuteness, meaning to picture the restlessness of men, and, perhaps, to justify his own, that, " were a
" number

"number of rats put into a basket, they would certainly eat their way out, unless the basket were continually shaken."

Toward the end of the year 1680, Muley Achmet, the nephew of Muley Ishmael, who had three years before retired from Morocco with the title of King of Dara, having entered into an alliance with a Shaik, of the kingdom of Suz, whose daughter he had married, aided by the advice and troops of his father-in-law, assumed the title of King of Suz. The intention of this prince, whose delight was only in war, was to invade the kingdom of Sudan, he having been promised aid by the Arabs of the desert.

Having assembled his forces, and collected the provisions necessary for crossing the desert, which separates the principality of Suz from the kingdom of Sudan, Muley Achmet began his march, and was joined by the Arabs of the neighbouring provinces. His army suffered much for want of water, and he lost about fifteen hundred men

men among the moving sands, which he was obliged to cross, and which, in this desert, vary their form according to the variations of the wind.

Muley Achmet, at length, arrived in Sudan, and layed siege to Tagaret, the capital of that kingdom. The negroes, who were shut up in the city, made some resistance; but, having only lances and javelins to oppose to fire arms, their defence was ineffectual, and the place surrendered at discretion, when it was on the eve of being stormed. The riches Tagaret contained were sufficient to load fifty camels: a great part of them consisted in gold dust.

Muley Achmet agreed that the son of the king of Sudan should give him ten thousand negro slaves, for his ransom, and that they should be sent to the frontiers of his states; which agreement was accordingly executed. After concluding this treaty, Muley Achmet returned toward Suz, and underwent his former difficulties in traversing the desert, where many of his followers perished, and where he loft several camels that bore a part of the riches he had taken. Once more fafely arrived at Tarudant, he fent meffengers to Muley Ifhmael, his uncle, announcing the fuccefs of his expedition, and with them a number of flaves, of both fexes, as a prefent.

Muley Ifhmael, ever forming new projects, and having no other amufement at Mequinez than what his wives and concubines, his buildings, and the exercife of his cruelties, could afford, wearied at this uniformity of life, undertook, in 1681, the conqueft of the caftle of Mamora, which was in the power of the Spaniards. Informed, by a fugitive, how entirely the place had been neglected, fince the death of Philip IV., and that the garrifon was daily weakened, by thofe difeafes which the humidity of the marfhes were the caufes of, the Emperor fent an order to the Alcaid Amar-Hadoo to affemble the troops in the province of Garb, and inveft the caftle.

Arrived before Mamora, that general foon deftroyed the lines, which were formed

formed only of ſtakes and paliſadoes. He likewiſe took two towers, facing the ſea, in which there were only twelve men, who, unequal to ten thouſand, capitulated, on condition their lives ſhould be ſaved. The general did more; he granted them their liberty, ſent them into the place, and bade them inform the governor and the garriſon, that, if they did not yield, they would all be put to the ſword on the arrival of Muley Iſhmael. The very name of this man ſo diſcouraged the ſoldiers that they rather choſe to encounter the loſs of liberty, than to expoſe themſelves to his barbarity, by defending a place ſo ill provided. In this extremity the governor ſaw himſelf obliged to ſurrender, and the garriſon were made priſoners of war.

Muley Iſhmael, who was encamped in the environs of Alcaſſar, received advice of the capitulation of Mamora, and marched thither on the morrow. Finding in the place near one hundred pieces of artillery, numerous arms, and much ammunition, he proſtrated himſelf to earth, and returned thanks to the Almighty for this conqueſt.

conqueſt. From this time, ambitious of ſeizing other places on the coaſt, he ſent the governor of Mamora to Laracha, there to inform the commander, and garriſon, they ſhould be treated with the utmoſt rigour, if they refuſed to ſurrender.

In the month of June, and the ſame year, the Chevalier de Chateau Renaud anchored once more in the road of Sallee, with a ſquadron of four ſhips; and, having deſtroyed ſome Corſairs, Muley Iſhmael ſent orders to Amar-Hadoo to conclude a truce. This negotiation, which was one continued chain of contradictions, not being brought to a concluſion, the Emperor reſolved to ſend the Hadgi Themin, governor of Tetuan, and Caſſem Menino, brother to the governor of Sallee, ambaſſadors, into France, on board the royal ſquadron.

Theſe Ambaſſadors arrived at Paris toward the end of December. It was the intention of Muley Iſhmael to equivocate; their miſſion, therefore, went no farther than to announce the deſire of, without

the

the power to conclude, peace. Every delay, of which this negotiation was fufceptible, and every new impediment, being an additional motive for new prefents, Muley Ifhmael was eager to renew the conferences.

The Emperor, conftitutionally ambitious, and admiring the fplendour of the reign of Louis XIV., who fingly refifted Europe, leagued againft him, appeared defirous of concluding a treaty of peace with this monarch. He therefore wrote to Louis XIV., requefting he would commit the negotiation to a confidential perfon, with whom he might treat, offering likewife to fend an ambaffador himfelf, fhould that be agreeable to the king.

In confequence of this invitation, Monfieur de St. Olon made a voyage to Mequinez, as ambaffador of France, which had no other effect than that of demonftrating the inftability of the court of Morocco, and the ambiguous character of Muley Ifhmael. Eager to feize on the prefents fent by the court of France, the Emperor eluded, cluded, by various specious pretexts, the motives of an embassy which he disavowed, although it had been made at his own request*.

Much about this time the English parliament, disgusted with the expence of maintaining Tangiers, from which the nation had imagined it should derive great advantages, and which, instead of profitable, was found burdensome, resolved to abandon the place. Consequently, in 1684, the English withdrew their garrison, stores, and artillery, and blew up the mole, and the fortifications which had been constructed by Charles II. This was new cause of triumph to Muley Ishmael, who affected to suppose that England had forsaken Tangiers, and restored it to him, from the dread they entertained of his arms.

Glorying in the conquest of Mamora, and the abandoning of Tangiers, the Emperor made preparations, in 1687, to be-

* Memoires de M. de St. Olon.

siege Laracha. After the neceſſary ſtores were collected, he marched, and laid ſiege to the place; in the following year he erected batteries on the ſouth ſide, and blockaded it by land. The town reſiſted his aſſaults during five months, but, at length, capitulated in 1689. It appears that the garriſon remained the priſoners of Muley Iſhmael, and was only allowed to be exchanged, on condition of reſtoring ten Moors for one Chriſtian.

Thus having the towns of Mamora, Laracha, and Tangiers, in his power, the next attempt of Muley Iſhmael was to take Ceuta. In 1694 he aſſembled more than forty thouſand men, and layed ſiege to this fortreſs; but, perceiving he ſhould be unable to vanquiſh it, unleſs he could render himſelf ſuperior by ſea, he contented himſelf with blockading it on the land ſide, and ſecuring his camp from ſurprize.

There were ſome ſkirmiſhes between the Moors and the Chriſtians, when the Spaniards made occaſional ſallies, but the loſs on both ſides was inconſiderable. The

Moors being, however, greatly disturbed by the bombs and grenadoes, which were thrown from the town, Muley Ishmael thought proper to encamp at a greater distance. He afterward left the command of his army to the viceroy of Garb, who merely lay a spectator of, without besieging, Ceuta.

The wars which happened in Spain at the beginning of the present century, after the death of Charles II., gave Muley Ishmael the hope of conquering the place with less difficulty. He therefore fortified the Moorish camp, erected houses for the commanders of his forces, huts for the soldiers, ordered the siege to be begun anew, and the place never to be forsaken.

The Moors had languidly lain more than twenty years before Ceuta, when Philip V. of Spain determined to drive them to a greater distance. In 1720 this prince sent an army thither, under the command of the Marquis of Leda, accompanied by a number of gallies and ships.

The

The Spanish army attacked the centre of the Moors, while the ships bombarded the wings, and with so much success that the Moors were thrown into disorder. The Marquis pursued his advantage with so much ardour that, in four hours, he not only drove them from their intrenchments, but also from one valley to another, without their daring to make further resistance. When the Spaniards returned to the Moorish camp, they found four Mortars, some pieces of artillery, four pair of colours, and many stores.

I have interrupted the order of the history of Muley Ishmael that I might present, under one point of view, all the attempts of that Emperor against Ceuta. Although the Moors, after his reign, never made any attack upon this town, their camp of observation has continued to exist, and, in despite of the good understanding which has lately been reciprocal, between the court of Spain and that of Morocco, the intercourse, between the camp of the Moors and the town of Ceuta, is mutually maintained with circumspection.

Not

Not by devaſtations, conqueſts, and ambitious projects alone, was the empire of Morocco, under Muley Iſhmael, agitated: as he advanced in years, his ſons whoſe numbers, ambition, and turbulence of character, led to new revolutions, and the commiſſion of new crimes, made him ſenſible, in the beginning of the preſent century, of all thoſe cares and vexations which he well might expect, from that reſtleſſneſs, and ferocity, of which he had given them an example.

Independent of the influence which the young princes began to acquire over provinces, the ſubjects of which, groaning beneath oppreſſion, were ever ready to change their maſter, domeſtic ambition, likewiſe, gave birth to domeſtic troubles. Secret intrigues were carried on by the wives of the Emperor, each of whom endeavoured to favour the intereſt of her own ſon, to the prejudice of the other brothers, and the provinces which theſe princes governed long ſuffered from their factions, and the perſonal animoſities with which ſuch factions were maintained.

Muley

Muley Mahomet, who, of all the sons of Muley Ishmael, most merited to be beloved, by the qualities he possessed, and the handsomeness of his person, was the one who gave his father the most chagrin. His mother was a Georgian, purchased at Algiers, who, by her accomplishments and beauty, had acquired some empire over the heart of this barbarous monarch. The pre-eminence he held in the public opinion had rendered Muley Mahomet audacious, and, regardless of the sacred asylum of the palace, consulting only the headstrong and illegitimate passions of youth, had entered the seraglio of his father, to the intrigues and violences of which he fell a sacrifice. A fate that the more certainly attends such intruders, because that these intrigues are carried on in silence and secresy.

One of the queens*, of negro origin, the mother of Muley Zidan, ambitious and

---

* In Morocco they indifferently give the name of queen, and that of Lela, or Lady, to the wives of the Emperor; whom they call Ladies only, and not queens, in the Seraglio of the Grand Signior.

intriguing,

intriguing, and who, by the art with which she could enflame the passions, shared the depraved heart of Muley Ishmael, determined to effect the destruction both of her rival and her rival's son, and, by this means, assertain the affection of the father for Muley Zidan. This queen, by her influence, and the natural ascendancy of her character, had acquired an authority over the other women, who, like herself, were jealous of the Emperor's partiality for the Georgian; she therefore induced them to conspire with her, confirm the suspicions she had raised of infidelity, and they thus obtained from Muley Ishmael, in an atrocious moment of love and rage, permission to have her strangled.

Grown cool, and left to reflection, the Emperor was much affected by her death, and his attachment for Muley Mahomet was increased. In order to remove him from the intrigues of Lela Zidana, whose powers of seduction he himself dreaded, he bestowed on him the government of Tafilet. This prince, who was governor of Fez, and who preferred that city as a

place

place of residence, eluded his departure, under a pretence of illness. His father, unwilling to control his repugnance, agreed to send him into the province of Suz to Muley Sharif, who had succeeded Muley Achmet.

Muley Mahomet had been but a short time in his government before, according to the Emperor's desire, he appeased insurrections raised near Tarudant, and the success of the prince, on this occasion, became the cause of his misfortunes.

Lela Zidana, who, with vexation, beheld that the conduct of Muley Mahomet gave him a farther claim over the affections of his father, set every possible engine in play to accomplish his destruction. She wrote a letter to the prince, to which she affixed the imperial signet, and therein commanded him to put a Shaik to death, who was most highly in the favour of the Emperor. The prince executed the order he received most reluctantly. Being summoned to Mequinez, there to justify himself concerning the death of the Shaik, he presented his father's letter, to which he had only paid obedience out of respect to the will of the Emperor.

Beholding his power thus abused, Muley Ishmael, at first, was furious; but Lela Zidana so successfully employed her arts that he sent back his son to Tarudant, and rewarded the children of the Shaik to recompense them for the loss of their father.

Muley Mahomet, after having been summoned to Mequinez, there to answer an accusation so malicious and so wicked, was inconsolable to behold the facility with which his father gave way to first impressions, and, knowing no means of counteracting the plots of Lela Zidana, whom he held in abhorrence, he rashly entertained projects of rebellion. Muley Ishmael, by letters he received, judged what were his son's intents; but, having undertaken an expedition against the regency of Algiers, and being on the eve of departure, he would not change his plan.

The

The monarch began his march, toward the commencement of the prefent century, with more than fixty thoufand men; the army of the Algerines fcarcely exceeded ten thoufand, but it was compofed of much better troops, and encamped itfelf on the frontiers, there to wait for the army of Muley Ifhmael, which, when it arrived, was harraffed by fatigue, and in want of all neceffaries. The Algerines began the attack with intrepidity, and without lofs of time; the army of the Emperor was routed, and Muley Ifhmael, who, for more than thirty years, had fought againft the Moors with unfailing fuccefs, was obliged to retire, and re-enter his ftates, after an ignominious battle.

Muley Mahomet took advantage of the impreffion which the defeat of his father had made on the minds of his fubjects, to render himfelf mafter of Morocco. He marched thither with near forty thoufand men, whofe fidelity was fecured by the perfonal qualities, fine figure, and bravery of their leader. The capital at that time was governed by the Alcaid Melek, who shut

shut the city gates, dispatched messengers to the king for succour, and caused the treasure of the palace to be secretly buried.

Muley Mahomet, who had no artillery, found it impossible to take Morocco, unless by surprise; he therefore divided his army into two corps, the one of which concealed itself near the city, while he began his march with the other as if retreating. Deceived by this stratagem, as the prince had foreseen, the Alcaid Melek made a sally with his forces to attack Muley Mahomet as he retired; and the other corps, leaving its place of concealment, fell upon the Alcaid in the rear, who was thus surrounded, and his army, in part, slaughtered, while the prince rendered himself master of the city. Muley Mahomet indulged his troops in pillage, as a reward for their valour, and seized himself on the treasures, buried by the Alcaid, which were immediately discovered to him by a young slave.

Muley Ishmael, on receiving the advice sent by the Alcaid of Morocco, ordered an army to march to the succour of that city, under the command of Muley Zidan, the son of that artful queen, who, by her fascinations, her intrigues, and plots, had occasioned the rebellion of Muley Mahomet. The latter prince, informed of his brother's march, retired to Tarudant, where he provided for his safety. Among his officers was an Alcaid, the kinsman of Lela Zidana, who informed the court of all transactions, and who, having been discovered, was beheaded.

When Muley Mahomet had assembled sufficient money and troops, he determined to march against Muley Zidan, who had a fine army. Muley Mahomet gave the command of his van to the Alcaid Melek, the former governor of Morocco, who had entered into his service. Melek suffered himself to be surrounded by the troops of Muley Zidan, which occasioned the loss of the battle.

Seeing the van of his army in the power of the enemy, Muley Mahomet was obliged to fly. The prisoners were conducted to Morocco, whence the chiefs were sent to the Emperor, who put them to tormenting deaths. The Alcaid Melek himself, who had been guilty of treachery only thereby to obtain pardon, was sacrificed to the vengeance of Lela Zidana. She would not forgive him for having, by order of the prince, beheaded her relation, who had acted as a spy. To render cruelty more infernal, this unhappy man was fixed to a board, and sawed down the back.

Muley Zidan, encouraged by victory, and the flight of Muley Mahomet, determined to march and besiege Tarudant; but having been repulsed in various sallies, made by the besieged, he was obliged to retire. Every artifice of treachery was then employed by this prince to ensnare his brother, and to corrupt his partisans. Having placed some troops in ambuscade to seize on him, one day, as he rode out, Muley Mahomet, notwithstanding all his efforts,

was

was taken and brought prifoner to Morocco, whence he was fent by Muley Zidan, under a ftrong guard, to the Emperor, in the year 1706.

After having afflicted the reader by an uninterrupted fucceffion of crimes and cruelties, I would it were in my power to omit fcenes ftill-more tragical, and, under an impenetrable veil, to conceal the atrocious acts of a violent and barbarous father, toward a rafh, unfortunate, and guilty fon.

Muley Mahomet approached Mequinez on his journey, when the Emperor went to meet him at the river of Beth, there to punifh his rebellion, and avoid all interceffions in his behalf. I fhall fupprefs the fhocking preparations which Muley Ifhmael made for the ferocious exercife of vengeance. They both arrived on the banks of the Beth on the fame day. The Emperor paffed four-and-twenty hours without admitting him to his prefence; when he, at length, fent for him, the prince fell proftrate to the earth, and fup-

P 4 plicated

plicated pardon for his errors in the moſt affecting terms. His father preſented him the point of his lance, and the prince, fearing death leſs than thoſe preparations which did but multiply its horrors *, again humbly conjured him to grant him pardon, and ever after to depend on his ſubmiſſion and fidelity.

The inflexible Iſhmael, who had ſo far forgotten all human pity as to be preſent at the puniſhment of his ſon, and the ſon whom he had moſt loved, commanded two men to ſeize him, and a third, a butcher, to cut off his right hand. The latter refuſed, preferring, as he ſaid, death to the ſacrilegious act of bathing his hand in the blood of a Sharif. Enraged at a ſentiment ſo generous, the Emperor ſtruck off the head of the butcher, and called another,

* Father Buſnot informs us that the Emperor was preceded by a guard of two thouſand horſe, and one thouſand foot; that fourteen Chriſtian ſlaves carried a cauldron, a hundred weight of tar, or pitch, and as much oil and tallow; and that they were followed by a cart load of wood, and ſix butchers, each with his knife in his hand. T.

who executed his will by cutting off the right hand, and the right foot, of the unfortunate prince.

" Now, doſt thou know thy father, wretch!" ſaid Iſhmael.

He then ſeized a muſket, and killed the Moor who had cut off the hand and foot of his ſon. Mahomet, groaning under pain as he was, could not forbear to remind him of the guilty inconſiſtency of a ſovereign, who equally murdered the man, who refuſed to execute his orders, and him who obeyed. Pitch was then applied to the leg and arm of the ſuffering prince as a ſtyptic, and the Emperor, ſtained with the blood of his ſon, commanded his guards to bring him living, under pain of inſtant execution, to Mequinez.

The recital of this tragical ſcene ſpread terror and conſternation through the city; the palace reſounded with lamentaions, groans, and ſhrieks, and Muley Iſhmael, unable to aſſuage their grief by the ſeverity of his orders, maſſacred ſeveral women
who

who had dared to difobey, till forrow, at length, was obliged to weep in filence.

The children of Muley Mahomet only were allowed to mourn, but were not admitted any more to fee their father. The prince lived thirteen days in torments, and demanded to be buried, not as a prince, but as a flave, for fo he had been treated by his father. Ifhmael, however, built him a maufoleum, and thereby preferved to pofterity a memento of his own barbarity.

After the defeat of his rival, Muley Zidan, with little internal caufe of happinefs, returned to Tarudant once more to befiege that city, in which the remainder of the revolted had fhut themfelves up, which he furrounded fo entirely that famine made dreadful ravages among the citizens, and it was obliged to furrender at difcretion. More ferocious, more avaricious, more inhuman, even than his very father, Muley Zidan, committed every kind of barbarity in Tarudant, and, by his cruelties, juftified the opinion entertained of him in his youth, that in him all the vices of the human heart were united.

The

The horrors, robberies, and maſſacres, commited by Muley Zidan in the city of Tarudant, being publiſhed, ſo terrified the Moors of the neighbouring provinces and towns, that they fled for refuge among the rocks, and no where ſuppoſed themſelves in ſafety. The town of Santa-Cruz was at the ſame time evacuted, that is to ſay, in 1712; and when this prince marched thither, to beſiege it, he found no perſon but an old woman and a blind Jew, who, becauſe of their infirmities, were unable to ſeek a hiding place. The ſoldiers of the prince finding no further reſiſtance, the Moors every where flying, enriched themſelves with pillage, and were indulged in every kind of licentiouſneſs.

The ſucceſs of Muley Zidan, his troops, and his treaſures, began highly to diſturb Muley Iſhmael, who was inceſſantly preyed upon by his paſſions; the Emperor repented ſomewhat too late that he had beſtowed the command of his army on his ſon, and invented various pretexts to recal him to Mequinez; but Muley Zidan, who meditated far other projects, delayed
his

his return from year to year, alledging that his prefence was ftill neceffary, totally to fubdue the infurgents.

The better to deceive his fon, Muley Ifhmael occafioned a report to be fpread that he was ill, and forbore to appear in public, at the fame time that he prevailed on the mother of Muley Zidan artfully to fend for her fon to Mequinez, in order that, in cafe of death, he might the more eafily poffefs himfelf of the government; but the prince, well acquainted with all the fubtleties of his father, fufpected the intelligence, and paid no attention to this advice. His mother wrote a fecond letter, telling him, that his father was at the point of death, and that, if he did not incontinently return, he would be too late to pay the laft duties of a fon. Whether my father live or die, replied the prince, I will not forfake the army, which, in cafe of his deceafe, will but the better afcertain my fucceffion.

The rumours of the illnefs of Muley Ifhmael, and the fear that he was in reality dead,

dead, gave rife to fome commotions in the provinces. The citizens of Mequinez were ripe for revolt, when Lela Zidana, who governed defpotically, under the pretence of the Emperor's illnefs, fallied from the palace with a lance in her hand, attended by a guard of armed foldiers, to re-eftablifh tranquillity, and even arrogantly commanded fome negroes, whom fhe encountered as fhe paffed, to be punifhed.

An event fo fingular, among a people where the women never appear in public, and under a government in which they are fuppofed to have no right to empire, aftonifhed the citizens, who, believing the king dead, imagined that this ambitious princefs, whom they fecretly detefted, intended to feize on the fovereign authority. This fuppofition fpread fo quickly, and excited fo great an alarm, that Lela Zidana was obliged to re-enter the palace.

The Emperor, who had not been feen in public during fifty days, informed of the commotion among the inhabitants of the city, inftantly left his retreat, and over-
awed

awed the people by his prefence, who teftifyed the fatisfaction they received to behold him alive. The pretended recovery of Muley Ifhmael was the caufe of public rejoicings, and he received the vifits of the Alcaids, the grandees, and deputies of provinces and towns, on the occafion, who brought with them the cuftomary prefents.

Highly regretting that he had not been able, by artifice, to inveigle Muley Zidan to Mequinez, the Emperor, confulting only the violence and ferocity of his character, now took other means to difencumber himfelf of this prince. He well knew how much he was addicted to drunkennefs, and that, in the fury of intoxication, he fo far abandoned himfelf to his cruelty that his very wives and concubines were not in fafety. Thefe he made his inftruments to obtain his purpofe. The wives of Muley Zidan had little reluctance in complying with the barbarous defire of Muley Ifhmael, for they had no other poffible means of freeing themfelves from the tyranny to which they were hourly subjected.

jected. Surrounding him in one of his fits of drunkenness, they smothered Muley Zidan between two mattresses, and thus delivered the world of a monster unequalled in depravity.

The body of the prince was taken from Tarudant to Mequinez by the command of his mother, and there interred. The Emperor, that he might conceal the part he had taken in his death, built a mausoleum, and a mosque, to his memory, in which an asylum is given to criminals; and thus, under a supposed idea of sanctity, is the memory of a prince held in veneration, who had abandoned himself to every vice, lived detested by the nation, a rebel to his father and his Emperor, and, contemning the laws of his religion, died in drunkenness.

After being informed of the death of Muley Zidan, Muley Ishmael, governed by that spirit of contradiction which, in him, was a characteristic quality, commanded the seven wives of this prince to be brought from Mequinez, and along with them the
Jew

Jew merchant, who had fupplied them with the brandy, by drinking which he had made himfelf drunk. Lela Zidana, as well worthy to be the wife of Muley Ifhmael as the mother of Muley Zidan, facrificed thefe eight victims to the barbarity of her revenge. Her cruelty was deteftably atrocious. She ordered the breafts to be fevered from three of thefe women, and obliged them to eat them previous to their being ftrangled.

Nero, Caligula, Heliogabalus, were abhorrent villains; yet Nero, Caligula, Heliogabalus, themfelves, were unequal to the fends of whofe acts I give but a partial relation.

The death of Muley Zidan happened in 1721, and his brother, Abdelmeleck, fucceeded to the government of the fouth, where he, at firft, behaved with difcretion; but the diftance at which he lived from his father, the ambition of reigning, the levity of the people, and the internal vices of the government, which, here combined, infpire rebellion among fuch princes, foon rendered

rendered him equally guilty with his brothers. Acting with despotic authority over the princes he governed, Abdelmeleck presently became suspected by his father, and even had the temerity to refuse paying him tribute.

The Emperor, whose great age no longer permitted him to traverse deserts that he might punish insurgents, possessing now no other arms than those of artifice, wrote his son letters, the most tender and confidential, that he might persuade him to return to court, in which he even insinuated it was his intent to abdicate the empire in his favour. Well acquainted with his father, Abdelmeleck answered with like art, and in the most respectful terms, that he might remove those suspicions which he appeared to have entertained. Muley Ishmael, disembling his vexation, feigned to be satisfied with the conduct of his son, and made no more intreaties; but, secretly nourishing hatred in his heart against this prince, he determined to leave his younger brother, Muley Achmet Daiby, his successor in sovereignty. Some have supposed it was the Emperor's intention to make the nation regret his memory, by leaving a successor unworthy of the sceptre, and incapable of government.

After reigning fifty-four years, continually agitated by inquietude, suspicion, or revolt, and sullying his sceptre by the most tragical scenes, Muley Ishmael died on the 22nd of March, 1727, aged eighty one. Active, enterprizing, and politic, this Emperor has tarnished the glory of his reign by his avarice, his duplicity, his oppressions, his injustice, and a continuation of barbarities, the relation of which would be dreadful, and the remembrance of which time only can efface.

Addicted to sensuality, Muley Ishmael had a prodigious number of wives, and, so numerous was his posterity, that, it is doubted whether he himself knew all his children. If the common opinion may be credited, he had more than eight hundred sons; and there still remains at Tafilet a confiderable body of the Sharifs, who are the defcendants of Muley Ifhmael, of his brothers, or his forefathers.

The Moors relate that the laft child of this fovereign was born eighteen months after the death of his father, and the Talbes decided that child birth, with refpect to him, had departed from the order of nature. The time of geftation, however, is certainly not longer in Morocco than in Europe; but phyficians, in the latter country, are lefs indulgent in their opinions.

Muley Ifhmael, who, among a number of vices, poffeffed fome good qualities, was ardent in the purfuit of his projects, artful in policy, and diftinguifhed his reign by his application to the forming of troops from the negro families, and their defcendants, whom he acquired from the coaft of Guinea. This population of foreign foldiers, whofe intereft was ever oppofite to that of the Moors, but ever connected with that of the monarch, has planted in the heart of the empire a new and diftinct nation. After the death of Muley Ifh-

mael,

mael, the number of the negro foldiers capable of bearing arms, amounted to about one hundred thoufand. This warlike and infolent foldiery, which was made the inftrument of the avarice of Muley Ifhmael, and by whofe aid he gratified all his paffions, had great influence in the revolutions, which, after the death of this Emperor, have fo much agitated Morocco. The Negroes might have fubjugated the empire in the fame manner as the Tartars have feized on China, had there been found among them ambitious leaders, as capable of forming as they were of executing projects fo great. During fuch tempeftuous intervals the empire became, for feveral years, the prey of this avaricious body, which never gave the fucceffors of Muley Ifhmael time fufficient to fecure their authority. They refembled the Roman legions, during the decline of that empire, they elected Emperors on one day, and dethroned them on the next.

CHAP.

CHAP. V.

Muley Achmet Daiby proclaimed by the Grandees and the Negroes. Duquella subjected. Avarice of the Emperor. Revolt of Abdelmeleck. Brutality, drunkenness, and indolence, of Muley Achmet. Abdelmeleck strangled. Death of the Emperor.

MULEY Achmet Daiby, the only son of Muley Ishmael who happened to be at Mequinez when his father died, behaved himself with so much prudence, by the council and aid of the governor of that city, that he disconcerted the projects of his brothers, Abdelmeleck and Abdallah, who, being both his seniors, had that claim to empire, and the confidence of the people, which age and experience give. The troops of the latter, while he was waiting

some

some revolution in his favour, voluntarily abandoned his party, which had not afcendancy fufficient to withftand his opponents.

The grandees, and the officers of the Negroes, being affembled, the day after the death of Muley Ifhmael, unanimoufly proclaimed Muley Achmet Daiby, and took the oath of fidelity. The new Emperor gave them two hundred thoufand ducats, about one million three hundred thoufand livres, or fifty-four thoufand pounds fterling, to diftribute among the troops; and they, encouraged by this generofity, marched againft the provinces that gave any tokens of infurrection, and that, after having loft Muley Ifhmael, fuppofed they no longer had a mafter.

The Moors of the province of Duquella, and of its environs, having taken up arms againft Muley Achmet Daiby, were entirely defeated and fubjected. This victory, which added to the afcendancy the Negroes had acquired, re-eftablifhed order and tranquillity in the other provinces.

Muley

Muley Achmet Daiby was only generous from policy: he was by character as avaricious as his father had been. In the very beginning of his reign he took all possible care to know and to increase his treasury. So little respectful was his avidity that he even stript the wives of his father, of the gold and silver jewels which they had received, in the moments of his caprice, or his liberality. The wealth left by Muley Ishmael was considerable, and Muley Achmet himself had been an œconomist, so that the treasury of the Emperor might amount to one hundred millions of livres, or near four millions two hundred thousand pounds. Yet did this mass of money, accumulated by time and oppression, soon after, disappear in an instant.

Dazzled at beholding such heaps of gold, Muley Achmet, as avaricious as he was intemperate, neglected the cares of government, and dedicated himself wholly to his pleasures. He yielded to the debauchery of drunkenness, without reserve; and this passion, which alienated the love of his people, was the source of his misfortunes.

In order to gain the affection of his subjects, in the beginning of his reign he issued an edict, by which he reduced all taxation to that of simply collecting the tenths, as prescribed by the law of Mahomet. Yet did not a regulation so wise produce effects which ought to have been the result, but rather served to manifest the abuse of authority among the governors, who profited by the vices of the imperial power to increase their extortions. The provinces became so much dissatisfied that the people, in many parts, took up arms to redress their grievances, and thus spread confusion throughout the empire.

The most of these provinces, beholding, with repugnance, the irregular conduct of Muley Achmet Daiby, were secretly inclined toward prince Abdelmeleck, who was a religious observer of the law. They, however, durst not openly testify their discontent. Muley Achmet being informed of the disposition of the people, and perplexed concerning the manner in which he ought to act, wished to secure the fidelity of the Negroes by his gifts, and almost

almoſt wholly confided the imperial adminiſtration of government, to the caprice and fickle avarice of his troops.

Such implicit confidence, prodigally beſtowed on foreign ſoldiers, whom the Moors deteſted, ſtill further alienated the minds of men, and the fermentation became general. Sedition firſt manifeſted itſelf at Fez, the governor of which, and near a hundred men of his party, were maſſacred by the people. The city of Tetuan, and its environs, followed the example; the governor was obliged to fly, and the furious people deſtroyed his houſe, his gardens, and ſubjected the city to all the horrors of a civil war.

Muley Achmet, ſunken in brutal intoxication, was incapable of yielding any remedy to ſuch diſorders, of which the people round him even kept him in igorance. So cruel was this emperor, when he was ſober, that his attendants and wives had no other means of ſafety than that of making him drunk. The governor of Mequinez, on whom he principally depended

for

for the administration of affairs, only rendered his master the more odious by his own negligence. Indolence and neglect pervaded the court. The debauched life of the king, the contempt in which his inactive government was held, and the murmurs of the people, rendered discontent so universal that it ended in revolt.

The provinces of the south were the first that reared the standard of rebellion. Muley Abdelmeleck, who had gained the hearts of the people, finding himself at the head of a powerful army between Suz and Morocco, was, of all those who aspired to empire, he who seemed to have the best founded claims; but he was guilty of an error, which became an obstacle to his good fortune and future elevation. In order to flatter his own army, composed of the inhabitants of the mountains and volunteers, who held the Negroes in abhorrence, this prince declared, that, should he ever arrive at empire, he would maintain no negro troops.

A declaration like this, which was exceedingly impolitic at such a moment, when the Negroes, accustomed to war, were in possession of all power, was for a time exceedingly favourable to the party of Muley Achmet, whose authority these same Negroes, proscribed by Abdelmeleck, saw themselves necessitated to maintain. The latter was not long before he felt the effects of his indiscretion, and the resentment of these troops. Morocco was already in his power; after having gained a battle, the provinces of the south were in his interest, as were the cities of Fez and Tetuan in the north, insomuch that he was almost master of the empire; but, having been defeated by the Negroes, whom he had provoked, he was obliged to abandon Morocco, and retreat, after having received three wounds, which occasioned the report of his death to be spread.

Having sustained some attacks from the forces of Muley Achmet Daiby, the city of Fez made peace with this prince, and acknowledged him Emperor. Muley Abdelmeleck made a proposition to lay down his

his arms, if his brother would cede him the half of the empire; and Muley Achmet was himself inclined to acquiesce, that he might have nothing farther to do, but drink and sleep. His ministers, however, his courtiers, and particularly his troops, who had great influence in these deliberations, firmly opposed any such division.

The dislike of the people to Muley Achmet continued the same, after he was thus recalled to empire, for his manner of life underwent no alteration. Totally neglectful of government, he knew not of those troubles which were incited in his provinces. His days were wholly spent in drinking, and his debauches were carried to such excess, that, to conceal them, from the public, was no longer possible. Going one Friday to the mosque to prayer, he was so drunk, that, when he prostrated himself, according to the custom of the Mahometans, he vomited up his wine; an indecency which was every where rumoured, and every where gave offence.

When

When he was brought back to his palace he treated his wives with exceffive cruelty, becaufe they made him fome remonftrances, till, impatient at fuffering his violence, they left the place, and uttered their clamors aloud, in the ftreets, againft the indolence and diffimulation of his minifters, and the commanders of his forces, who had no refpect whatever for religion. So general was the difcontent, that the foldiers themfelves, prejudiced as they were againft Abdelmeleck, joined the natives, and Abdelmeleck was once more proclaimed.

This proclamarion made, which happened in the month of March, 1728, the principal Alcaides, affembled at Mequinez, fent deputies to Abdelmeleck, preffing him to haften his arrival. His fon, who was at that time in Mequinez, was appointed regent, in expectation of the coming of his father; and the young prince, by fome well-timed gifts, very prudently fmothered thofe difcontents which the party of Muley Achmet at firft teftified, in confequence of this election.

Muley

Muley Abdelmeleck arrived at Mequinez, and made his public entry on the 10th of April. In the barbarity of his religious zeal, it was his intention to have put out the eyes of his brother, but he satisfied himself with banishing him to Tafilet, remonstrances having been made to him that, Muley Achmet having been found unworthy of the throne only in consequence of his debauchery and indolent conduct, he did not merit any other chastisement than that of being deposed.

After this first act, Abdelmeleck, austere, arrogant, and choleric, began to treat his ministers, and the Moors in general, with so much severity, haughtiness, and contempt, that he universally alienated the minds of his subjects. Scarcely had he reigned three months before the Negroes, recollecting the declaration which Abdelmeleck had publicly made concerning them, formed a party, and sent a detachment to Tafilet to solicit pardon of Muley Achmet Daiby, and to invite him once more to put himself at their head, and assume the reins of government.

Attended

Attended by some troops in addition to the Negroes, the Emperor began his march, and presently found himself at the head of eighty thousand men. Abdelmeleck, who, by the excess of his pride, had deprived himself of partisans, was obliged to shut himself up in Mequinez, where he was besieged, and the city, taken by assault, was exposed to pillage, and every horror which vengeance and barbarity could inspire.

During the confusion, Muley Abdelmeleck escaped to the city of Fez, where he was again besieged. Unable to take this city by storm, Muley Achmet resolved on a blockade, and, as there were not sufficient provisions in Fez to sustain a siege, the inhabitants, at the end of three months, determined to capitulate. The sole condition which the Emperor exacted from them was, to yield up his brother. Abdelmeleck was accordingly delivered over to the conqueror, who, for a moment, dissembling the ferocity of his character, thought proper to send him, under a strong guard, to Mequinez, where he

some-

sometime after commanded him to be strangled.

Muley Abdelmeleck had been executed but a few days before Muley Achmet Daiby himself died, in March, 1729, of an incurable dropsy. Such was the end of a prince, become brutal by indolence and intemperance, and who, despised by his subjects, never was capable of making his power respected.

CHAP.

CHAP. VI.

Accession of Muley Abdallah, his cruelties; power of the Negroes, their insatiable avidity, and consequent revolutions. Muley Abdallah a sixth time proclaimed Emperor; the negro troops enfeebled, and the power of the Emperor rendered more stable. Character of Muley Abdallah, his depravity, vices, and intolerable barbarities.

AFTER the death of Muley Achmet Daiby, the sceptre, which the army disposed of at will, was frequently removed from prince to prince; and the empire of Morocco, which, in its birth, had so often been the prey of fanaticism, was now at the mercy of the negro soldiers. Muley Booffer, the son of Muley Achmet, who was the immediate heir to the throne, firſt preſented himſelf as his father's ſucceſſor; but his party was not ſufficiently powerful. Lena Coneta, the mother of Muley Abdallah, an artful and intelligent princeſs, knew ſo well how to gain the minds of the people, and treated the Negroes with ſo much generoſity, that her ſon was by her means proclaimed.

Muley Abdallah, though, perhaps, as capricious as, and not leſs cruel than, his father, Muley Iſhmael, was generous even to exceſs. Six times depoſed, and ſix times remounting the throne, in the commencement of his reign he was the ſport of fortune, the victim of his people's fickleneſs, and the avarice of his ſoldiers. Muley Booffer, his nephew, conteſted with him for empire; but Booffer's ſole reſources were in a Marabout, held in veneration by ſome followers, whom the ſpirit of fanaticiſm had aſſembled; his faction therefore was ſoon defeated and diſperſed by the Negroes, and he was himſelf taken, as was the Marabout, who had become his counſellor, protector, and guide.

Muley

Muley Abdallah pardoned his nephew, and granted him his liberty; but, regardlefs of the prejudices of the Moors, he commanded the Marabout to be beheaded, and treated him as an impoftor; for, faid he, had this Marabout been really a Saint, the fabre that ftruck at him would have been edgelefs.

Muley Abdallah afterward marched againft Fez, which had declared in favour of Muley Booffer, and laid fiege to the city. It fuftained a blockade of fix months before it furrendered; and, irritated at the obftinacy of the inhabitants, the Emperor intended to have deftroyed and wholly erafed its foundations. Remonftrances, however, were made to him, that it had been built by a defcendant of Mahomet, and a founder of the empire, and that he would expofe himfelf, by fuch profanation, to the wrath of Heaven, and the hatred of the people.

The little religion Muley Abdallah demonftrated, in thus manifefting his intention to deftroy a city confecrated by the

Moors to devotion, and the violent and sanguinary character his actions already had announced, so alienated the minds of men that there were indications of sedition in various provinces of the empire; the Brebes of the mountains of Tedla were the first who took up arms. Prompt and vindicative, Muley Abdallah hastily assembled some native Moors to march and reduce these mountaineers, without reflecting that he endangered his own glory, and disgusted his other troops by so ill-judged a selection.

Having attacked the mountaineers at the head of twenty-five thousand men, the Emperor lost the half of his army in the battle, and returned to Mequinez to wreak his vengeance, and add to the shame of his defeat, by odious exhibitions of barbarity. A multitude of the inhabitants were put to death on the slightest pretext, himself aiding the murderers. Desirous of shewing him the detestable absurdity and inhumanity of such actions, his mother remonstrated, and he replied — " My subjects have no other right to
" their lives than that which I think pro-
" per

"per to leave them, nor have I any other pleasure so great as that of killing them myself." More abominable in cruelty than even his predecessors were, this Emperor seemed anxious to add to the infamy of his hereditary ferocity.

The tragical barbarities of Muley Abdallah occasioned the tribes of the mountains of Tedla to revolt; and, proud of the advantage they had already gained against the monarch, they drew over the neighbouring provinces to their party. Grown prudent by experience, and listening to the advice of his mother, the Emperor engaged the Negroes to take part in his meditated vengeance, and, by some acts of liberality, induced them to forget the neglect with which they had been treated. He now marched at the head of thirty thousand new-raised troops, who were followed by as many Negoes. In July, 1730, he arrived among the mountains of Tedla, and proceeded through a country full of brambles and underwood. Unfortunately these took fire near his camp, and he lost many men, horses, and camels, with all his provisions,

visions, and was himself in danger. The superstitious soldiers considered this accident as an evil prognostic, and the Negroes, who had testified some indications of inconstancy, were disgusted. Muley Abdallah, however, prevented them from abandoning him, by promising them three hundred thousand ducats (or upward of eighty thousand pounds sterling) at the end of the campaign.

The army having received a new supply of provisions, it once more began its march, in two columns, each at some distance from the other, thereby to surround the insurgents. The Emperor who commanded the van attacked them with the greatest valour; and the Negroes, who followed, seconded this attack so effectually that the rebels were cut off, and their country totally ravaged. The troops of Muley Abdallah took a vast number of horses, camels, herds, and flocks, contenting themselves with killing the sheep, that they might carry off the wool. The very women and children were stripped of their clothing, and turned naked into the country;

try; but the Emperor gave them wherewith to cover their nakedness; and this was the first act of humanity he had ever been known to perform.

Muley Abdallah passed the remainder of the campaign in the province of Hea, where his troops were indulged in repose, and whence he sent a detachment into that of Dara. His arms here were unsuccessful; the commander, who had been sent on this expedition, brought back to Mequinez, to which place the king had returned, not more than the tenth part of the forces, with which he had been entrusted; he had fought with equal prudence and valour, and was vanquished, because overpowered by numbers.

Muley Abdallah basely put this general to death, together with the soldiers who had returned with him, and not only presided himself a witness of, but was the chief executioner at, this scene of blood. Perceiving that those who put these wretches to death performed their task ill, he took the sabre himself, to shew them the manner in which it ought to be used. Thus perished, by the hand of a vile executioner, called an Emperor, men who, in any other country, would have met the rewards due to their services.

To keep his subjects busy, and not give them time to reflect on his barbarities, Muley Abdallah built new fortifications and new walls at Mequinez, to secure it from the incursions of the Brebes. The inhabitants, be their rank or condition what it would, were all obliged to assist at raising these walls. At the conclusion of the year 1732, he left this work to march against the mountaineers of the environs of Tetuan, who gave tokens of insurrection, and who, intrenched among their mountains and precipices, firmly waited his approach, without even defending the passes. Having imprudently entangled himself in a defile with thirty thousand men, the Brebes suddenly appeared on the heights, and attacked the army of the Emperor with so much success that it was put to the rout, and Muley Abdallah could with difficulty secure himself and a few soldiers,

leaving

leaving his baggage the prey of the victors.

The spirit of insurrection having spread itself almost throughout the whole empire, Muley Abdallah passed the following year in the province of Tafilet, there to quell a revolt. The success of this campaign was by no means prosperous; the Emperor wanted not intrepidity, but was unskilful and imprudent; and, having rashly attacked the rebels before he had been joined by his whole army, he was vanquished, and obliged to retreat. As the remainder of his forces advanced to join his army, he caused their officers to be seized, and commanded them to be dragged by mules along the road, that he might revenge upon them the disgrace of his own imprudence and defeat.

The mother of Muley Abdallah, perceiving she had lost all influence over the mind of her son, and seeing herself exposed to his contempt, unwilling longer to be a witness of his blood-thirsty acts, asked permission to quit the court, and go on pilgrimage

grimage to Mecca. The Emperor, on her return, testified little affection for this princess, nor did he fulfil those duties prescribed by propriety and custom, after a journey consecrated to religion. His mother, however, shewed much tenderness for him, and presented him with four beautiful slaves whom she had bought, hoping, by their means, to inspire him with the love of women, and extirpate an unnatural passion, to which this depraved wretch had addicted himself. This worthy mother continued to give her son advice, concerning his government; but, deaf to her counsels, and listening only to his own impetuosity and caprice, he wholly lost the affection of his subjects.

That he might the more easily subjugate the Negroes, who, in consequence of his dissipation, had become intractable, and whose avarice and fickleness he dreaded, Muley Abdallah formed the project of cutting off their general, and those among their officers who most influenced the resolutions of this soldiery. The secret, however, having been discovered by the interception

ception of letters, the negro corps, ever in arms, and conscious of its own power, rendered the project of Muley Abdallah abortive, by publicly deposing him, on the 29th of September, 1734; and Muley Ali, one of his brothers, was elected in his stead.

Being informed of what were the intentions of these troops, Muley Abdallah sent them three hundred thousand ducats, hoping thereby to appease them; but the Negroes received the money in part of payment of what had been promised, and no way changed their determination. The Emperor then, as a last expedient, shut himself up in Mequinez, there to defend himself; but, after having made his preparations, he fled among the mountains, accompanied by six hundred horsemen, and left his mother, his wives, and children, to the mercy of his enemies.

From Mequinez to Tarudant, Muley Abdallah visited all the mountains, among the inhabitants of which the Negroes were held in aversion, and by this means raised himself

himself a party. Had he been susceptible of reflection and prudence, he might have re-established his power; but, equally impetuous in prosperity and adversity, he continually acted with violence: the very tribes that had testified their attachment to him soon felt the caprices of his character, and cruelty; he, with his own hands, ill-treating and killing those among them who came to make him remonstrances: so that, at length, he was detested and execrated by all the provinces, which no longer would interest themselves in his behalf.

Muley Ali, who was at Tafilet when he was called to empire, arrived at Mequinez, in October 1735. The first of his cares, after his entrance, was to inform himself concerning the state of the treasury, which he knew had been left rich by his brother, Muley Achmet Daiby. Seeing it reduced to a very trifle, he, avaricious and barbarous like his predecessors, indulged his ferocity; and the mother of Muley Abdallah, beholding one of her own female attendants assassinated in her arms, and fearing herself to fall the victim of his fury, gave him some infor-

information concerning a part that had been concealed, but which, however, was of small value.

Anxious to preserve a crown, for which he was indebted to the preponderating power of the Negroes, this prince distributed among them all the money that remained in the treasury; and, without foreseeing the consequences, further promised them, as soon as he should be able to pay it, the sum of two hundred thousand ducats, or between fifty and sixty thousand pounds sterling. Hitherto the cities of Fez and Mequinez, and their dependencies only, were under the obedience of Muley Ali; the remainder of the empire was to be acquired by the valour of the Negroes.

Their general, the same whom Abdallah intended to have cut off, went, at the head of thirty thousand men, to besiege Morocco, took it by assault, put the garrison to the sword, and gave up the city to be pillaged by his soldiers. Actuated by resentment, this general proposed to march and give battle to Muley Abdallah himself; but, perceiving indications of irresolution among his troops, that had so often experienced the capricious generosity of this Emperor, he was determined to march with his army into the province of Beni-Haffen, whence it carried off the flocks and herds, and ravaged the environs of Sallee; which place refused to open its gates.

However high the resentment of the Negroes might be against Muley Abdallah, still their desire of money soon made them forget his cruelties, recollecting only the profusion of his gifts. Muley Ali was poor, and this to them was a feeble recommendation; their general, who was in the interests of the latter, insensibly lost the confidence of his soldiers. Influenced by their own avidity, and the intrigues of the mother of Muley Abdallah, who promised each man thirty ducats if they would proclaim the Emperor once more, they, in May, 1736, deposed Muley Ali, who had for some time past stupified himself by the immoderate use of the Achicha, which had benum-

benumbed his powers of body and mind*.

Informed of the reftoration of Muley Abdallah, Muley Ali retreated in his turn among the neighbouring mountains of Tremecen, accompanied by his family, and only fome forty men, who refolved to follow his fortunes.

A fecond time called to the throne, Muley Abdallah received at Teza, where he then was, a deputation of the officers of the Negroes, at the head of two thoufand men, to announce the revolution, and efcort him to Mequinez. Although the Emperor treated this deputation with demonftrations of gratitude, he ftill refufed to return to Mequinez, unlefs the Negroes would deliver up their general, Selim Doo-

---

* This plant greatly refembles hemp, and, mixed with other drugs, produces the fame kind of intoxication as opium. Some of the Moors take it continually; it infpires them with agreeable reveries, and, though exceffively heating, it benumbs the fenfes. In fome conftitutions, it renders thofe who take it furious.

quelli;

quelli; and he then promifed to recompenfe them by a gift of four hundred thoufand ducats, (or upward of a hundred thoufand pound fterling) which he had concealed.

Covetous as they were of money, yet the delivering up of their general was repugnant to the Negroes; befide, they perceived that the plan of Muley Abdallah was to weaken their power, and no longer to remain dependent on the influence they had acquired in the election of Emperor. Selim Dooquelli, an artful man, and beloved by the foldiers, was fo powerful in perfuading them that they did not hefitate once more to renounce their election of Muley Abdallah, and to proclaim Muley Mahomet, Ool Del Ariba*. The general expedited a courier to the latter at Tafilet, and fent him a detachment to efcort him to Mequinez. Thus was Muley Abdallah, by his imprudence, depofed

---

* That is to fay, the fon of the Ariba, which was the family name of the queen, his mother.

either the fame, or nearly the fame day, on which he was once more elected.

This precipitate proceeding, notwithstanding, gave birth to quarrels among the foldiers, who were not all of the fame opinion. They took to their arms, the party of Muley Abdallah became victorious, and he was a third time proclaimed before the arrival of Muley Mahomet. The latter, being then on the road, found himfelf obliged to ftop at Old Fez, where he was received and treated as Emperor. Sovereignty, in times fo perilous, was a very precarious and temporary poffeffion, which depended entirely on the moment and its accidents, on the character of the commanders and the caprices of the foldiery.

The officers of the Negroes, having reinftated Muley Abdallah on the throne, interefted themfelves in behalf of their general, and obtained a promife of pardon by the mediation of the Emperor's mother. Selim Dooquelli, who had taken refuge in an asylum, left this hospitium on the word of the Emperor; but he informed his soldiers of the fear he had, that he should become " the victim of the deceit of this subtle and sanguinary fox, who, said he to them, only wishes to deprive you of your chief, that he may destroy you with the greater facility."

His fears and forbodings were justified by the event. Having been conducted to Teza, covered by the cloth of the sanctuary, to which he had fled, he prostrated himself before Muley Abdallah; the Emperor kissed the holy cloth, that far paying respect to custom, and ordered it to be taken from the general, but, regardless of the asylum of religion, or his pledged faith, buried his lance in his body, and called for a cup that he might drink his blood. He afterward cut off the persons attached to this general, and even his children, whom he caused to be strangled in his presence.

This thirst of blood, this disrespect of his word, and of the prejudices of the nation, incited general indignation against
Muley

Muley Abdallah. Not only is the sanctuaries of their Saints confidered, among the Moors, as a certain afylum, which guards the culprit againſt the firſt efforts of authority, and yields him the means of juſtifying himſelf, but a like reſpect is alſo paid to the very habit of the faint, to whom any fuch hoſpitium is confecrated. To act contrary to this cuſtom, to treat the public opinion with contempt, and thus to violate the facred rights of the holy place of refuge, was to deprive the nation of all protection from the power of deſpotiſm; yet Muley Abdallah, acknowledging no other rule than his arbitrary will, took a pleaſure in contemning theſe hoſpitiums and their Marabouts, for which and whom the Moors have fo much veneration. Defirous of preventing the refentment which his ill faith muſt infpire among the Negroes, the Emperor departed from Teza for Mequinez, under the pretext of paying them the four hundred thouſand ducats which they had been promiſed. In order to gain time, and the better to deceive the foldiers, he commanded the earth to be dug up, in certain places which he

described

described, and affected the utmost' astonishment when no money was found. Having, nevertheless, promised to pay the Negroes before he made his entrance into Mequinez, and being arrived there without the power of fulfilling his promise, Muley Abdallah knew not how to act. The sum of four hundred thousand ducats, and the gratification which had been before stipulated with his mother, amounted to near two millions of ducats; all the money he had possessed had before been dispersed, and he was obliged to sell his arms, his horses, and jewels; but, though this sacrifice proved his desire to pay, it did not produce the quarter of the sum he had promised.

Never had Muley Abdallah more need of circumspection, and resource in his own understanding, than at this instant. Secretly detested by his soldiers, who were enamoured only of his prodigality, he had the more to dread from their inconstancy because that he was at no great distance from Muley Mahomet, and to whom only he had been preferred in the hope of reward.

ward. The Emperor once more entered into treaty with the Negroes, and promised to pay them in the space of two months, while these soldiers, on their part, determined to remain neuter during that interval, and neither interest themselves in his behalf nor in behalf of Muley Mahomet, who was shut up in Fez.

Thus we behold a despotic sovereign capitulating with his soldiers; yet, being themselves the instruments of despotism, it is no wise astonishing to see them sometimes thus acting as arbitrators.

This resolution of the Negroes determined Muley Abdallah to lay siege to Fez, accompanied by the Brebes of his party. The city made a most vigorous resistance, and the sallies of Muley Mahomet were so successful that the Brebes, wearied and and disheartened, determined to raise the siege.

The two months, which the Negroes had granted to Muley Abdallah, being expired, they sent to demand their money, as a creditor sends to demand a debt. The Emperor made excuses, pleaded present circumstances, and once more paid them with promises. The Negroes, whom money alone might render tractable, now recollected all the vices of Muley Abdallah, his cruelties, his ill faith, and hatred to them; nor could they find any being so odious as this Emperor, when he no longer had any thing to give.

The murmurs of this turbulent body, whose resentment and ferocity were dreaded by Muley Abdallah, determined him to escape with what he could collect most precious, and retire among the mountains, accompanied by his mother, his son, and a few soldiers. Astonished at the flight of the Emperor, and irresolute themselves concerning the manner in which they ought to act, the Negroes, in October 1736, once more named Muley Mahomet Ool Del Ariba, at the solicitations of the deputies of Fez, who engaged to pay, in behalf of this prince, the four hundred thousand ducats, which had been promised them by Muley Abdallah.

Muley

Muley Mahomet, dreading his brother as a rival, and the fickleness of the soldiery, sent an army, against Muley Abdallah, among the mountains in which he had taken refuge; but this army dared not to attack the Brebes in their fastnesses, and was impelled to retreat. After raising a more numerous army, Muley Mahomet marched thither in person, but with no better success; his cavalry being incapable of acting among mountains and precipices, he was obliged to renounce his enterprize, and to content himself with ravaging the country, and destroying some castles in the environs. His army, having afterward been attacked by the Brebes in a defile, was beaten, and thrown into disorder. Muley Mahomet was himself wounded in the arm, and in danger of being taken, having fought personally, and with great valour.

After these acts of hostility, the Negroes, much more occupied concerning their own interests than the maintenance of the sovereign power, began to make remonstrances concerning the four hundred thousand ducats, which the deputies of Fez had undertaken to pay; the latter having eluded the payment of this sum, the soldiers no longer could dissemble their resentment. These restless and avaricious troops indicated so much indifference concerning Muley Mahomet, that this prince, who was mild, just, and the enemy of tyranny, was on the eve of laying down his authority voluntarily, that he might no longer subject himself to the phantasies of these forces*. The Negroes, perceiving the sovereign they had chosen possessed not that spirit of vexation which alone might gratify their rapacity, suddenly stripped him of the authority they had bestowed, and, in 1738, named his brother, Muley Zin Lahabdin, as his successor.

The reign of Muley Zin was but momentary. Muley Abdallah, who had gone

---

* This prince has been dead about ten years; he lived like a private man near Mequinez, where I had the honour of being acquainted with him and his sons. Like the princes of the Arabs, they supported themselves on the revenues of their lands, flocks, and herds. They were very polite, and exceedingly affable in society.

toward Morocco, where he had made himself a powerful party, was a fourth time proclaimed Emperor by the provinces of the South, that had taken arms to counteract the power of the Negroes. Made wife by the viciffitudes of fortune, to which he had been expofed by his own vices and diffipations, and by the avidity and inconftancy of his troops, the Emperor felt the neceffity of weakening thefe infolent Negroes, who difpofed of empire at their pleafure.

He long remained encamped under Mount Atlas with an army of Brebes, fuppofing that the Negroes would march to attack him, and intending there to give them battle: but, finding this project did not fucceed, he began his march for Mequinez, where, on his arrival, his election was confirmed. The Negroes had confented to this, becaufe they perceived no better means of acting; they, neverthelefs, did not behold with pleafure a monarch on the throne, who, prodigal as he had been in his gifts, had yet fo often deceived them, and who, contrary to the faith of promifes

pledged,

pledged, had sacrificed their general and principal chiefs to his policy and his vengeance; but they were obliged to dissemble their discontent.

As the avarice of these troops favoured the intrigues of all those who aspired to sovereign power, the secret dissatisfaction of the Negroes soon found an opportunity of making itself manifest. The mother of Muley Mustadi, who clandestinely negotiated with their general, so well succeeded that she disposed them to favour her son, who, in 1740, was proclaimed Emperor, and Muley Abdallah was once more obliged to retire among the mountains. Such and so incessant were these revolutions; for, as they depended on the cupidity and inconstancy of an armed mob, these raised up Emperors and pulled them down, almost in the same moment.

Muley Mustadi, unwilling to depend on the caprice of his soldiers, thought he acted wisely in uniting himself with the province of Beni-Hassen, and with the Bashaw of Tangiers, who governed that of of Garb. This alliance, by which a union was again effected between all the north of the empire, inſpired the troops with jealouſy; and, that they might not give Muley Muſtadi time ſufficient to ſtrengthen his party, they once more recalled Muley Abdallah.

Muley Muſtadi, however, was not depoſed with the ſame eaſe as his predeceſſors had been. Each party maintained and defended his election by the force of arms. Various actions happened between the two armies, and many fell on both ſides. At length, Muley Abdallah, ſupported by the Negroes, the Ludaya, and the moſt warlike tribes, was victorious over the factions of the two provinces, which, powerful as they were, could not withſtand an army compoſed of ſoldiers inured to war. Muley Muſtadi, on his part, without wholly renouncing empire, thought proper to retire to Arzilla, where he carried on a conſiderable commerce in grain with the Spaniards.

The

The empire at this time was, for a short space, divided between Muley Muftadi and Muley Abdallah; the latter, defirous of obliging his brother wholly to abdicate the throne, marched with an army to poffefs himfelf of Tangiers, and to cut off the Bafhaw, Achmet Ben Ali, who was governer of the city, and who fuftained Muley Muftadi, by his credit, his money, and his troops. The Bafhaw having been killed in battle, the city was taken, and his palace was pillaged; but his fon, Mahomet Ben Achmet, had time to efcape to Gibralter, whither he carried all his wealth.

Muley Muftadi profited by this momentary diverfion to go and ravage the environs of Fez. On his return from this expedition, he was attacked near Alcaffar by Muley Abdallah, and, having been deferted in the battle by a part of his forces, he found himfelf obliged to retreat to Sallee, where, notwithftanding his defeat, he was received and acknowledged Emperor.

The town of Rabat, which is only separated from Sallee by a river, having refused to own his authority, a civil war arose between the two places, which long continued, and which was equally ruinous to both by the facility they mutually had to injure each other. Sallee and Rabat, having become feudatory towns of the empire, under Muley Ishmael, formed at that time a kind of republic, under a municipal government: restored to the monarchy, they might, by their wealth, and the character of their inhabitants, favour the factions that distracted the empire.

Muley Mustadi, for fourteen months, besieged Rabat; but, finding himself unable to take the place, he retired to Tedla, where he was arrested and put in chains by the Brebes, of the party of Muley Abdallah. The Brebes of the casile of Oordega carried him off in the night, and transported him into the hospitium of Sidi El Mati, a sacred asylum, the saints of which family had inherited the veneration of the people. Sidi El Mati escorted Muley Mustadi to Sallee, where the Bashaw,

shaw, Fenis, received him with so much the more eagerness inasmuch as that town, devoted to this prince, was totally averse to Muley Abdallah.

Muley Mustadi, however, finding that he was incapable of resisting the faction of the Negroes, or of restoring tranquillity to an empire ever in revolt, renounced the throne, and once more went to Arzilla, where he lived like a private person, and continued to trade with Europe.

Muley Abdallah thus, at length, was for the sixth time, master of the empire, and the Negroes, enfeebled by so many divisions, became less insolent in proportion as there were fewer candidates for sovereign power; beside, it was no longer possible to set up the crown to the best bidder, or to gratify the avarice of the soldiers, because of the exhausted state of the treasury, and of the difficulty with which contributions might any longer be raised in the provinces, which had been entirely laid desolate by such a succession of revolutions.

Become

Become more prudent and circumfpect by experience, and full of refentment againft the Negroes, the inconftancy of whom he had fo often experienced, Muley Abdallah determined to fupprefs this audacious foldiery, from whofe aid he had nothing more to hope, and from whofe infolence he had every thing to fear. He artfully took every occafion to involve the Negroes in quarrels with the mountaineers, and, by his fecret intrigues, endeavoured to render them odious to all the provinces. Under the pretence of forced contributions, the amount of which he was to receive, he often fet the Negroes at variance with the Brebes, by whom they were held in abhorrence; keeping up a correfpondence with thefe mountaineers, the Emperor himfelf would fend faithful troops, that the Negroes might be put between two fires, and thus facrificed to the public hatred, his private vengeance, and his future repofe. By fuch acts of barbarous policy, which had, in fome fort, become neceffary, in confequence of the avarice, ficklenefs, and preponderance of the Negroes, thefe turbulent forces, that had fo often

often put up the empire at auction, loft that afcendancy they had acquired.

The Negroes being thus reduced, the Emperor recovered his power, and the empire a part of its tranquillity. Muley Abdallah was firmly eftablifhed on the throne, and remained thus in peaceable poffeffion till his death. Yet did not all the varieties of fortune he had felt make any change in the manners of this Moor; he ftill preferved the fanguinary and cruel character he from the firft had teftified, and ftill infpired no other fentiments than thofe of fear and terror. Ingenious in refining on barbarity, not a week paffed, perhaps not a day, that did not behold fome one immolated to his choler, or his caprice.

It muft, notwithftanding, be acknowledged that, cruel and frantic as were the acts which difgraced his reign, he ftill gave tokens of fome principles of equity and difintereftednefs, which, though they cannot excufe, feem, in fome degree, to foften his ferocity. When any Moor whatever had committed a crime, Muley Abdallah caufed him

him to be punished with the utmost severity, without seizing on his wealth. An Alcaid, after having been imprisoned and condemded to death, offered to give him his riches, which were very considerable, would he only grant him his life. "Thy riches," answered the Emperor, "belong to thy " children, who are not guilty; but, as " thou art, it is but just that thou shouldest " perish."

Muley Abdallah having, at length, suppressed those revolutions, by which his reign had so often been disturbed, he alternately made Mequinez and Morocco his places of residence, that he might occasionally be present at each boundary of his empire, and overawe, with the greater ease, the provinces, whose inconstancy he feared. He afterward commanded the palace, called Arbiba, to be built near New Fez, in which he passed the latter years of his life.

Heir to all the caprices and barbarities of Muley Ishmael, he neither possessed his prudence

prudence nor his policy. More generous than his father, and less a slave to the prejudices of his religion, he did not resemble him in his dislike of Europeans: he soon concluded treaties of peace with the English and the Dutch, who, in the beginning of the present century, enjoyed almost the exclusive commerce of Europe; the confidence of foreign powers, under his reign, was so far established that several commercial houses were settled at Tetuan, Sallee, Saffi, and Santa Cruz; and the merchants, as well as the ships of nations that were not at peace with the empire of Morocco, there enjoyed all the rights and good faith of asylum.

After the example of his father, Muley Abdallah employed the slaves, whom the fate of battles gave into the power of his corsairs, on the public works; and, though he treated them with barbarous rigour, chastising and putting them to death on the slightest pretence, he still held it contrary to the principles of humanity to refuse their being redeemed; many of them were released under his reign, and thus,

amidst

amidſt the moſt exceſſive cruelties, did he ſeem to be impreſſed with ſome ſentiments of humanity and juſtice.

The plague, which had laid waſte the ſtates of Morocco, under the reign of Muley Iſhmael, again committed new ravages under that of Muley Abdallah, and made its appearance in 1752, being communicated to the Moors from Algiers and Tunis, whither it had been brought from Turkey*.

It was at the commencement of the reign of Muley Abdallah, in 1732, that

---

* The plague was almoſt general in Turkey in the year 1751, and Conſtantinople loſt a third of its inhabitants. The ravages of this ſcourge of man were, in ſome degree, foretold by the old people, who, ſeeing the quantity of ſnow that fell in the winter of 1750 and 1751, foreboded, from experience, that the plague would become very fatal. Their prophecy was juſtified by the event, though it had by many been regarded as vague and idle. It might happen that the nitrous particles, with which the air was impregnated, increaſed the fermentation of the blood, and rendered the contagion more quick and poiſonous. I have allowed myſelf to write this note, which, perhaps, may deſerve indulgence from the accurate obſervers of nature.

the Duke de Riperda, renowned for his high rank and adventures, paſſed over to the court of Morocco. Born in the province of Groningen, and become miniſter of Spain, under Philip V., this Duke, after his diſgrace, was expoſed for a time to numerous viciſſitudes of fortune. After eſcaping from Segovia, where he was impriſoned, he went to England and Holland; his reſtleſs and turbulent temper made him liſten to the inſtigations of the Alcaid, Perez, who, at that time, reſided as ambaſſador at the Hague, and turn his thoughts toward Morocco.

Full of animoſity againſt the court of Madrid, the Duke formed the project of beſieging Ceuta, thinking he ſhould thereby involve the court of Morocco in his reſentment. He met a very kind reception from Muley Abdallah; but the ſtates of the Emperor being conſtantly a prey to revolutions, and he himſelf inconſiſtent, the Duke went to Tetuan, and made that the place of his reſidence.

Here

Here he formed various projects to dissipate his weariness, and animate the Moors against Spain; but his motives of resentment, and plans of revenge, were wholly ineffectual at a court which never acted from any fixed system, and which was itself too much divided to concern itself with foreign interests. By nature turbulent, the Duke afterward entered into the projects of Baron Neuhof, who, under the name of Theodore, was for a moment king of Corsica.

Desirous of prevailing on the court of Morocco to unite itself with the people of Tunis, who were disposed to give aid to this rising kingdom, he made many journies to the court at Mequinez, where his plan appeared to be approved; but he was amused only with hopes, in order to obtain presents, and his political views were very little regarded. It is not, however, true that the Duke de Riperda became a proselyte to Mahometanism; nor did he ever command the armies of Morocco, as some writers have affirmed. Some Moors of the country, who were particularly acquainted

quainted with him, have affured me that he ended his life and romantic adventures at Tetuan, toward the end of the year 1737, without either changing his drefs or his religion.

Muley Abdallah having paffed the greater part of his life in one continued agitation, never, during the firft years of his reign, tafting repofe, it may be that this erratic and troublefome life might contribute to the brutal ferocity of his character, and to that depravation of manners which made him contemned by his fubjects. His whole pofterity confifted but of two male children; the eldeft having died in the caftle of Rabat, while heading his father's party againft Muley Muftadi, there only remained Sidi Mahomet, the prefent reigning Emperor.

This circumftance prevented the divifions, which always arife on the death of an Emperor, to obtain the fucceffion; for, as the rights of feniority and birth are not fufficiently eftablifhed to give unequivocal claim, all the fons of the late fovereign, anxious to
poffefs

poſſeſs a crown, form parties; and the empire becomes the inheritance of him who is the ſtrongeſt and moſt wealthy.

Sidi Mahomet, deſirous of fixing the public opinion concerning himſelf and accuſtoming the people to obedience, obtained from his father the government of Saffi, where he paſſed a part of his youth. Several European merchants had ſettled in this city, which, at that time, was the moſt commercial on the whole coaſt; and this prince, who was exceedingly eaſy of acceſs, and whoſe views were equally to employ his time agreeably and to gain valuable information, frequently converſed with theſe merchants concerning the cuſtoms of Europe, the commerce of its nations, their taxes, and their mode of adminiſtration. At this time it was that Sidi Mahomet acquired thoſe general, vague, and imperfect ideas, which ſince have unfolded themſelves during the courſe of his reign, and which have given Europeans an advantageous opinion of his abilities. Theſe are, perhaps, held in higher conſideration among foreign nations than in his own empire,

empire, where, however, the beft judgement may be formed of his principles, by an actual view of their confequences.

Defirous of fhewing himfelf in the provinces of the empire, Sidi Mahomet, while prince, pretended it was neceffary he fhould journey through them, in order to make the fovereign authority refpectable, which authority he infenfibly appropriated to himfelf: he traverfed thofe of Duquella, Tedla, and Temfena, where he levied many contributions, to his own profit, with a high hand. At his return, his father, who had retired to Fez, entrufted him with the government of Morocco, and there he refided with one of his coufins, Muley Dris, an enlightened prince, who, in the firft advances of Sidi Mahomet toward empire, aided him by his advice and abilities.

Of all the princes who had difputed fovereign power with Muley Abdallah, Muley Muftadi was the only one who, whenever his brother fhould die, might raife an infurrection in the provinces of the North.

Sidi

Sidi Mahomet, in order to prevent any such attempts, sent him notice to quit Arzilla, and to go and reside at Fez, where he, a short time after, died.

The better to establish his authority in the north of the empire, Sidi Mahomet left Morocco, in 1755, accompanied by an army, and presented himself, during the month of August, before Rabat and Sallee, which places, since the reign of Muley Ishmael, had been governed by a special administration of their own, and formed a kind of republic. This regency, though feudatory to the empire, appeared to prescribe limits to the sovereign authority. The inhabitants of these combined towns, known by the name of Saletines, or Sallee rovers, fitted out corsairs at their own expence, and were in possession of the gains of piracy, and the advantages of commerce, which, by the situation of those towns on the sea shore, and the industry of the people, had become considerable.

The wealth and independence of these two cities afforded motives sufficiently powerful

powerful to enflame the ambition of the prince, covetous as he was of riches, and defirous of empire. Sidi Mahomet had further cause of enmity against these places, arising from the wavering state in which they remained during the revolutions that had disturbed the reign of his father. This was remembered with rancour by the prince, and thus had the recollection of the wealth they contained, their independence, and the part they had taken in behalf of Muley Muftadi, long excited his avidity and his resentment.

Rabat and Sallee, though united by a confederation, which situation, mutual convenience, and contiguity, rendered necessary, were, nevertheless, disturbed by that spirit of restlessness so natural to the Moors, and by a diversity of interests, which were continual and unceasing causes of quarrels and dissensions. On the approach of Sidi Mahomet, however, they united their forces, and resolved to refuse entrance to the prince.

Rabat,

Rabat, faithful to its engagements, obstinately defended its walls; but the Bashaw, Fenis, who commanded at Sallee, desirous of obtaining the favours of the prince, and by his submission of conferring an obligation on Sidi Mahomet, as he had before done on Muley Muftadi, repaired, in company with the principal men of the city, to the camp of the prince, on the 26th of August, there to supplicate for clemency and reward. Sidi Mahomet pardoned the Bashaw, Fenis, and sent him back exceedingly well satisfied, but, some time after, took an opportunity to effect his destruction, and had him stoned to death in his presence.

After the reduction of the city of Sallee, that of Rabat, which found a difficulty of preventing communication by the river, was also obliged to submit. Sidi Mahomet imprisoned the principal persons in the government, behaved to them like a haughty victor, and obliged them to pay heavy contributions. One of the inhabitants, whose name was Misteri, exceedingly wealthy, and at the head of the confederants, en-

gaged

gaged to fupply the place with food himfelf during a year; but the brother of this republican betrayed him to the prince, whom he informed of the ftate of the place. Mifteri was ftripped of his property, as a punifhment for his firm refiftance; and his brother was made governor of Rabat, as a reward for his treachery.

All the inhabitants of the city were made to feel the refentment of the prince. Three merchant's houfes, two French, one Englifh, and a Spanifh convent, were not excepted. The monks, who had no property, were made flaves, and where afterward ranfomed. The merchants themfelves were not releafed till each of them had firft paid ten thoufand piaftres, and thefe were paid in effects, which were eftimated at fo low a price that their ranfom amounted to double the fum. The Englifh merchant, for having fold gunpowder to Muley Muftadi, was treated with ftill greater rigour; and, after having been expofed to various humiliations and violences, hung himfelf in defpair. The taking of Rabat and Sallee

expofed

exposed the inhabitants of these two places to very considerable impositions, but cost none of them their lives, the Bashaw, Fenis, alone excepted, who was put to death some time afterward, and who was the sole victim the prince appears to have sacrificed to his resentment. Perhaps this is the only act of cruelty with which he can be reproached; and, for the commission of which, he has himself testified his repentance.

By that contradiction which is either natural to man, to the character of this prince, or, perhaps, to arbitrary power, Sidi Mahomet chastised Sallee for having received, and Rabat for not having received, Muley Mustadi. He, with greater reason, reproached the inhabitants of the latter place for their conduct toward his brother, whom they had besieged and almost starved to death, in the castle where he had shut himself up, when defending the rights and interests of his father, Muley Abdallah.

After

After having subjected the cities of Rabat and Sallee, Sidi Mahomet marched into the North of the empire, where he obliged the Alcaid, Lucas, Governor of Tetuan, to render up an account of his administration. This Alcaid, who had taken advantage of the distance of the court, and the feebleness of the government, in the latter part of the reign of Muley Abdallah, to extend his own authority, was stripped of his property and power.

Sidi Mahomet reformed various abuses during the life of his father, with whom he almost divided the empire, till, at last, Muley Abdallah, worn out by age, and still more by the troubles he had met with during his reign, died on the 12th of November, 1757, in his palace at Fez, where he had only preserved the shadow of authority.

Exposed as he was himself, in the first years of his reign, to all the caprices of fortune, and as his subjects were to all those of his own temper, this Emperor still had some good qualities, which were clouded by
a much

a much greater number of vices. He poſſeſſed courage, judgment, and generoſity; but was violent, ſanguinary, and addicted to drunkenneſs, and to a depraved and infamous vice, which he made faſhionable at his court. The ferocity of his character ſeemed to be the conſequence of an atrabilarious conſtitution, and which diſplayed itſelf periodically, occaſioned, perhaps, by the greater or leſs agitation of the blood.

He one day made a preſent of two thouſand ducats to a confidential domeſtic, and adviſed him to go and live far from his preſence, that he might not be expoſed to the effects of his fury. The attachment to his maſter was ſo great that the ſervant refuſed, and, in one of his barbarous fits, Muley Abdallah ſhot this faithful ſervant, reproaching him with his folly for not having left him as he had been adviſed.

As he was paſſing the river of Beth on horſeback, at the place where it falls into the Seboo, the Emperor was in danger of being drowned, when one of his Negroes

ran

ran to his succour and preserved his life. The slave congratulated himself for having saved his master, when the Emperor, drawing his sabre clave him down, and exclaimed, " Here is an infidel! To suppose " that he had saved me! As if God stood " in need of his intervention to save a " sharif."

Without publicly neglecting the rites of the law, Muley Abdallah paid little respect to popular prejudices, and put to death several Moors, whose sanctity had been held in veneration. He one day killed two Marabouts, who came from the neighbourhood of Tunis, and who informed him they were saints. " You " saints!" said the Emperor. " You are " no saints. You are impostors, who, " abusing the credulity of the people, " come here as spies." After which he fired a musket at each, and laid them dead at his feet.

A saint, revered throughout the country, having come to the court of this prince to remonstrate to him concerning his mode of life,

life, so contrary to the laws of Mahomet, said to the Emperor: " The prophet him-
" self has ordained me to come, on his part,
" and speak to thee thus ——— And did the
" prophet tell thee in what manner I
" should receive thee?— Yes, he told me
" that you would be affected by the words
" which he commanded me to speak, and
" that you would employ them to your
" advantage—Then he has deceived thee,"
said the Emperor, discharging at the same moment his piece, which laid the saint lifeless; and, farther to punish his temerity, he would not permit his body to be buried.

An Alcaid, who had been guilty of disobedience, having come to the court of Muley Abdallah to implore pardon, the Emperor commanded him to be beheaded. He then ordered dinner to be served to the officers who had accompanied this Alcaid, and to place in the dish of Cooscoosoo, out of which they were to eat, this bloody head, that they might not soon forget the punishment disobedience merited.

Thus did this prince make his crimes and executions his amufement. Enough has been faid of him; it were but to infult humanity to add more traits of the cruelty of his character.

BOOK

BOOK V.

The reign of Sidi Mahomet—Commercial regulations—Administration, public and domestic—Insurrections—Wars, Locusts, Famine—Character of the Emperor—Commerce of the Empire—Duties, Coins, Weights, and Measures.

INTRODUCTION.

After the death of Muley Abdallah, his only son, Sidi Mahomet, who, during the life of his father, had already accustomed the people to respect his authority, succeeded to the empire without opposition.

The reign of this Emperor has not been varied by revolutions, or victories; neither is it fullied by thofe acts of violence, and barbarity, which fo dreadfully ftained the fceptre of his predeceffors. I have imagined, the beft mode of giving a clear idea of his reign would be briefly to examine the feveral regulations attending it, and the principal events. Thefe combined will prefent a faithful picture of the character, the genius, and the views of Sidi Mahomet, and of the prefent ftate of the empire of Morocco. I fhall therefore fpeak feparately of the difpofitions and plans of this Emperor, relative to commerce and taxation, to the general adminiftration of the government, the domeftic and œconomical affairs of the palace, the few infurrections that have happened during his reign, and the events by which it has been diftinguifhed.

CHAP.

CHAP. I.

The dispositions and views of Sidi Mahomet relative to commerce and taxation.

THE empire having been so long disturbed by revolutions, under the reign of Muley Abdallah, the distant provinces lived in a kind of independence. The governors had usurped more authority, and the treasury had been exhausted by the avidity of the soldiers, and the capricious manner in which money was squandered by that Emperor. Sidi Mahomet, ripened by age and experience when he ascended the throne, applied himself to find means of quickly re-establishing the finances, and supplying the state treasury; and with the care of making arbitrary power respected throughout the provinces; which power had been

been somewhat enfeebled by the concussions of the late troublesome reign.

The information he had acquired, concerning commerce and taxation, occasioned the Emperor to perceive that, of all political advantages, that which tended to revive commerce in a nation could alone augment its revenues, and repair its losses. The profits arising from piracy, an occupation which was exposed to real losses and uncertain gains, might, on the one part, provoke the resentment of nations, the maritime forces of which were daily augmenting, while, on the other, the barter of the productions of the empire would ascertain to him those more abundant resources of wealth which accrue from agriculture.

Reflexions like these determined Sidi Mahomet to make peace with the powers of Europe. After confirming that already made between Morocco, England, and Holland, he, in the beginning of his reign, concluded treaties with Denmark and Sweden succeffively; and, in the following years,

years, with the republic of Venice, France, Spain, and Portugal. In 1782, the Emperor and the Grand Duke of Tuscany made peace, and the other powers of Italy enjoy a kind of truce with the empire of Morocco.

Before the reign of Sidi Mahomet the nations of Europe had formed commercial connections on the coast of Morocco, and those who were not at peace with the empire still enjoyed the safety of asylum. True it is that the instability of the government somewhat diminished the confidence of nations; and the little security the roads of Morocco afforded, in winter, was an obstacle to the increase of navigation. At that time there were only a few safe ports on the coast of the empire. They were dangerous from the impediments of bars, and the ignorance, avarice, or evil intentions, of the pilots.

In order to aid commerce, and encrease the glory of his reign, Sidi Mahomet caused the town of Mogodor to be built in the south part of his empire, where nature had formed a port a port accessible in all seasons. The Emperor encouraged foreign merchants to erect houses in this new city, by giving them to suppose the duties of the customs should be lessened. The Moors and the Jews also built houses there to please their Master; and Mogodor, as I have already observed, is built with more regularity than any other city of the empire.

After having thus founded Mogodor, the principal expence of which was supported by foreign commerce, the Emperor, who began to take delight in building, ordered the fortresses of Laracha and Rabat to be repaired, embellished each of these cities with some edifices and public markets, and, at the same time, made additions to his palace at Morocco, for which he has a degree of predilection. After he had extended the circumference of this palace, he caused new pavillions to be added, built with taste by European masons.

In 1773, Sidi Mahomet commanded the foundation of the town of Fedale to be laid, which was then begun, but which has never

never been finished. These undertakings have been neglected, pursued, or again abandoned, according to the temporary change of circumstances, or, perhaps, because the revenues of the Emperor are insufficient to support such expences. Neither do cities seem so necessary, in these temperate climates, where the people are habituated to a solitary country life, as they are in latitudes less mild.

The confidence which the regulations, political views, and personal character, of Sidi Mahomet inspired, among foreign nations, at first multiplied mercantile establishments on the coast of Morocco. Merchants settled at Santa Cruz, Mogodor, Saffi, Rabat, Laracha, and Tetuan. There were even too many, and their purposes were subverted by their own eagerness. The Emperor successively increased the duties, hoping thereby to augment his revenues; but this oppression, however, produced an effect the very reverse. Shackled thus by taxation, commerce grew languid.

The

The Emperor, pretending to give it new animation, became a merchant himself; and this did but increase the evil, for it did but increase restraint. Obliged to sell their wares a d to purchase the country products at such prices as the despot pleased to fix, merchants became merely his factors, and were constrained to remove from port to port in his empire, wherever he chose to indicate, as best suited his convenience, or to those to which he gave the preference.

By this means the channel of trade was interrupted. The farmer and the foreign trader, reaping no fruit from the labours of their industry, and unable to resist the current of authority, are wholly discouraged; the fields lie waste, the markets are deserted, and, of all the mercantile houses dispersed over the coast of Morocco, there scarcely remain six. United at Mogodor, and accustomed to the variations of the government, they have to struggle against the extortions excited by the spirit of interest, and which, at one moment increased, creafed, at the next relaxed, are never certain.

More enlightened than his predeceffors, Sidi Mahomet, in 1766, made a regulation which betokened extenfive views; but, not being directed by invariable principles, its effect was merely momentary. At that time there was a confiderable quantity of corn amaffed, in the maritime provinces, which long had been inclofed in Matamores*, and there expofed to perifh, exportation being prohibited by the law. The Emperor, whofe fyftem was more humane and more œconomical, wifhing to conciliate the wants of the nation with its prejudices, and give his plan a legal fanction, affembled the learned in the law, and propofed to them his difficulties concerning the exportation of corn.

---

* Corn can only be preferved in fuch kind of pits in hot countries; and it appears probable that the reafon is becaufe the corn, there, is firm and hard. The wheat reaped in the northern countries of Europe, which is called foft corn, could not be fo preferved. Yet this difference in the grain is accidental, and relative to the nature of the foil and the climate, and not to its own inherent qualities.

" I have

"I have need," said the Emperor, "of arms and ammunition, for the defence of our religion; but, by purchasing them, I must exhaust the treasures of the state. Would it be contrary to our law to procure these things, by giving in exchange corn which we cannot eat ourselves, and which, in time, must perish?"

The proposition was so clear, and the necessity also of approving the will of the despot so great, that the assembly concluded such barter would be entirely legal, and the exportation of corn was permitted in exchange for mortars, cannon, and gunpowder. The Emperor, at length, received money for it, because that, with money, arms and ammunition may be bought. In a short time he had collected not only artillery, bombs, and mortars, but some millions of livres, while the provinces that had sold their corn had this additional resource to pay their enforced contributions, which, in the Empire of Morocco, is the usual consequence of wealth, a tax on their ficklenefs, and the pledge of their

their fidelity. Thus did this excellent regulation benefit the Emperor alone.

The exportation of corn from the coaſt of Morocco would become an inexhauſtible ſource of barter and wealth, to the ſubject and to the ſtate, were only a moderate taxation impoſed, which might encourage agriculture. But, in free ſtates only, and governments that ſeriouſly are active to procure happineſs to man, are ſuch advantages well underſtood; therefore do we only behold the lands rich and fruitful in thoſe happy countries where agriculture is encouraged; while the provinces of Morocco, naturally fertile, yet overrun with brambles, are little better than deſerts, and where the generations of men languiſh and inſenſibly diminiſh.

CHAP. II.

Of the public Administration under Sidi Mahomet.

IT has before been shewn that the government of Morocco is wholly subordinate to the will of the despot, and that he confides the regulation of the provinces and cities of his empire to his Alcaids and Bashaws. It has likewise been observed that the Emperor himself, three times a week, gives public audiences to enforce justice, and at which all his subjects, without exception, are heard. This system, which cannot be too much admired, prevents malversation, and the abuse of authority among the chiefs. It gives the sovereign an opportunity of knowing the truth, which it is the interest of his courtiers to conceal, of becoming acquainted with

whatever

whatever paſſes in his ſtates, even to their utmoſt boundaries, and enables him to ſuperintend the adminiſtration of juſtice.

After the acceſſion of Sidi Mahomet, this judicious Emperor, deſirous of effacing all recollection of the caprices of his father, wholly employed himſelf in the reſtoration of order, of re-eſtabliſhing rules for government, and uniformity in the deciſions of juſtice. Well knowing the talents and penetration of Muley Dris, his relation, with whom he had paſſed a part of his youth, he made him his friend, repoſed entire confidence in him, and almoſt raiſed him to the rank of his aſſociate in the empire.

Muley Dris was a penetrating and enlightened prince. Though covetous of riches, he ſtill was generous to his Maſter. Subtle, ſagacious, and fertile in expedients, he ſoon brought all affairs to paſs through his hands, and almoſt governed the empire under the ſhadow of the monarch. That he might conform to the taſte of the Emperor, he appeared in public with the utmoſt

moſt ſimplicity. But, for this abſtinence, he amply recompenſed himſelf in his palace and in his gardens, where he lived voluptuouſly.

Muley Dris almoſt excluſively appropriated to himſelf the adminiſtration of European affairs. This was to him a ſecret ſource of wealth, which, by his management and addreſs, became inexhauſtible. Not one perſon at the court of Morocco could treat ſuch ſubjects with greater dexterity, or could ſo artfully varniſh, or give effect to, his good or his ill offices. Full of diſſimulation with foreigners, who came to viſit him, he oſtentatiouſly diſplayed his cabinets, richly ornamented with ſilver plate, china, and jewels, which he had re-received as preſents from various courts. Like a cunning courtezan, who knows artfully to ſtimulate the generoſity of her lover, he, with ſubtlety, inſinuated to one nation how much he had received from another, to excite emulation, and the deſire of pleaſing him, by the largeneſs of their gifts. Thus acquainted with the human heart, he ſported with the vanity of individuals,

individuals, and raised a rivalship between nations.

The wealth which Muley Dris had thus accumulated has had a similar fate to that of all other individuals, in Morocco, who have preceded him, or survived. Acquired as it was by the influence of the sovereign, it has become a part of the treasures of the state, which must, at length, insensibly engulph the whole riches of the empire. This prince was, various times before his death, stripped of a part of his property, and the Emperor took care to secure what remained after his decease, fearing lest his children, who were young, might make an ill use of their money.

Muley Dris, after having indulged in pleasure to excess, died in March, 1772, of a dropsy, which appeared to be the consequence of his irregularities. He made an immoderate use of the Achicha, which is of a nature so heating, and which rendered him so choleric and ferocious, that there was no barbarity he was not capable to commit during his intoxication. He had inherited the vices of his anceſtors, was intemperate, covetous, and cruel; and, had fortune raiſed him to power, he would have walked in the paths of Muley Arſhid, Muley Iſhmael, and Muley Abdallah.

After the death of this prince, Sidi Mahomet having no confidential perſon whom he entruſted, indulged his own character more freely. Some of his ſelfiſh agents, whom he appoints or depoſes at pleaſure, are charged with the execution of his orders. They are become the inſtruments by whom all buſineſs muſt be tranſacted, and negociations are now more tedious and more uncertain. Each new reſolution is expoſed to thoſe variations which muſt be the reſult, under a government the ſyſtem of which is to conſult the intereſt of the moment.

CHAP.

CHAP. III.

Of the domestic affairs and interior œconomy of the palace.

SIDI Mahomet does not awe the spectator by any oftentation of magnificence. The friend of fimplicity, and without the leaft inclination for luxury, this Emperor is only diftinguifhed from the grandees of his court by being on horfeback, and protected from the funbeams by an umbrella, which, in Morocco, is the diftinctive mark of fovereignty. The numerous retinue of officers, foldiers, pages, and fecretaries, who appertain to the court, befpeak the prefence of the monarch, who never appears in public but on horfeback, or in his calefh. He is never feen on foot, except in his palace, at his devotions, or, on fome few occafions, in his gardens. He never travels in a carriage, becaufe of the bad ftate of the roads.

The Emperor of Morocco, only on days of ceremony, or when he holds his Mefhooar, that is, his council, or audience, appears with all his pomp, which then rather confifts in the number than in the fplendour of his train. When he leaves his palace, for his amufement or to vifit the public works, he difplays no pomp; and he has been fometimes feen in a fhallop, on the Sallee river, with not more than two attendants.

The cuftoms of the court of Morocco, and thofe of the Ottoman court, bear no refemblance. The latter is remarkable for its magnificence, the former for its ruftic fimplicity. At the court of the Grand Seignior, the adminiftration of the government, and that of the palace, are entrufted to a number of minifters, who themfelves live in great ftate, and poffefs great power. At Morocco, the Defpot grants his fubjects only fleeting and momentary confidence. They attend on him but to execute

cute his commands, without possessing any stable or permanent authority.

Female negro slaves have the care of the palace, and of the kitchen. The Emperor has occasionally sent for European cooks and bakers; but, wanting the conveniences to which they had been accustomed, unacquainted with the manners of the Moors, ignorant of the language, and not easily habituating themselves to a kind of wandering life, these Europeans never settled at the court of Morocco. The monarch being, also, naturally temperate, troubles himself little concerning such things. He has not so much as any fixed hour of dinner.

The table of the palace is served with great uniformity. The Moors eat only to live, and are unacquainted with that multitude of dishes, and that variety of sauces, which, in Europe, are objects of so much industry and expence. Sidi Mahomet generally eats alone, and those officers who personally attend on him are afterward served from his table. Each of the Emperor's wives

wives has a separate table, which is sufficiently supplied to suffice for all her attendants. Coofcoofoo, which has been described in its proper place, is the chief dish of the Moors, as well in the palace of the Emperor as in the hovel of the subject; and this is dressed in such quantities that the vessel that contains it is sometimes carried on a kind of chairman's horse.

The palace of the Emperor contains numerous servants of both sexes, who are new cloathed once a year. On this occasion all the taylors in the city are summoned, who usually are Jews, and they are obliged to labour gratis. This is a species of corvée, or tax, for which they indemnify themselves, when they can, by filching. Most trades are obliged to work gratis for the Emperor. The proprietor of a lime kiln must set apart a tenth for the service of the monarch; each article of merchandize, or industry, which is subjected to a like taxation, becomes more dear in proportion, and what the prince does not pay the purchaser must. The Emperor is served by slaves, who receive no other wages than what arise

from

from the profits or perquisites of the business they transact. He is at no expence, except that of feeding and cloathing his family, and which yet is defrayed out of the product of the tenths, and the custom-house duties, so that he seldom has any occasion to disburse money.

In the palace of the Emperor is a guard of women, with their female commanders, who are called Harriffa, and who form a kind of court, the province of which is the chastisement of women. These Harriffa are sent over the country to put the wives of the grandees to the torture, when the latter are imprisoned, and to make them confess all they know concerning the wealth of their husbands.

The luxury of the ladies of the palace is not very great. They depend on the generosity of the sovereign, which, in Sidi Mahomet, is wholly actuated by the greater or less degree of love they inspire. Such women as have not greatly pleased the monarch are often neglected, forgotten, and left in one imperial city, when the Emperor removes to another. This practice gives credibility to the opinion that access to the palace of the Emperor, in Morocco, is not so difficult as at Constantinople, where the women are shut up, and guarded with greater austerity. The women at the court of the Grand Seignior are kept in much greater splendor, and are held in much higher esteem than in these southern climates, where the Seraglio is renewed so often that they can only inspire a fleeting passion. The present Emperor has been known to send back to a Bashaw one of his daughters, to whom he had been only married six months.

The wives of the Emperor of Morocco, who are legally espoused, are not slaves, but are generally either princesses, the daughters of Sharifs, the daughters of the governors of provinces, or of private individuals. The Great Queen, for such is the title they give to the first wife, was the daughter of Muley Soliman, and grand daughter of Muley Arshid. This princess, who, by right of priority, had precedence over all the other women of the palace, enjoyed,

enjoyed, during her life, by the rights of birth and perſonal merit, a very high aſcendancy over the mind of the Emperor. The very ſame reaſon, alſo, enſured to her the attachment and veneration of the people, ſhe having ever, with the utmoſt prudence, attended to the government of Morocco, when the monarch was abſent. The regret of the empire, at her death, was equal to her merit and her virtues.

Sidi Mahomet has a great number of children. His daughters, married to ſharifs, have diſtricts aſſigned them, and, during the life of the Emperor, reſide in the palace, where they are miſtreſſes of their own actions. In order to provide for his ſons, as ſoon as they are married the Emperor beſtows upon them the governments of provinces and cities, where theſe young princes, indulging all the intemperance and follies of youth, and yielding to the advice and rapacity of their ſervants, inflict every kind of vexation, while the ſubjects have neither the fortitude nor the liberty to complain. Thus, in the adminiſtration of their offices do they imbibe the art of oppreſſing the people,

people; and, when their extortions raife univerfal difcontent, which can no longer be concealed, they are punifhed by confifcation for the benefit of the public treafury. After this difplay of juftice, oppreffion once more recommences; the treafury fwells, and the miferable people are the eternal victims.

CHAP. IV.

Revolutions that have happened during the reign of Sidi Mahomet.

NOTWITHSTANDING the restless spirit of the provinces, under the ever-agitated reign of Muley Abdallah, the tranquillity became great, when Sidi Mahomet ascended the throne. That discontent, which ever must arise from public wretchedness, may often have brooded in secret, but has since seldom burst forth. This Emperor has maintained a calm throughout his states, by occasionally going in person to their utmost boundaries. Wherever he appeared, some pretext for levying contributions generally has attended him; either originating in complaints against the governors, or in the prejudices and divisions which are unceasing, among those tribes which

which inhabit the provinces. The paſſions by which the Moors are tormented are never ending motives for inflicting pecuniary puniſhment. All their quarrels, their reconciliations, all acts of authority, of mercy, or of juſtice, are inceſſantly concluded by the payment of ſome quintals of ſilver. Such trifling diſputes give the monarch no inquietude; they do but draw his attention for a moment. It is even a part of his policy to maintain and provoke theſe miſunderſtandings; they are the ſafeguard of the deſpot, and ſeldom fail to turn to the advantage of his treaſury.

Sidi Mahomet had reigned fifteen years, when, in 1772, ſome ſeeds of thoſe revolutions, which had ſo often overthrown this empire in its birth, began to appear. A Marabout, whoſe enthuſiaſtic imagination was enflamed by pride and fanaticiſm, departed from the ſouth, which had been the cradle of all the ancient dynaſties, accompanied by a number of his diſciples, united by the ſpirit of bigottry.

Theſe

These visionaries, amounting to about three thousand, went to Morocco, and informed the Emperor that the end of his reign approached, and that their chief was to become the sovereign. The only arms of the companions of this Marabout were fanatic predictions, and clubs, which they, in the extravagance of their phrenzy, prophesied should be transformed into guns, while the arms of their adversaries should, on the contrary, be metamorphosed into clubs.

It so happened, however, that their prophecies were not fulfilled. The enthusiasts were hewn down, and put to flight, like cowards, by a few soldiers; and their chief, who had encouraged them in their reveries, having been seized in a mosque, was led before the Emperor at his public audience. The Marabout answered all interrogatories with the fortitude and impudence of an inspired person, and the Emperor commanded him to be put to death, at the Meshooar, as a disturber of the public peace.

From that time, till the year 1778, the provinces gave no figns of fedition fufficient to infpire fear. Thofe of the north, according to the cuftom of this people, began to be a little troublefome when the Emperor was in the fouth, and thofe of the fouth did juft the fame when he was in the north; but the prefence of the monarch, and pecuniary fines, brought them back to obedience; and thus did the Emperor at once increafe his wealth and confirm his authority.

The treafury was exhaufted, in 1774, by the fiege of Melilla, and a fucceffion of calamities having prevented the Emperor proportioning his expences to his revenues, and again filling his coffers, he found himfelf obliged to increafe the old taxes, and even to add new. The Negroes, the arrears of whofe pay progreffively increafed, murmured againft thefe new taxes, and, at length, in October 1778, drove the tax gatherers from Mequinez, and feized on the city.

After

After an act of such open rebellion, the Negroes sent a deputation to Muley Ali, at Fez, the eldest son of Sidi Mahomet, to offer him the empire. This wise prince, incapable of failing in the respect he owed to his father, rejected the proposal, endeavoured ineffectually to calm the minds of the people, and thought proper to retire to Rabat, that he might not provoke the insolence of the Negroes by a more obstinate refusal.

Muley Ali having thus declined, the Negroes determined to apply to Muley Yezid, who did not betoken the like repugnance to the throne, and this prince, beloved by the soldiers, was publicly proclaimed at the hour of prayer. This revolution caused an insurrection at Mequinez. The governor of that city found a difficulty in escaping, amid the firing of muskets, and his house was pillaged and pulled down.

Muley Yezid, notwithstanding, thought proper to inform his father of what had happened, and make excuses concerning the facility with which he had yielded to

the

the defire of the foldiers, hoping by that means once more to reduce them to obedience. This conduct of Muley Yezid, and fome mifintelligence among the Negroes, relaxed the progrefs of the revolution, which would have been effected, had the prince, who was neither pofieffed of money nor credit, marched at the head of his troops to Rabat. Reinforced as he would have been by eight thoufand Negroes, who were there affembled, he might eafily have made himfelf mafter of the treafury, which had, very injudicioufly, for fome years, been diftributed in the cities of Rabat, Laracha, and Tangiers. The poffeffion of thefe places, which might have been taken in a week, would have rendered Muley Yezid mafter of the empire. The firft effervefcence of tumult over, as is the cafe in all popular commotions, fedition weakened in confequence of reflection, of the inexperience of the prince, and the irrefolution of the foldiers, who, themfelves, had only a confufed idea of the infurrections their predeceffors had fo often raifed, in the beginning of this century. A calm fucceeded this flight tempeft, and the revolt

volt at Mequinez ceafed of itfelf without farther progrefs.

Informed of this rebellion, the Emperor departed from Morocco with his troops, and, on his march, fecured the fidelity of thofe who were at Rabat. He then continued his way to Mequinez, where he was received as a fovereign. Each party, equally agitated by fear, gave contradictory relations of what had paffed.

From Mequinez the Emperor went to Fez. This city, which, from its extent and antiquity, has fome preponderance in the affairs of the empire, had adopted fimilar ideas to thofe of the foldiers, had ftrengthened their diffatisfaction, and given it importance. The principal citizens, and men of the law, being reproached by the Emperor for their difobedience to his orders, replied, with like firmnefs and refpect, " That the city of Fez meaned not to dif- " obey him, nor ever fo could mean, but " that the taxes laid on provifions, the in- " creafe of duties on merchants, and the " new

" new imposts which had been laid, and
" which Musselmen regarded as contrary
" to their customs, and inimical to reli-
" gion, were considerations that, to a
" prince so just and so religious, might ex-
" cuse the general murmur and discontent
" of the people."

Sidi Mahomet, yielding to circumstances, prudently dissembled all resentment; but, being convinced by intercepted letters that his son, Muley Yezid, maintained a correspondence with the Brebes, which was susceptible of dangerous interpretation, he caused him to be confined, and afterward sent him on pilgrimage to Mecca, by that means to calm his unbridled passions, and render him more circumspect. Grown wiser by age and experience, the prince reaped those fruits from this voyage which are the usual consequences of the study of men, and the knowledge gained by visiting foreign nations.

However inclined to clemency, Sidi Mahomet could not forget the audacious conduct of his negro soldiers at Mequinez, and

and accordingly took measures to rid himself of these turbulent troops, the impatience of which daily became more burdensome, and whose fickleness and avarice had so frequently been experienced by his father.

The exhausted treasury could with difficulty supply the pay of the troops. The country, ravaged as it had been by locusts, in 1779, and by three successive years of dearth for want of rain, which increased its wretchedness, no longer permitted the people to pay those imposts which time and circumstances had multiplied. There were not above ten millions of livres, or somewhat more than four hundred thousand pounds, in the treasury, and four of these millions were necessary for the support, in these calamitous times, of thirty, or thirty-five thousand negro cavalry.

In this embarrassing situation the Emperor determined, in 1780, to reduce a part of these forces, from whose unquiet spirit he had every thing to dread. That he might disguise his intention, and prevent those inconveniences which might otherwife have been the result, he sent these Negroes away by detachments, pretending they must go and be quartered in the provinces; and, by an after order, sent still stronger detachments to disarm the first, and appoint them lands, in different countries, sufficiently distant from each other for him not to live in fear of their communication. A part of them, the fidelity of whose chiefs he was assured of, were still maintained; thus, in the course of sixty years, the hundred thousand armed Negroes, whom Muley Ishmael had left, and their posterity, are reduced to about fifteen thousand soldiers. All the remainder have disappeared.

CHAP.

CHAP. V.

Of the Wars, Locusts, Famine, and other events, under the reign of Sidi Mahomet.

THE Emperor having employed the beginning of his reign to re-establish commerce throughout his states, he afterward made various incursions into the provinces bordering on the mountains, there to confirm and render his power respectable. These expeditions, undertaken from motives of interest, conciliation, and peace, never were of that impetuous and cruel kind with those by which the people had so often been afflicted, under the barbarous government of his predecessors.

Scarcely had this Emperor collected, in 1767 and 1768, a quantity of artillery, than, in the beginning of 1769, he made preparations for the siege of Mazagan, which the Portuguese had resolved to evacuate, and which surrendered in the month of march, in the same year.

Flattered by this conquest, Sidi Mahomet, who thus inspired Europe with a greater idea of his puissance, and his people with higher awe, meditated projects still more ambitious. Having permitted farther exportations of corn, from the year 1771 to the close of 1773, he still farther increased his train of artillery; and, in order to conceal his intentions, he went into the north of his empire, and took up his residence for some time at Rabat and Sallee. The dislike which the Emperor had entertained to these two cities, which, in times of former revolutions, had thrown off their allegiance to his father, served as a pretence to make researches concerning the effects and houses that had appertained to the royal domain, and he recovered that vast inclosure which, since the reign of Jacob Almonsor, after having so often had new masters,

masters, had been embellished by gardens and a fine vineyard.

When this vineyard flourished, six pounds of exceeding good grapes might have been bought for a blanquil, worth about seven farthings. In 1775 a single pound of grapes cost six blanquils, or ten pence, so that the price was increased in the proportion of thirty six to one.

Beside this estimable inclosure, the inhabitants of Rabat farther lost several houses, and were even exposed to the licentiousness of the soldiery, which, during this time of prejudice, stole, with impunity, their flocks, their fruits, and corn. Sidi Mahomet caused the ground plot of a new town to be marked out, in a place called Guadel, which, in the idiom of the country, signifies reserve, and to which town he gave this same name, and caused it to be inhabited by five thousand of his Negro troops.

Guadel, which this monarch caused to be embellished with various mosques and public

public edifices, is at prefent deferted, and the houfes have all gone to ruin fince the time when, from political motives, the Negroes were reduced and difperfed. Scarcely built in 1776, this town was no more, in 1781, than a frightful heap of ruins, which feemed to have efcaped the fury of men and of the elements. The monarch afterward, more juft, fuffered each individual to reclaim his property. But the remembrance of oppreffion fo recent has difgufted the inhabitants of Rabat, who are little anxious to recover poffeffions the limits of which they do not know, and the titles to which are no longer in their own power.

The project which the Emperor fecretly meditated was not difcovered till the year 1774. He then affembled, in the heart of his empire, troops, artillery, and ammunition, and, after having mafked his views, under pretext of hoftilities, at one time againft the city of Fez, at another againft the mountaineers, he began his march to lay fiege to Melilla. The Emperor pretended, for fuch were his expreffions, that he he was only at peace by sea with his friend Don Carlos, which he was very desirous to maintain, but that they were not at peace by land.

This distinction, characteristic of the Moors, and which originated in the hope of success, gave great offence to the court of Spain, which sent speedy succour for the defence of Melilla, and broke off all correspondence with the court of Morocco. Sidi Mahomet might easily have taken the place, had he at first attacked it vigorously, because that, depending on the faith of treaties, it was then but feebly garrisoned. But General Sherlof, having entered Melilla with between seven and eight hundred men, made so courageous a defence that the Emperor had cause to repent of an enterprise, the success of which failed, which had cost him vast sums, and which the Moors seemed secretly to have disapproved.

Sidi Mahomet was obliged to remove his camp farther from the walls, the cannon of which

which thundered upon his army. It was also annoyed by some frigates, which, notwithstanding the narrow space they had to act in, manœuvred very ably. The Moors were so discouraged that, could the Spaniards have attacked them with any considerable force, they must have put them to flight, and taken the baggage and artillery.

The siege of Melilla had occasioned expences, and met with impediments that had not been foreseen. The cannon and ammunition were to be transported across the lesser Atlas, a mixture of vallies and mountains, among which there scarcely was a path. These stoney and ill-cultivated countries were also unable to supply provender, and this was obliged to be brought at such an excessive expence that the keep of a horse amounted to half a crown per day. The soldiery must likewise be encouraged by gratifications, so that the whole of these expences sunk more than thirty millions of livres, or one million two hundred and fifty thousand pounds sterling, which was an immense sum for a state

state so poor and exhausted. The Emperor saw himself obliged to abandon his undertaking; and, that he might prevent those impressions which his retreat might make on the Moors, he caused it to be rumoured, through the provinces, that the King of Spain would yield him up Melilla, as soon as he could quell the discontents of the Monks, who highly disliked the cession of that place. Rejoicings were made on the receiving of this news, and Sidi Mahomet returned to Mequinez, in the beginning of 1775, exceedingly chagrined with his own proceedings, and highly dreading the resentment of the court of Spain, and the formidable armament that was then preparing, not knowing that it was intended against Algiers. The Emperor was, in effect, in the utmost perplexity, and with reason, at beholding the gathering storm; nor was he more tranquil till he knew the true destination of that fleet, and heard of its failure.

After having thus provoked the resentment of the court of Madrid, the monarch employed all possible means to effect

fect a reconciliation; but the Spaniards, for some time, preserved that rancour which a conduct so perfidious had inspired. A change in the affairs of Europe having occasioned explanations between the courts, peace was re-established in 1780, and, during its negociation, Sidi Mahomet did every thing which he supposed might be most agreeable to the king of Spain, and might induce him to forget the past.

When Sidi Mahomet prepared for the siege of Melilla, he declared war against Holland, finding the present sent by the republic, on some extraordinary occasion, not equal to his expectations. Hence it may be judged how little confidence ought to be placed in the friendship of a monarch who sets his friendship up to sale, as actuated by whim, or interest. Holland fitted out ships for the protection of her commmerce, and, after a defensive war, when she might have done much better, renewed the peace in 1778, and increased her largess.

During

During the reign of Sidi Mahomet, the locusts, which so often afflict the southern climates, have various times ravaged the empire of Morocco; but never so generally or so fatally as after the year 1778. In the summer of that same year, such clouds of locusts came from the south that they darkened the air, and devoured a part of the harvest. Their offspring, which they left on the ground, committed still much greater mischief. Locusts appeared and bred anew in the following year, so that in the spring the country was wholly covered, and they crawled one over the other in search of their subsistence.

It has before been remarked, in speaking of the climate of Morocco, that the young locusts are those which are the most mischievous; and that it seems almost impossible to rid the land of these insects, and their ravages, when the country once becomes thus afflicted. In order to preserve the houses and gardens in the neighbourhood of cities, they dig a ditch two feet in depth, and as much in width. This they pallisade with reeds close to each other, and

and inclined inward toward the ditch; so that the infects, unable to climb up the slippery reed, fall back into the ditch, where they devour one another.

This was the means by which the gardens and vineyards of Rabat, and the city itself, were delivered from this scourge, in 1779. The intrenchment, which was, at least, a league in extent, formed a semicircle from the sea to the river, which separates Rabat from Sallee. The quantity of young locusts here assembled was so prodigious that, on the third day, the ditch could not be approached because of the stench. The whole country was eaten up, the very bark of the fig, pomegranate, and orange tree, bitter, hard, and corrosive as it was, could not escape the voracity of these insects.

The lands, ravaged throughout all the western provinces, produced no harvest, and the Moors, being obliged to live on their stores, which the exportation of corn (permitted till 1774) had drained, began to feel a dearth. Their cattle, for which they make no provifion, and which, in thefe climates, have no other fubfiftance than that of daily grazing, died with hunger; nor could any be preferved but thofe which were in the neighbourhood of mountains, or in marfhy grounds, where the re-growth of pafturage is more rapid.

In 1780, the diftrefs was ftill farther increafed. The dry winter had checked the products of the earth, and given birth to a new generation of locufts, that devoured whatever had efcaped from the inclemency of the feafon. The hufbandman did not reap even what he had fowed, and found himfelf deftitute of food, cattle, or feed corn. In this time of extreme wretchednefs, the poor felt all the horrors of famine. They were feen wandering over the country to devour roots, and, perhaps, abridged their days by digging into the entrails of the earth in fearch of the crude means by which they might be preferved.

Vaft numbers perifhed of indigeftible food and want. I have beheld country people in the roads, and in the ftreets, who
had

had died of hunger, and who were thrown acrofs affes to be taken and buried. Fathers fold their children. The hufband, with the confent of his wife, would take her into another province, there to beftow her in marriage as if fhe were his fifter, and afterward come and reclaim her, when his wants were no longer fo great. I have feen women and children run after camels, and rake in their dung to feek for fome indigefted grain of barley, which, if they found, they devoured with avidity.

Let us not dwell too long on woes which thus afflict humanity, and of which fo many thoufands, whofe hearts are rendered infenfible of pity by plenty, have no conception. The mifery would have been much greater, had not Spain and Portugal, where the harvefts had been tolerably abundant, permitted the exportation of oil, butter, dried fruits, and other provifions, and particularly the corn of the north, which happily, at that time, was plentiful at Cadiz and at Lifbon. This corn, which had paffed through fo many hands, was fold in the markets of Sallee at one hundred

dred and twenty livres, or five pounds, the measure, which measure corresponds with the Setier of Paris*. Bad oil and rancid butter were worth one hundred and eighty livres, or seven pounds ten shillings, the quintal. Peas, beans, and lentils, which abound in these countries, were become objects of so much luxury that they were counted out by grains, and twelve or fifteen were sold for a denier. During three or four years of dearth, the people ate bread which, by the mixture of the species of grain, and its bad quality, was exceedingly heavy, and difficult of digestion. Good bread was worth from six-pence to seven-pence halfpenny the pound, and other articles of subsistence in proportion.

Afflicting and extreme as the calamities of the empire at this time were, the awful resignation of these unhappy people, to the

---

* According to the author's estimate (See page 328 of Vol. I.) that the Setier of Paris weighs two hundred and a half, this measure will contain somewhat under four bushels. T.

decrees of Providence, could not be beheld but with aftonifhment; they fupported their afflictions without complaint, becaufe that, according to their faith, all things are decreed by the Moft High, and nothing happens but as pre-ordained by his will. Europeans, lefs refigned, more reftlefs, or, perhaps, more accuftomed to confide in the cares of an adminiftration the province of which is to provide for all their wants, are impatient and clamorous during times of fcarcity; and, fufpecting abufes, which fufpicions may be fometimes well founded, they charge their governors with carelefs- nefs or guilt. Plenty, or fcarcity, never- thelefs, depend moft evidently on the fer- tility or intemperance of feafons; when not occafioned by monopolies, or the excefs of exportation and importation.

The miferies the empire of Morocco underwent, in confequence of the fore- going evils, made it impoffible for the Moors to pay their taxes; the efforts of commerce flackened, and the revenues of the ftates diminifhed in proportion.

The

The roads soon became unsafe, travellers were obliged to be provided with escorts, the provinces were in a state of warfare, reciprocally to rob each other of what had escaped from the ravages of locusts, and the unfavourableness of the seasons. From the districts of Rabat and Sallee to the Morbeya, the whole of the provinces of Temsena and Tedla were, for the space of two or three years, exposed to depredations, which the public calamity might excuse, since they were not excited by the spirit of sedition. Such troubles, which resemble passing storms, are soon appeased, without the interference of government, when plenty restores tranquillity, and once more cools and bridles the restlessness and rapacity of the people.

In the year 1783, the Emperor made an excursion to Tafilet, with a detachment of troops; that city, and its environs, inhabited by numerous Sharifs desirous of power, had for some time been exposed to civil commotions, which were entirely appeased by the presence of the sovereign. Sidi Mahomet levied, in the province and on the eastern borders of the greater Atlas, heavy contributions, to punish the turbulence of the people.

While the Emperor was at Tafilet, the whole empire suffered a great loss by the death of Muley Ali, the eldest of his sons, who died at Fez, at the age of forty four, in consequence of a relapse of a neglected or ill-cured fever. This prince possessed all the qualities necessary to render his people happy; he had not inherited from his ancestors that impetuous and cruel character which, without constituting the happiness of kings, never fails to render nations miserable. Appointed by his father to the government of Fez, which is one of the most considerable in the empire, Muley had behaved with so much prudence, and disinterestedness, that, the Emperor having commanded him to render up an account of all he possessed, the city of Fez consented to pay the sum the sovereign exacted, that the prince might be maintained in his government, and continue in the good graces of his father.

The difinterestedness of Muley Ali, which was a very high recommendation to him among the people, had, perhaps, weakened the affection of his father, who had not the same manner of thinking. Sidi Mahomet having laid a tax on his son, which was to be paid for the benefit of his brothers, commanded him to raise the sum required on the community of the Jews, who, not being, he said, in the road to salvation, merited no pity.—" Sire," replied Muley Ali, " the Jews are so poor that they
" are incapable of supporting their present
" taxes, and it is impossible I should exact
" from them new ones. Should you so
" please, you may dispose of the revenues
" of my government for the benefit of
" my brothers; but I earnestly suppli-
" cate you will not require me to op-
" press these people, and thus oblige
" me to increase wretchedness already
" too great."

Such anecdotes prove with how much reason the people regretted the loss of this prince. I was well acquainted with his worth;

worth; the confidence with which he honoured me often made me a witnefs of his benevolence, and a judge of his heart.

CHAP.

CHAP. VI.

Character of the reigning Emperor.

SIDI Mahomet, endowed with penetration and judgement, would have been fusceptible of all the high qualities necessary to govern men, had education brought to perfection those gifts which nature had bestowed. His age is somewhere about seventy six*, his heighth five feet eight inches

---

* It is not customary among the Moors to register the birth of children, not even that of princes; their age is remembered by certain accidents, or events, which the parents commit to memory. A Moor very naturally says, he was born in the dry summer, the wet winter, or mentions any other similar accident.

The reigning Emperor was at Mecca, in 1727, when Muley Ishmael died; he was not then married, and, as he has always perfectly remembered this journey, it may well be supposed he was at that time about sixteen or eighteen,

inches, his symmetry tolerable; he squints a little, which gives his aspect some severity; his constitution being naturally strong, and his mode of life sober and frugal, his body is become very capable of supporting the fatigue of a life so laborious as the government of this empire requires. He is tolerably easy of access; foreigners he receives with politeness, and converses with them willingly; but the cool, or warm, reception he gives, alike, are directed by some motive of personal interest. His favour is not constant, but varies according as such like interested sensations vary.

However marked the attachment of Sidi Mahomet to riches may have been, he has seldom employed those means, for the accumulation of them, which violence or cruelty might have suggested. This Emperor will not leave so rich a treasury at his decease as his love for œconomy might fore-

---

and that he must have been born in or near the year 1710. This is the mode I have taken to calculate his age, in which I am confirmed by the oldest people in the country.

bode,

bode, and that because his reign has been exposed to heavy expences; his empire, gradually exhausted, has no longer in itself the same resources. Independent of the heavy sums expended on the siege of Mazagan, that of Melilla, and the maintenance of his forces, Sidi Mahomet has also built towns and fortresses, mosques and public markets, exclusive of his palaces, which he has embellished. He likewise purchased, in Malta and the Italian states, numerous Mahometan slaves, in 1782, the greatest part of whom were not his subjects; and he has further sent to Constantinople, in 1784, more than four million of livres, (or a hundred and sixty-six thousand pounds) which it is supposed he, out of respect to his religion, either appropriated to the temple of Mecca or the defence of the Ottoman empire, for which, knowing the ambition of its neighbours, he seems to have some fears.

Covetous as he appears to have been of wealth, Sidi Mahomet will leave little to posterity, except these monuments of his devotion, his charity, and his precaution.

More

More humane, more acceffible, and lefs exigent than his anceftors, Sidi Mahomet has ever treated the Chriftians, whom the fate of war has put into his power, with compaffion, and on fome among them he has beftowed marks of his confidence. After the taking of Mazagan, he fent thirty-eight flaves to the Grand Mafter of the knights of Malta, who were fubjects of the Grand Duke of Tufcany, and the Grand Mafter returned a like number of Moors.

Quick and penetrating, this Emperor has often made very juft obfervations on the characters of nations, judging by the flaves whom he had in his poffeffion, and who happened to be about his perfon. Perceiving how active the French were in their labours, he chofe them in preference for the execution of any fudden project; obferving, at the fame time, that they were reftlefs and turbulent, he held it neceffary they fhould be employed, that they might neither quarrel among themfelves nor with the other flaves. It cannot be faid that, under his government, flaves have been worked

worked to excess; it will likewise be perceived that monarchs, who number the ransom of slaves as one part of their revenues, have an interest in their preservation.

During thirty years that Sidi Mahomet has sat on the throne, his reign has been happy. It would be rash to prophesy what shall happen after his death: although it be true that similar causes will produce similar effects, we must not always judge of the future by the past; the smallest difference of circumstances, either in the times, or the characters of those men who head insurrections, will change the state of things, and decide on the destiny of nations. Nevertheless, when we behold in Morocco a multitude of princes, each desirous of governing, each having nearly an equal claim to govern, it should seem that like dissentions may well again be feared, and like revolutious to those which, under preceding reigns, so often have rent this empire.

The

The fucceffion is not fixed in Morocco, either by law or cuftom, but depends entirely on concurring accidents. It is well underftood, among the Moors, that the eldeft fon ought to inherit the crown, becaufe that his experience renders him the moft proper to govern; but, as there is no determinate law on this head, and as there is neither divan nor council in the empire to deliberate on affairs of ftate, the election of the Emperor depends entirely on chance, on the character of the candidates, the opinion of the people, the influence of the foldiery, the fupport of the provinces, and moft particularly on the poffeffion of the treafury. He who has money may have foldiers, and he who has foldiers can make himfelf feared.

We have feen that, under Muley Abdallah, one province and one faction would elect this fovereign, another that; and like anarchy may well be expected, whenever there are a great number of candidates for the throne; at leaft, unlefs the governors of provinces fhould all unite to protect one alone. This is a thing moft difficult to be

accom-

accomplifhed, among the Moors, where men do nothing, and where Providence regulates all.

Of ten or twelve male children, to whom the Emperor is father, there are feveral who are capable of government; nor can I doubt but that, informed as they muft be of former revolutions, they all afpire with equal confidence to that crown to which birth, the voice of the people, or a concatenation of incidents, may give each an equal right.

CHAP.

CHAP. VII.

Of the commercial intercourse between the Empire of Morocco and the nations of Europe.

WHEN the spirit of industry began to effect a change in Europe, in the power of kingdoms, and the manners of their inhabitants, monarchs felt the necessity of naval armaments, and, by their maritime forces, to secure to their subjects the progress of their commerce, and the freedom of the seas.

Before the discovery of the rout to the East Indies, round the Cape of Good Hope, and even for some time after, Europe had no communication with Asia, except by the Mediterranean, and over this sea a considerable trade was carried on through Spain, France,

France, Italy, the Levant, and the northern shores of Africa, which latter, even at that time, were invaded by bands of freebooters. Tripoli, Tunis, Algiers, Morocco, usurped by multitudes of soldiers, whom religion had armed, enemies as they were of the Christian religion, from bigotry, became still more so from interest; their inhabitants were poor, little addicted to labour, without commerce, pirates from inclination and necessity, and had no means of becoming of some importance, except by the licentiousness of freebooting.

Europe, which had formerly been armed against these common enemies by the zeal of religion, presently found itself divided in its own political interests. Nations, ambitious of power and of wealth, individually employed by the efforts of industry, and the barter of their products, consulted only their individual conveniency, and, in the hope of acquiring a greater ascendancy in commercial and maritime affairs, determined to make treaties with these usurpers of the shores of Africa; which treaties have

have been more or lefs obferved, according to the opinion entertained of their refpective force, and the reciprocity of their interefts.

Such were the motives, fuch the principles, of friendfhip, between the powers of Europe and the regencies of Barbary. The rivality, or the feeblenefs, of fuch commercial nations, occafioned thefe regencies afterward to acquire thofe means of power, the difadvantage and incumbrance of which have fince been fo often felt; the conditions by which their friendfhip muft be purchafed have imperceptibly become more humiliating, more intolerable, and lefs ftable.

It was not fo much for the promotion of trade, on the northern fhores of Africa, as to favour the growth of maritime power, and commerce in a different channel, that the nations of Europe have entered into thefe friendly treaties with the Barbary regencies, and the empire of Morocco. This empire itfelf, though rich in its native products, is not capable of any extenfive trade; the inftability of its laws is an obftacle stacle to the industry of its inhabitants, and to the confidence of foreigners. Neither are the wants of the Moors multiplied by their mode of education, or by the temperature of a climate where nature requires but little; and imaginary wants have been further suppressed by government, which, by depriving the people of the means of luxury, must necessarily enfeeble the activity of commerce, of which luxury is the Primum Mobile.

Thus, some trifling barter excepted, the safety of the sea has been the cause why the nations of Europe have made treaties with the empire of Morocco. I shall speak more particularly of these their treaties, and their interests, according to the priority of their dates, and shall bestow a separate chapter on those that relate to France.

England is the first power which concluded treaties of friendship and commerce with the Emperors of Morocco. Being in possession of Tangiers, which had been ceded to her by Portugal in 1662, she occasionally

casionally felt those inconveniences that result from the turbulency of the Moors, which she overlooked, and even gave up certain points, that she might, with the greater ease, maintain the garrison of that town, which, because of its distance, at length became a burthen to the nation.

England having, even at that time, acquired an extensive foreign commerce, she made propositions of peace to Muley Ishmael in 1675, which the caprices and contradictions of that Emperor rendered ineffectual. A truce, however, was concluded for four years in 1681, but was broken before the term expired; the Moors pretended that the peace had only related to the garrison of Tangiers, and did not extend to the protection of the British flag.

A distinction like this, worthy an Empire where treachery is native, gave birth to explanations. Muley Ishmael sent ambassadors to London at the commencement of the present century. This was a new pretext for new presents, and the treaty of peace was, at length, renewed under George

George I. After the death of Muley Iſhmael this treaty was confirmed, and renewed, in 1728, by Muley Achmet Daiby, and a little time after by Muley Abdallah.

The immenſe navigation and trade of the Engliſh gave them ſufficient motives to make peace with the Emperor of Morocco; and they had further a political reaſon, which was, to re-victual, with freſh proviſions, their garriſon of Gibraltar with facility, which place has been under their government from the beginning of the preſent century. Sidi Mahomet, more intelligent than his predeceſſors, has derived all poſſible profit from this circumſtance; and the Engliſh nation, haughty, jealous, and ever ready to take offence, has continued, and ſtill continues, to overlook all that inequality of conduct to which the ſpirit of avarice gives birth, on the part of the court of Morocco. The Engliſh have long maintained a trade on the coaſt of that empire, where they ſell coarſe cloths, ſerges, linens, pewter, lead, mercer's commodities, and the iron which their ſhips bring from Biſcay.

They receive in return sometimes oils, gums, wax, elephants-teeth, and have often sent, in French bottoms, to Marseilles, oils, raw hides, and wool, the consumption of which is greater in our southern provinces than among the more northern nations.

They have also exported a number of Mules to North America; but the dismemberment of that part of their dominions has greatly decreased their trade with Morocco, which before was not very considerable. England can only have a confined trade with Morocco, not having a sufficient market for the commodities she returns. The commercial relations which exist between kingdoms always depend on their mutual wants, and the facility with which barter can be made to mutual advantage.

In 1732 an ambassador was sent by Muley Abdallah into Holland, and the republic then made its peace with that Emperor; but the revolutions by which his reign was disturbed gave but little stability to the treaty. Holland was the first power which renewed

renewed treaties of peace with Sidi Mahomet, who then was only prince and governor of Saffi, but who, being the sole heir of the empire, had arrogated to himself the chief part of the authority. Independent of the safety of navigation, Holland had further a political motive, which was early to make peace with the Emperor, that she might the better profit by her neutrality during the war of 1755.

Having been informed that this republic treated the regency of Algiers with greater generosity than himself, Sidi Mahomet complained of the States General; and, notwithstanding the compliance that was shewn, the Emperor declared war against the Dutch toward the end of 1774, pretending that an extraordinary present, which they had sent him, and which he kept, was not sufficiently magnificent.

The republic sent numerous vessels into the Straits for the protection of trade and navigation; few of them appeared upon the coast, and that so seldom that the corsairs of Morocco took three Dutch ships, two of them as they left the port of San Lucar, within sight of Cadiz. These advantages were counterbalanced by the losses of the Emperor of Morocco. A Dutch frigate, which did but begin to chace two Corsairs of Sallee, caused them to be shipwrecked, even without following them, the one at the entrance of the river of Laracha, and the other at the mouth of that of Mamora. Holland renewed the peace in 1778, was more generous in her gifts, and, if so she shall please, may continue it by the like means.

Holland carries on a certain trade with the coast of Morocco, and custom has almost rendered her importations necessary. She there vends quantities of Silesian linens, called platillas, many of the coarse linens of the Baltic, and others, some few spices, drugs, tea, timber, iron of Biscay, and quantities of the cutlery and mercery wares of Germany.

Holland receives from the coast of Morocco, in return, sometimes oils, wax, gums, and elephants-teeth; but, as those returns,

returns, which suit the Dutch merchants, are insufficient to balance the quantity of merchandize they send thither, they have almost continually profited by the facility with which they can run for the French ports, to send oils to Marseilles, wools, and raw hides, which there find a readier sale than in the north. Had not Holland this liberty, she would imperceptibly have been obliged to renounce a trade, which must have become disadvantageous, when she could no longer freight her ships by barter, or be paid in money.

The court of Denmark began to negotiate with Sidi Mahomet in 1755. That kingdom is so distant from Morocco that the Danish ministry had not any just ideas concerning the government of this empire. Deceived by a Jew, who was the instrument and interpreter of the negotiations of Denmark, she supposed she might, without impediment, build a fortress at Santa Cruz, that she might there protect a mercantile settlement, which she intended to establish. The Jew agent disguised the intentions of the court of Denmark;

nor was there any knowledge in Morocco of the intended fort, till the materials for building it were landed. The Emperor, offended at feeing himfelf treated like the princes of Senegal, imprifoned the ambaffador of Denmark, and his retinue, pretending he would treat them as flaves. Some time was neceffary to rectify this miftake. Denmark again undertook to negotiate in 1757, a ranfom was agreed upon, new prefents were made, and a new peace concluded.

The late king of Denmark, occupied by commercial projects, gave his confent at that time for the forming of a royal African company, which, on paying an annual tribute of fifty thoufand piaftres, obtained from the Emperor of Morocco the exclufive commerce of his coaft, for the term of ten years, in the ports of Sallee and of Saffi, where two mercantile fettlements were made. The oppreffions and embarraffments which this monopoly incited, the expences occafioned by the forming of thefe eftablifhments, and the want of œconomy in fome foreign directors, to whom the adminiftration ministration of the company's affairs were confided, rendered this attempt unsuccessful. The monopoly extended only to the ports of Saffi and Sallee, the trade of which declined in consequence of other establishments, at the ports of Mogodor and Laracha, whither, by lessening the duties of the customs, the Emperor had drawn the chief products of his domains, which freighted the returning European ships.

This company, beside, were merely concerned in a carrying trade, as uncertain in its success as ill judged in its principles. Denmark itself contains no product necessary for the coast of Morocco, nor can the products of that empire find any market in Denmark; so that this company was but a clog upon the industry of the intermediate nations, and could derive no other advantage than that of affording employment to some Danish ships, which often arrived on the coast of Morocco loaded, and returned empty back. The Danish African company soon saw its capital sunk by ill-timed speculations, and by the gifts which the

compli-

compliance of its directors, and the necessity of satisfying the Emperor, did but multiply.

This company continued busied in the liquidation of its debts, after the accession of Christian VII. to the throne of Denmark; it was suppressed in 1767, at which time the court of Denmark freed itself from the annual burthen of fifty thousand piastres, a price paid for a monoply, which the royal African company ought to have enjoyed, but did not. The Danes only, however, could obtain the continuation of peace by annually paying the sum of twenty-five thousand piastres. Denmark has not itself any direct trade with that coast.

The Swedes concluded peace with the Emperor of Morocco in 1763. The present Sweden sent consisted of cannon, masts, and timber; she likewise agreed to make an annual present of twenty-thousand piastres, which she meant to pay in her own native products, but which the Emperor insisted on receiving in ready money. In the year 1771, Gustavus III., who then ascended

ascended the throne of Sweden, refused all kind of tribute, reserving to himself the liberty of making voluntary presents, without any determinate time or value. It was, at length, agreed, as a means of continuing the former good understanding between the courts, that the king of Sweden should send an ambassador and a present once in two years, to the Emperor of Morocco. The Swedes have no commercial intercourse with this empire.

The republic of Venice made peace with the Emperor of Morocco in 1765. She sent a very handsome present in money, and agreed to pay an annual tribute of about a hundred thousand livres, (or upward of four thousand pounds.) This republic having treated the regency of Algiers still more liberally, the Emperor was offended at the distinction, and sent a Genoese, who was in his service, to Venice to complain. His envoy having been received with great coolness by the Senate, and having returned with an answer that did not satisfy Sidi Mahomet, he gave further tokens of his discontent to the republic in 1780,

1780, and, inventing certain imputations, obliged the Venetian conful to depart from his ftates; but the republic having acquiefced in the wifhes of the Emperor, in 1781, the conful returned, and was very favourably received at the court of Morocco. The republic of Venice has no commercial intercourfe with this empire, and therefore, like the courts of Denmark and Sweden, pays this tribute folely for the fafety of navigation.

The court of Spain, as well as that of France, made peace with the Emperor of of Morocco in 1767. Sidi Mahomet was the firft to fend an ambaffador to Spain, and affected to give this kingdom fo much the preference that the confidence placed in his profeffions were too great. After having received very high proofs of the generofity of the court of Spain, and having, in fome meafure, difpofed of his arfenals for the repair of her fhips, this monarch took occafion to deftroy the good harmony which then exifted between the two powers, without breaking the peace, which, according to him, was merely confined

fined to the liberty of navigation. He marched with an army, about the end of 1774, to lay siege to Melilla, which place, instead of defending, he supposed Spain would abandon.

This proceeding, contrary to the faith of treaties, was the occasion of a rupture, between the court of Spain and that of Morocco. The Moor, having failed in his enterprize, took every possible means to re-establish peace; but the court of Madrid, deeply resenting his conduct, deferred concluding any treaty, and was satisfied with remaining in a kind of truce.

The quarrel between France and England having changed the political situation of Europe, the court of Spain thought that a favourable moment to treat with the Emperor of Morocco; and Sidi Mahomet renewed peace, in 1780, by the mediation of his ambassador, Ben-Otman, eagerly acquiescing in whatever the Spanish court demanded. The Emperor not only consented to refuse revictualing the garrison of Gibraltar, the siege of which was meditated

tated by Spain, but the Spaniards were, in a manner, masters of Tangiers, where they victualed their army, and which place served as an asylum to such of their ships as were stationed near the Straits. Their posts of observation beyond the castle, and as far as Cape Spartel, were so well regulated, that their signals from place to place communicated along the whole coast of Andalusia.

Their can be no continued trade between the coast of Spain and that of Morocco, for the corn trade, which varies according to circumstances and seasons, must only be considered as casual. The products of Morocco, their provisions excepted, are wholly useless in Spain; nor does Spain itself afford many articles of consumption for Morocco, cochineal excepted, which is used to dye Morocco leather, and the exclusive trade in which the Emperor has reserved to himself. The iron of Biscay, and the Barcelona handkerchiefs, which are in general use, might, indeed, be imported, but foreign nations buy up the first in exchange for their several products,

and

and the trade in the second is not of sufficient extent to maintain a continual intercourse.

For some years after the peace, conluded in 1767, the harvests having failed in Spain, the Spaniards bought up considerable quantities of wheat and barley on the coast of Morocco. This, however, was a forced trade, and not reciprocal; they took their money thither to buy provisions, poultry, and fruits, wherewith to supply Andalusia, where, because of the heat of the climate, men are little inclined to labour, and where the inequality of the seasons renders their harvests very uncertain.

Politically considered, this trade was only advantageous to the Emperor of Morocco, since Spain was not only dependent on him for supplies, but that, likewise, the facility with which these supplies were obtained did but further increase the indolence of the farmers of Andalusia. Hence resulted a great circulation of piastres in the empire of Morocco, and, perhaps, two million of livres

livres (or upward of eighty thousand pounds sterling) of increase to the revenue. Between the years 1770 and 1774, Spain transported from Morocco quantities of wheat and barley; but she again rendered the very same aid to Morocco, from 1779 to 1781, when a part of that empire was afflicted by famine.

In February, 1769, the court of Portugal lost the town of Mazagan, on the western side of Morocco, which it had preserved, and where the arms and the commerce of Portugal were so eminently successful at the beginning of the sixteenth century. This town, situated in the centre of a fertile province, clandestinely supplied Portugal with some provisions and cattle. After the loss of Mazagan, the court of Lisbon, desirous of possessing its former resources, and wishing to acquire greater safety for its flag and guard its ships from the corsairs of Morocco, to which the peace between Spain and Morocco gave more frequent opportunities of approach to the coast of Portugal, thought proper, in 1773, to conclude a treaty with the Emperor.

peror. There is no continued trade between Portugal and Morocco, and the intercourse of the two courts is simply confined to testimonies of friendship. The Emperor of Morocco sends a few horses, and many compliments, to the court of Lisbon, which returns demonstrations of good will somewhat more substantial.

Toward the end of the year 1782, Sidi Mahomet sent an ambassador into Tuscany, who, in 1783, departed thence for Vienna to conclude a peace with both these courts; but the trade between Morocco and these nations is only accidental, and the treaty has no other utility than that of the safety of navigation for Tuscan and Imperial ships, and of thus giving a greater degree of stability to commerce, which these powers wish to encourage throughout their states.

The republic of Genoa enjoys only a kind of truce with the empire of Morocco, which is wholly unsupported by any treaty. A Jew subject of Morocco, whose name was Ben-Amor, made a voyage to Genoa by order of his master, and treated with a noble Genoese concerning commercial connections with the Emperor, who on this occasion, voluntarily made very great advances. The senator formed a commercial company, and sent his agents, in 1769, with splendid presents, and a numerous train. This company enjoyed a momentary fame, and afterward as suddenly declined. It did but resemble a flash of lightning in a clouded and gloomy night.

The Emperor of Morocco, thus at peace with the principal commercial nations, and desirous of being so with all the Christian powers, hoping thereby to extend the commerce of his empire, and to profit by the rival spirit of nations, publicly manifested, by letters, in 1777, " That he granted " entire liberty to all ships to trade with, " and enter, his ports, being desirous of " peace with the whole world." This general notice produced no effect, either because those nations which it most interested had not sufficient confidence in his promises, or because they wanted such products and resources as were necessary to maintain

maintain a trade with the coast of Morocco.

Notwithstanding that the Emperor had declared he held himself to be at peace with all Europe, he nevertheless pronounced a ship from Ragusa, taken by one of his corsairs, in 1779, a legal capture. The cargo, worth more than a hundred thousand livres, (or upward of four thousand pounds) was the property of the Maltese, and was confiscated; and yet, from some inexplicable caprice, the Maltese sailors were restored to their freedom, while those of Ragusa were made slaves.

The dispute this occasioned, and which was rendered still more intricate by a diversity of interests, was very tedious, and liable to numerous incongruities. The Ottoman Porte claimed the sailors of Ragusa as its vassals, and by the same title protected the freedom of the Ragusan flag. The dispatches of the Porte, written in the Turkish language, although the Moors could not read them, were not received with the less deference; the Ragusan sailors,

lors, detained in flavery, were reftored to the Envoy of the republic, and the Emperor dictated fuch terms of peace as Ragufa could neither accept nor durft refufe. The fufpence and inconveniences that arofe gave occafion to new explanations, which did not filence the fears of the Senate of Ragufa; a ftate fo feeble, and in fo precarious a fituation, can enjoy but little certainty.

The United States of North America, after fecuring their independence by wife laws, and concluding various commercial treaties with the powers of Europe, were further defirous of adding new means of advantage, and increafe, to their induftry and navigation. In confequence of this, they, during the year 1786, profiting by the pacific difpofition which the Emperor of Morocco announced to all commercial nations, concluded a treaty of peace with this monarch.

CHAP.

CHAP. VIII.

Of the commercial intercourse between the kingdom of France, and the empire of Morocco.

IN the beginning of the present century, France was possessed of colonies, manufactures, mercantile establishments, in foreign nations, and a maritime commerce, which, in its birth, betokened the extent of which it was susceptible, from national industry, and the vigilance of the ministry; her navigation began to appear respectable, in consequence of her naval forces, under the reign of Louis XIV.; but the wars she was obliged to maintain, toward the conclusion of this reign, greatly retarded the progress of her foreign trade.

So rapid was the growth of this trade, under the following reign, that her rivals, jealous of the empire of the sea, took umbrage at her maritime prosperity. The late success of her arms has effaced the remembrance of those humiliations to which she was subjected, in consequence of the war of 1756; and the influence which this success ought naturally to acquire should, each returning day, give new strength to her commerce.

The first efforts of France to extend her navigation incited the cupidity of the regencies of Barbary, that were in the neighbourhood of her southern ports. After having several times chastised their temerity, France, at length, made peace with Algiers, Tunis, and Tripoli. She also held momentary negotiations with Muley Ishmael, but found no possible means of fixing the wavering temper of that Emperor, and of obviating those difficulties which might well be feared from his want of good faith. This monarch being dead, the empire of Morocco, become the prey of rebellions, was continually changing

its

its masters. Its ports, also, were under the government of particular and local laws, and the difficulties of treaties of peace were increased, because that, during a state of such anarchy, it was impossible to assign any duration to such treaties.

These obstacles were removed when Sidi Mahomet ascended the throne, and France profited by the dispositions of this Emperor to enter on new negotiations; but they were subject to so much incertitude, and so many variations, that, in order ultimately to bring the Moor to a firm determination, she thought proper, in 1765, to send a squadron, of one ship of the line, eight frigates, three zebecks, one bark, and two bomb ketches, to the western coast of Morocco. This squadron, of greater force than was necessary, was impeded by a concatenation of circumstances, which were not sufficiently foreseen, because a sufficient knowledge of the coast had not been obtained. The bomb ketches played upon Rabat and Sallee with little success. The squadron next proceeded to Laracha; the frigates occasioned a corsair to be stranded

stranded upon the coast, and the smaller vessels of the squadron, after being detained two or three nights by a diversity of opinions among the captains, and the difficulties of the passage, at length entered the river of Laracha, and there burned a ship.

This advantage was balanced by the loss of many brave men. Obliged, in the river, to give battle to a multitude of Moorish soldiers, who had had time to assemble, because of the delays to which this expedition had been subjected, the French lost near two hundred men on that occasion, forty-five of whom were made slaves, without enumerating the wounded. But this loss was no sufficient counterpoise to that of the Emperor of Morooco, many of whose soldiers also fell. This monarch was enabled to judge, by the valorous defence of the French, that, on some future opportunity, this valour might be more successful, and he proposed a suspension of arms. A truce was, at length, agreed on, and this truce was prolonged that reciprocal explanation might be more precise. The preliminaries of peace were definitively

tively concluded toward the end of the year 1766, by the intervention of the Sieur Jean Jacques Salva, a French merchant, settled at Saffi.

In the spring of 1767, the Comte de Breugnon, a captain in the navy, was appointed ambassador to conclude the peace, and sailed to Saffi with a squadron under his command. The Comte took with him a present, worthy of the magnificence of his monarch, for the Emperor of Morocco. The French flag was saluted at Saffi by the whole artillery of the castle; and the ambassador met, on shore, and during the rest of his voyage, the most distinguished reception, according to the custom of those people.

France, however, had proof that, though the character of a nation may vary according to circumstances, in reality it is ever the same. At the very moment when the Moors made those warm professions, which an interested court will ever testify for its new friends, a corsair of the Emperor took three French merchant ships in the

the Straits, which, though there was no difficulty in proving the injury, were sometime before they were restored. The Emperor disclaimed this act of hostility, and the corsair was condemned never to sail more. The signing of the peace was itself delayed, because that explanations were necessary, and the preliminaries, which had been agreed on between the two courts, and sent to Versailles, written in Arabic, to be signed, were laid aside: proceedings were all again to be begun, and the treaty, concerning which the two powers had been mutually agreed, was once more to be discussed, and almost wholly altered.

Previous to the peace between France and Morocco, the French had two mercantile establishments settled there on the faith of asylum. After the peace their mercantile houses became numerous. This was the error of the French; there were too many of them for the trade, and their numbers were not only injurious to their own interests but, probably, excited the avarice of the Emperor, who, estimating the

the advantages of their trade by their eagerness, was defirous it might become more profitable to himfelf, and therefore impofed heavier duties. The trade then began to decline; merchants were difcouraged by thefe new fhackles, by rules which defpotifm prefcribed, by the neceffity of conforming to thefe rules, by the removal of their trade from one port to another, and by all the various means which the abufe of power, the fpirit of avarice, and the convenience of the moment, could fuggeft.

France, perhaps, is the only nation which is capable to maintain an uninterrupted trade with the empire of Morocco, mutually beneficial. She is enabled herfelf to fupply all the wants of that empire, and the products of Morocco find at Marfeilles a more certain fale than at any other port. According to the beft and moft exact information, it is demonftrated that her trade, on the coaft of Morocco, might not only become capable of increafe, but that the reciprocal conveniences, which muft refult to the two powers by the barter of
their

their respective products, ought to be considered as a political motive for the mutual maintenance of peace.

If France, by living in good harmony with Morocco, should unite to the benefits of commerce that of the safety of her flag, Morocco would, on her part, acquire a very essential advantage from this connection, by the great facility with which she could vend her native products, which constitute the sole wealth of nations, and the ultimate resources of a state. It must be acknowledged that, at first, it would not be possible to give any degree of stability to this trade, because of the difficulty there must be of fixing the ideas of a despot, whose motives all originate in momentary conveniences, on any determinate point. This, however, may be remedied in time; wants and circumstances every where prescribe laws, and every where, soon or late, teach men the necessity of conforming to these laws.

France would insensibly and exclusively engross the trade of Morocco, if, profiting by by her advantages, she should subject that trade to the same laws which have so successfully procured her the exclusive trade of the Levant, and the republics of Barbary. Endeavours at improvement, and, perhaps, the spirit of innovation, have caused the voice of freedom to raise itself against prohibitory laws. Such laws may be wrong, in particular cases; but the application of this rule should not be universal; they may, in general, be beneficial to a nation, which, possessed of native products and colonies, having a maritime force to preserve, manufacturers to encourage, and multitudes of workmen to employ, is interested to procure to itself, exclusively, such branches of commerce as may best obtain these ends. She would act contrary to her interests, were she to suffer her rivals to become the carriers of her products, while they refuse her a similar and reciprocal freedom.

The French vend, on the coast of Morocco, much of the linnen of Brittany, and of other places, some raw silk for the manufactures of Fez, unspun cotton, Biscay iron, common papers, mercery goods, some few silks, cloths, sugars, and coffee, and as much sulphur as the Emperor requires, the trade in which he has reserved to himself.

They receive in exchange, wool, oil, raw hides, wax, gums, and elephants' teeth. The balance, being against France, is paid in Spanish piastres, or in merchandize brought from some foreign nations; yet we ought not to suppose the trade of Morocco disadvantageous to France, since she does not send her ships thither for objects of luxury, but supplies necessary to her manufactures, and such as may animate national industry, by renewing the materials of exportation, and procuring the commodities of trade and commerce.

After having explained the commercial intercourse of the European nations with the empire of Morocco, enumerated what shackles are imposed by government, and what result from local circumstances, I think it proper to speak a word concerning the custom which the Emperors of Morocco have in suffering the ships of nations, with whom

they

are at war, to trade to their coaſt. This political toleration appears to do honour to theſe monarchs; but the abſurdity of the Europeans, in making uſe of this permiſſion, is not the leſs evident, ſince Morocco enjoys the double advantage of trade and of piracy.

Neither can it be ſaid Europe, in this reſpect, has a like advantage, for there is the following difference. The empire of Morocco cannot ſupply its own wants, yet has the balance in its favour, by its commerce with Europe; therefore it grants the freedom of its ports only from neceſſity, and that it may diſencumber itſelf of products, for which it has no conſumption, and receive others, of which it is in abſolute need. Hence, it would be much wiſer, were the European nations, eſpecially thoſe that find the quickeſt market for the products of Morocco, to renounce this freedom, and to avail themſelves of the neceſſity of that empire to barter its commodities, and thereby oblige it to remain quiet. For one nation to ſupply another, with which it is at war, and to carry on a trade beneficial

to

to that other, is, by fair deduction, to pay tribute, without enjoying the advantages of peace.

CHAP.

CHAP. IX.

Custom-house duties, coins, weights, and measures.

THE duties, coins, weights, and measures, in Morocco, are almost as variable as the opinion of the Emperor; yet, notwithstanding this fluctuation, I have thought proper to terminate my observations, on what concerns this empire, by giving an abstract of their present state.

The duties of exportation and importation have been much altered. Those of importation, which are paid in effects, and not in money, have risen from eight to fifteen per cent., iron excepted, which pays the fourth, or the third, of its value. Those of exportation, which I have several times feen raifed, are entirely arbitrary; the articles do not each pay in the fame proportion. The duties on fome amount to as much as the prime-coft.

Merchant fhips are fubjected to an anchorage duty, which has alfo undergone many variations; neither is this duty the fame in all the ports of the coaft, which ports do not all equally enjoy the freedom of trade and navigation.

The coins, which are current over the coaft of Morocco, are thofe of the Emperor, and thofe of Spain. The coins of the Emperor are in gold, filver, and copper. Their feveral values are not fixed, but the variations, to which they are fubject, do not there influence the price of provifions and goods, as they would in Europe, where money is properly confidered only as the fymbol of wealth.

The gold ducat, which is very fcarce, and therefore little in circulation, is worth fifteen ounces, which correfponds to ten

French

French livres, or eight and four pence English.

The silver money is the current ducat, the ounce, and the blanquil. The current ducat is worth ten ounces, the ounce four blanquils, and the blanquil twenty-four flus. The flus is the only current copper coin. The value of the blanquil is three sous four deniers of France, or nearly seven farthings English; consequently the ounce is worth thirteen sous four deniers, or six pence three farthings, and the ducat six livres thirteen sous four deniers, or five shillings and six pence three farthings[*]. The Spanish piastre is current in trade, and in general its value is fixed; it may, however, vary according to the convenience of the Emperor, and the interest he may have to render piastres scarce or common.

The weights, by which they buy and sell in Morocco, are equivalent to the weights

---

[*] The English is the third part of a farthing above the exact estimate in all these three cases. T.

of Paris; that is to say, to the *Poids de marc*, or pound of sixteen ounces; the subdivisions of which are, at both places, the same. Merchandize is in general sold by the quintal of one hundred pounds; but some commodities are sold by the great quintal, or one hundred and fifty pounds.

Corn is measured, after different manners, along the coast of Morocco. In the southern provinces, known by the name of the kingdom of Morocco, wheat is sold by the Garara and the Mood, which is the modus of the ancients, whence the French have derived their Muid. The garara contains forty mood, and the mood weighs from eighteen to twenty pounds; hence the garara must be nearly eight hundred weight. In the kingdom of Fez, from Sallee to the north, corn is sold by the Saffa, the Sahah, and the Mood. Four mood make one sahah, and sixty mood one saffa; hence, the mood weighing from eighteen to twenty pounds, the weight of the saffa must be twelve quintals. Three sahah, or twelve mood, are nearly equivalent to the measure of Marseilles, called the

charge,

charge, which also nearly corresponds to the Setier of Paris. It is necessary to observe that the corn measures are liable to be varied, according to the will of the Emperor.

The measure by which cloths, linen, and woollen, are sold, is called coode, which is the cubit of the ancients. The coode, which is in use throughout all the empire, and which never varies, contains nineteen inches four lines. There are forty-four inches in a French ell, consequently two coodes and a quarter are equal to an ell, the fraction of half an inch excepted.

THE END.

INDEX.

A.

ABDA, province of, I. 9.
Abdalharaman, revolt of, II. 45.
Abdallah, first of the Benimerins, II. 36.
——— son of Abu Said, reign of, II. 49.
——— affassinated, II. 50.
Abdallah, Muley, son of Muley Ishmael, generosity of, II. 242.
——— ——— persuaded not to destroy Fez, II. 243.
——— ——— defeated by the Brebes, II. 244.
——— ——— barbarous maxim of, *Ibid.*
——— ——— cruelty of, II. 245.
——— ——— money promised by, to the Negroes, II. 246.
——— ——— insurgents quelled by, *Ibid.*
——— ——— clothes the naked, II. 247.
——— ——— general, basely put to death by, *Ibid.*
——— ——— performs the office of executioner, *Ibid.*
——— ——— obliges people of all ranks to build the walls of Mequinez, II. 248.
——— ——— project of, to subject the Negroes, II. 250.
——— ——— deposed, II. 251.
——— ——— flight of, *Ibid.*
——— ——— first restoration of, II. 255.
——— ——— hatred of, to Selim Dooquelli, *Ibid.*
——— ——— deposed the day of his election, II. 257.

Abdallah,

[392]

Abdallah, Muley, frantic cruelty of, II. 258.
———— ———— artifice of, to amuse the Negroes, II. 259
———— ———— obliged to sell his horses, arms, and jewels, II. 260.
———— ———— second flight of, II. 262.
———— ———— a fourth time proclaimed, II. 265.
———— ———— projects of, against the Negroes, *Ibid.*
———— ———— recalled by the Negroes, II. 267.
———— ———— a sixth time Emperor, II. 270.
———— ———— anecdote of the justice of, II. 273.
———— ———— not inimical to Christians. II. 274.
———— ———— allows the redemption of slaves, *Ibid.*
———— ———— few children of, II. 278.
———— ———— character of, II. 286.
———— ———— anecdotes of the cruelty of, II. 287.
———— ———— Saints despised by, II. 288.
Abdelmeleck, son of Ishmael, made a governor, II. 224.
———— ———— artful behaviour of, II. 225.
———— ———— a strict observer of the Koran, II. 232.
———— ———— impolitic declaration of, II. 234.
———— ———— defeated by the Negroes, II. 235.
———— ———— again proclaimed Emperor, II. 237.
———— ———— religious barbarity and character of, II. 238.
———— ———— flight of, from Mequinez, II. 239.
———— ———— besieged in Fez. *Ibid.*
———— ———— strangled, II. 240.
Abdelmeleck, Muley, first Emperor, II. 103.
———— ———— character of, *Ibid.*
———— ———— assassinated when drunk, II. 104.
Abdulmomen, acts of, II. 21 to 25.
Abdulmomen, Muley, assassinated, II. 96.
Abu-Artab, II. 41.
Abu-Hennon, rebellion and reign of, II. 46.
Abul-Hassen, II. 41.
———— ———— subjects Tremecen, Sugulmessa, Algiers, and Tunis, II. 42.

Abul-

Abul-Haffen, defeated near Rio Salado, II. 44.
———— fleet of, defeated, II. 45.
Abu-Said, reign of, II. 40.
———— fucceffor of Abu-Hennon, II. 47.
———— affaffinated, II. 49.
Abu-Teffifin, II. 13.
Achica, intoxicating properties of, II. 255.
Acorns, remarkable, I. 104.
Acton, Chevalier, remarkable action of, I. 318.
Africa, interior, and Morocco ancient trade between, I. 108, 324.
Agmet, city of, I. 55, 64.
Aguadir, or capé Aguer, I. 47.
———— Toma, city of, I. 54.
Alcaid, foot of an, cut off by Muley Arfhid, II. 146.
Alcaffar, battle of, II. 99.
Alcaffer-Quiber, city of, I. 83.
———————— remarkable ftory of its foundation, I. 84.
Alcaffar-Seguar, built by Almonfor, II. 29.
Algerines defeat Muley Ifhmael, II. 211.
Algefira, rebuilt by Ben-Jofeph, II. 40.
———— taken by Abdelmeleck, II. 42.
———— retaken, II. 45.
Algiers and Morocco jealous of each other, I. 304.
———— letter of the Divan of, to Muley Ifhmael, II. 195.
Alhabid, El-Monfor, II. 10.
Ali, fon of Jofeph Teffifin, II. 19.
Ali, Soliman, II. 124.
Almedina, ruins of, I. 37.
Almond harveft, I. 103.
Almonfor, acts of, II. 28 to 33.
———— cities founded by, II. 29.
———— faying of, II. 32.
———— ftrange difappearance of, II. 33.
Alms, giving, I. 198, 199.
Alphonfo III. vanquifhed, II. 31.

Alphonfo

Alphonso X.—II. 39.
Ambaffador bare-footed, anecdote of, I. 349.
Ambaffadors fent from Morocco to France, II. 200.
Amulets, I. 200.
Anafa, or Dar Beyda, town of, I. 36.
Anchorage, the beft, in the road of Sallee, I. 34.
Anecdote, *vide* Abdallah Muley, Alcaid, Alcaffar, Ambaf-
  fador, Affaffin, Avarice, Bofville, Butcher, Can-
  non, Captive, Chriftian, Coofcoofoo, Cruelty,
  Fifh, Gallant, Governor, Ifhmael, Lela, Liar,
  Lion, Marabout, Mazagan, Meffiah, Moors,
  Mofque, Muley Arfhid, Muley Daiby, Negro
  Slave, Prayer, Pudding, Renegado, Saint, Storks,
  Spaniard, Thieves, Teeth, Walnuts.
Antelope, I, 170.
Appeals to the Emperor, I. 216.
Apples, enchanted, I. 370.
Aqueducts, rude, at Morocco, I. 63.
Arabic, the language of Morocco, I. 241.
——— the moft extenfive of living languages, I. 242.
Arbiba, palace of, built by Muley Abdallah, II. 273.
Arga tree, and its almond, I. 102.
——— oil of, I. 103.
——— fruit of, how eaten by goats, *Ibid.*
Armament, French, fent againft Morocco, II. 375.
Arzilla, town of, I. 22.
——— taken by Don Alphonfo of Portugal, II. 51.
Afs, eaten raw by Saints, I. 183.
Affaffin, juft reward of an, II. 97.
Aftrology ftudied by the Talbes, I. 239.
Atlas, mount, fcite of, I. 12, 62.
——————— riches of, I. 14, 106.
Audience given to all ranks, good effects of, II. 302.
Augury from the heart of a Sheep, I. 197.
Avarice, allegory concerning, I. 250.
——— of the Moors, *Ibid.*

Avarice,

Avarice, anecdotes of, I. 251. Note, and 252.
Azamore, town of, I. 36.

B.

Barbary fig, I. 101.
Barbers shops, the rendezvous of newsmongers, I. 264.
Bashaw, what, I. 262.
Bastinado, guilty and innocent equally liable to, I. 217.
Battle, Moorish, order of, I. 308. II. 76.
——- of the Seven Counts, II. 18.
——- of Alarcos, II. 31.
——- lost by Muley Oatas, II. 77.
Beard, ceremony of swearing by, II. 69.
Beating the high road to preferment, I. 368.
Beef salted by the Moors, I. 164, 271.
Bees wax, I. 104.
Bellote, or Acorns, I. *Ibid.*
Beni-Hassen, or Habat, I. 7.
Beni-Oatas, II. 53.
Ben-Joseph, reign and acts of, II. 36 to 40.
Beth, river of, I. 26.
Betting, forbidden the Mahometans, I. 258.
Black, peculiarities of the colour of, I. 281.
Boar hunting, I. 342.
Boccari, al, or el, troops, consecrated to, I. 306. II. 191.
Bones liable to be mistaken at the day of judgement, I. 351.
Bonfires of Saint John, I. 292.
————————- conjectures concerning, I. 293.
Booffer Muley, rival of Muley Abdallah, II. 241, 242.
Booffega, river of, I. 18.
Bosville, Mr., anecdote of, I. 217.
Bougie, derivation of, I. 272.
Brahem, last of the dynasty of Morabethoon, II. 19.
——- throws himself headlong from a rock, II. 21.
Brambles, camp of Abdallah fired by, II. 245.

Brandy

Brandy made from dates, I. 91.
Bread of Morocco, excellent, I. 346.
Brebes, I. 117.
―――― diflike, and are more independent than, the Moors, I. 118.
―――― have a language of their own, I. 119.
―――― vigorous, have fine teeth, *Ibid*.
―――― hunt the lion and tiger, I. 120.
―――― valour of, II. 182, 185.
―――― ftrange notions of, concerning Chriftians, II. 185.
Bridges, Moorifh, I. 90.
Budobus, defeat of, II. 37.
Buhafon, valour of, II. 77.
―――― ―――― active conduct of, in Fez, II. 79.
―――― ―――― league of, with Salah Reis, II. 85.
―――― ―――― Fez, taken by, II. 88.
―――― ―――― victory of, over Muley Abdallah, II. 90.
―――― ―――― killed in battle, II. 91.
Bulahuan, tremendous caftle of, I. 87.
―――― ―――― faid to have been built by Abdulmomen, II. 25.
Burial fervice, Moors, fing at, I. 292.
―――― opinion of the Moors, concerning, II. 32.
Butcher, a merciful, II. 216.
Butter, how made, I. 346.
Buttons cut from the clothes of an ambaffador, I. 348.

C.

Cafiles, what, I. 119.
Caliphs, caufes of the decay of the power of the, II. 2.
Camel, I. 165.
―――― engendering of the, *Ibid*.
―――― flefh of, eaten, I. 166.
―――― milk of wholefome, *Ibid*.
―――― ftomach of, I. 167.
―――― hardinefs of, I. 194.

Camel,

Camel, dead, given to poor pilgrims, I. 195.
——— sacrifice of, II. 183.
Camp, Moorish, before Ceuta, II. 205.
——— fired by brambles, II. 245.
Camps, how chosen by the Moors, I. 308.
Cannon founderies, I. 309.
——— anecdote of a, II. 181.
Cape Spartel, I. 22.
Captive and Lion, anecdote concerning, I. 340.
Captives, French, ransomed, II. 105.
Carra, Alcaid, killed by Muley Ishmael, II. 152.
Carubin, mosque of, II. 7.
Castles, walled, but without artillery, in most of the provinces, for the Bashaws, I. 86.
Cats, forty, of Muley Ishmael, I. 339.
Cavalry, Moorish, I. 307.
Ceuta, town and harbour of, I. 19.
——— taken by Don John of Portugal, II. 47.
——— siege of, II. 203.
Chabanets, *vide* Shabanets.
Chess and Hazard, Moorish games, I. 258.
Children, how taught to read, I. 131.
——— run naked to the age of nine or ten, *Ibid.*
Christian and Saint, story of, I. 357.
Christians, hatred of the Moors to, I. 352.
——— degeneracy of, in Morocco, I. 353.
Circulation, exceedingly slow, I. 331.
Cities, little need of, in Morocco, II. 297.
Climate of Morocco, I. 93, 96.
Climi, city of, I. 54.
Clubs, fanatic prediction concerning, II. 317.
Coffee-houses of Constantinople, I. 264.
Coin debased, I. 331.
Coins of Morocco, II. 386.
Cold, degree of, I. 96, 344.
——— and heat, remark concerning, I. 344.

Cooks,

Cooks, European, at Morocco, II. 309.
Coofcoofoo, preparation of, I. 123.
——————— nutritive and agreeable, *Ibid.*
——————— how eaten, I. 271.
——————— bloody head in a difh of, II. 289.
——————— dreffed in vaft quantities, II. 310.
Corn, manner of grinding, I. 123.
——— preferved, I. 285.
——— exportation of, allowed under Sidi Mahomet, II. 299.
——— quality of, *Ibid.*
——— exchanged for artillery, II. 300.
——— price of, during the famine, II. 337.
Corfairs purfued by a Dutch frigate and wrecked, II. 358.
Corvée, *vide* Jew-tailors, II. 310.
Court of Morocco, fimplicity of, II. 308.
Courtfhip, how performed, I. 275.
Cowdung, burnt, I. 132.
——————— ufed medicinally, *Ibid.*
Crefcent, form of the, for the order of battle, I. 308. II. 76.
Crom el Hadgy, character of, II. 107.
——————— maffacred by his bride, II. 108.
Cruelty, remarkable anecdotes of, I. 363. II. 121, 134, 146, 178, 214, 216, 224, 258, 287, 288, 289.
Cuftom-houfe duties paid in kind, I. 333. II. 385.
Cuftom-houfe duties of Morocco, II. 385.

D.

Dates plentiful in Tafilet, I. 91.
Day of judgement, odd opinion concerning, I. 351.
Days, length of, I. 96.
Dead, the, not buried in mofques, I. 291.
——————— when interred, I. 292.
——————— wept over on Friday, *Ibid.*
——————— queftioned by the Moors, I. 351.
——————— fuppofed capable of pain, *Ibid.*

Dearth

Dearth at Tafilet, II. 115, *vide* famine.
Death counterfeited by Abdelmeleck, II. 43.
Denmark, court of, deceived by a Jew, II. 359.
———— ambaffador of, feized, II. 360.
———— royal African company of, *Ibid.*
———— tribute paid by, to Morocco, II. 362.
Dervifes, I. 179.
Defert, danger of croffing, II. 197.
Defpotifm, effects of, I. 247.
Dews, corrofive, will ruft metal worn in the pocket, I. 97.
Difcipline, ill ftate of, I. 306, 307.
Dogs, numerous, in Morocco, I. 339.
Don Ferdinand, II. 30.
———————— king of Caftile, II. 38.
Don Sancho III.—II. 26, 40.
Douhars, what, and how regulated, I. 121.
Doum, or wild palm, made into hats, bafkets, &c. I. 105.
——— fruit of, *Ibid.*
Dra, province of, I. 11.
Dris, Muley, the friend of Sidi Mahomet, II. 280.
——————— power and abilities of, II. 303.
——————— cunning of, II. 304.
——————— death and character of, II. 305.
Dromedary, fwiftnefs of the, II. 148.
——————— white, I. 339.
Dubudu, town of, I. 86.
Ducat, current value of, I. 335.
Duquella, province of, I. 9.
———— inhabitants of, large, robuft, and mercantile, *Ibid.*
Dynafty of Morabethoon, II. 13.
———— of the Moahedins, or Almohades, II. 23.
———— of the Benimerins, II. 36.
———— of Fileli, II. 117.

Eating,

E.

Eating, Moorish, mode of, I. 271, 347.
Eclipses, terrible, to the Moors, I. 237, 238.
——— strange notion concerning, I. 239.
Edris, adventures of, II. 5.
——— expulsion of, II. 8, 9.
——— veneration of the Moors for, II. 112.
Edrissites, who, II. 2.
Education, I. 227.
——— of the sons of Muley Ishmael, I. 371.
Eels, manner of catching, in the lakes of Mamora, I. 25.
Elcaisseria, what, I. 58.
El-Edrissi the geographer, II. 9.
El-Hadgy, Mahomet, subdued by Muley Ishmael, II. 177.
El-Mohadi, revolt of, II. 9, 10.
El-Valid, Muley, character and reign of, II. 104.
——————— suffers French captives to be ransomed, II. 105.
Emperor, despotic power of, I. 203, 204.
——— has no first minister, I. 206.
——— gives audience to people of all ranks, I. 213.
——— title of, first assumed in Morocco, II. 103.
Emperors hold it derogatory to keep their word, I. 208.
Empire of Morocco, ancient wealth of, I. 324.
——————— extent and boundaries of, I. 1.
England, ambassador of, to Muley Ishmael, II. 159.
——— first made peace with Morocco, II. 353.
English merchant, suicide of, II. 284.
Enigmas, a Moorish diversion, I. 229.
Escura, or Ascora, province of, I. 12.
Eunuch, behaviour of a, I. 360.

F.

Famine, dreadful, in Morocco, II. 335.
——— effects of, II. 339.

Fatimites,

Fatimites, II. 2.
Fedala, road and town of, I. 35.
Fenis, Bashaw, befriends Muley Muftadi, II. 270.
—— gives up Sallee to Sidi Mahomet, II. 283.
—— is stoned to death, *Ibid.*
Fertility of Morocco, I. 98, 343, 344.
Festivals of the Moors and Mahometans, I. 196.
Fevers, common, I. 232.
—— hot and cold fits of, occasioned by a fiend, *Ibid.*
Fez, province of, I. 12.
Fez, city of, I. 70.
—— when founded, *Ibid.*
—— formerly held holy, I. 72.
—— learning of, I. 72, 228.
—— profligacy of, I. 73.
—— manufactures of, I. 73.
—— florid, but false description of, by Leo Africanus, I. 76.
—— cannot be entered without an order from the Emperor, I. 78.
—— romantic situation of, *Ibid.*
—— fickleness of its inhabitants, I. 79.
—— founded by Edriss, II. 6.
—— taken by Muley Mahomet, II. 82.
—— privilege of, II. 86.
—— taken by Muley Buhafon, II. 88.
—— cruel treatment of, by Muley Mahomet, II. 92.
—— revolt of, under Muley Daiby, II. 233.
—— makes peace with Muley Daiby, II. 235.
—— intended destruction of, by Muley Abdallah, II. 243.
—— citizens of, repulse Muley Abdallah, II. 261.
—— spirited answers of the citizens of, II. 321.
Fez, New, when and by whom built, I. 80.
Fight between lions, wolves, and dogs, I. 340.
Figs soon worm-eaten, I. 100.
Fileli, dynasty of, II. 117.
Fish, strange reason for prohibiting the eating of, I. 352.

Fleet, French, under Renaud, II. 193, 200.
Fort Charles abandoned, II. 193.
Foxes, I. 170.
Fruits, early, I. 94.
—— what native in Morocco, I. 100.

G.

Gallant, story and punishment of a, I. 268.
Ganger, what, I. 145.
Garb, or El-Garb, province of, I. 6.
Gardens of the Moors, I. 263.
Garet, province of, I. 5.
Gayland, Alcaid, II. 128.
—— bravery and death of, II. 154.
Gayroan, I. 119.
Gazia, II. 18, 30.
General, a treacherous, put to death, II. 164.
Genoa, treaty of, with Morocco, II. 369.
Genoese company, failure of, II. 370.
Geography of Morocco, inaccurate, I. 4.
Georgian, beauteous, strangled, II. 208.
Gesula, province of, I. 11.
Gibraltar taken by the Moors, II. 42.
—— victualling of, II. 355, 365.
Gold dust taken at Tagaret, II. 197.
Golius, in Morocco, II. 103.
Government of Morocco, what, I. 202, 359.
—— feudal, I. 298, 300, 301.
Governor put to death by Sidi Mahomet, I. 211.
—— of Fez, anecdotes of, I. 221.
—— condemned to sweep the town he had governed, I. 262.
Governors stripped by the Emperor, I. 213.
Grandees, reason of, convoking in Morocco, II. 187.
Grapes, large and delicious, I. 100.
Guadel- brief and remarkable history of, II. 327.

Gum-

[403]

Gum-Sandarac, I. 103.
—— transparent, *Ibid.*
Gunpowder, game of, I. 265, 341.
——————— of Morocco, bad, I. 310.

H.

Hadgy, what, I. 191.
Haicks, how made and worn, I. 125.
Hameda, story of, I. 374.
Harami, what, I. 275.
Hares, good, I. 170.
Harriffa, office of, II. 311.
Harvest, early, I. 94.
Haffen, tower of, I. 32.
Hats first worn in Africa, I. 153.
Hazar, a kind of Cedar, I. 8.
Hea, province of, I. 9.
—— inhabitants of, restless, uncivilized, and factious, I. 10.
Head served up in a dish of Coofcoofoo, II. 289.
Heads cut off without the owners' knowledge, I. 348.
Historians, itinerant, I. 264.
Holland and Morocco, war between, II. 332.
—— quarrel of Sidi Mahomet with, II. 357.
Horsemen, Moors excellent, I. 337, 341.
Horses, numerous and good, I. 167.
—— studs of, kept by the Emperor and Grandees, *Ibid.*
—— Moors imagine the Christians have no, I. 338.
—— revered as Saints, *Ibid.*
Houses seldom more than one story high, I. 142.
—— mode of building, *Ibid.*
—— road over the tops of, I. 364.
Hunting the boar, I. 342.

Infantry,

I.

Infantry, weak state of, I. 307.
Inheritance, laws of, I. 275.
Inoculation practised, I. 233.
Insurrections, frequent, I. 302.
―――――― how promoted and punished by Sidi Mahomet, II. 316, 318.
Interregnum of the kingdom of Fez. II. 49.
Isac, son of Brahem, strangled, II. 24.
Ishmael, Muley, accession of, II. 148.
―――――― avarice of, I. 369, 370.
―――――― hypocrisy of, I. 369.
―――――― cruelty of, I. 370.
―――――― guilty conscience of, I. 373.
―――――― mean appearance of, I. 374.
―――――― caprice of, I. 375.
―――――― opposed by his nephew, Muley Achmet, II. 150.
―――――― victories of, over Muley Achmet, II. 151, 157.
―――――― conquers Fez, II. 155.
―――――― cruelty of, I. 340, 358, 362, 363, 366, 368. II. 152, 158, 179, 216, 224, Passim.
―――――― avarice of, II. 158, 172.
―――――― anecdotes of the deceit of, II. 160, 171, 220.
―――――― attempted to be assassinated, II. 164.
―――――― repulsed at Santa Cruz, II. 165.
―――――― perfidy of, II. 168.
―――――― rage of, at entering Morocco, II. 175.
―――――― revolt quelled by, II. 177.
―――――― sends ten thousand heads to Fez and Morocco, II. 178.
―――――― concubines of, II. 179.
―――――― repulsed by the Brebes, II. 182, 185.

Ishmael,

Ishmael, Muley, passion of, for building, II. 191.
——— ——— Christian captives, how punished by, II. 192.
——— ——— remarkable saying of, II. 195.
——— ——— rebellious sons of, II. 306.
——— ——— defeated by the Algerines, II. 211.
——— ——— anecdotes of the caprice of, I. 338, 339, 366, 367, 368. II. 218.
——— ——— pretended illness of, II. 220.
——— ——— murders his son, II. 222.
——— ——— character of, II. 226.
——— ——— numerous descendants of, *Ibid.*
——— ——— anecdote of, *vide* Messiah.
——— ——— and Spaniard, anecdote of, I. 367.

J.

Jacob Almonsor, palace of, at Rabat, I. 29.
——— ——— and fisherman, story of, I. 84.
Jew of the mountain massacred by Muley Arshid, II. 123.
——— tailors, how treated, II. 310.
Jewels, uncommon, I. 145.
Jews in Morocco, formerly much more numerous, I. 157.
——— ill treated and despised, *Ibid.* 157, 353.
——— understand trade better than the Moors, I. 158.
——— employed by the Emperor, *Ibid.*
——— of Morocco, superstitious, I. 159.
——— of Morocco, all know Hebrew, I. 160.
——— Shrieks and lamentations of hired women at the funerals of the, I. 161.
——— the tax-gatherers, I. 326.
——— taxation of the, I. 327.
——— strange reason why their prayers are granted, I. 346.
——— two rival, anecdote of, I. 358.
——— generously protected by Muley Ali, II. 341.
——— wives of the, handsome and gallant, I. 143, 159.

John, Saint, conjectures concerning the festival of, I. 293.
Joseph, Ben Jacob, II. 41.
Joseph Teffifin, II. 15.
————— ——— conquers the kingdom of Fez, II. 16.
————— ——— alliance of, sought by the Mahometans of Spain, II. 17.
————— ——— gains the battle of the seven Counts, II. 18.
Joseph, son of Abdulmomen, acts of, II. 26.
Judges follow the letter of the law, I. 220.
Justice, ridiculous parade of, I. 339.

K.

Knight of the Ass, a usurper, called the, II. 11.
Knowledge, state of, among the Moors, I. 226.

L.

Lances darted into the air and caught, I. 341, 368.
Language of the Brebes, Shellu, and Moors, compared, I. 244.
Laracha, town of, I. 23.
————— river of, I. 24.
————— taken by Muley Ishmael, II. 203.
Law, men of the, powerless, I. 219.
—— for the safety of travellers, I. 133. II. 140.
Laws, code of religious, I. 215.
Leather, the table and table cloth of the Moors, I. 347.
Legs thought handsome when thick, I. 151.
Lela, what, II. 207.
Lela, Zidana, character of, II. 208.
————— ——— wicked intrigues of, *Ibid.* 209.
————— ——— inhuman cruelty of, II. 214.
————— ——— daring ambition of, II. 221.
————— ——— anecdotes of the cruelty of, II. 224.

Lena,

Lena, Coneta, mother of Muley Abdallah, prudence of, II. 242.
————— ————— mercy and wisdom of, II. 244, 245, 250.
————— ————— pilgrimage of, II. 249.
————— ————— female slave assassinated in the arms of, II. 252.
————— ————— money promised by, to the Negroes, II. 254.
Liar, anecdote concerning, I. 349.
Limbs amputated, how dressed, I. 269.
Lions not uncommon, I. 170.
——— feed on young boars, I. 171.
——— manner of hunting, *Ibid.*
——— one-and-twenty killed by one Moor, *Ibid.*
——— taken alive, I. 172.
——— and Brebe, story of, *Ibid.*
——— kept for state by the Emperor, I. 174.
——— slow to attack man, *Ibid.*
——— mode of entrapping the young boar, I. 175.
——— flesh of, eaten by the Moors, I. 176.
——— fighting of, I. 340.
Locusts, I. 95.
————— eat by the Moors like red herrings, *Ibid.*
————— dreadful ravages of, II. 333.
Loueti, the Alcaid, influence of, II. 127, 133.
Loyalty of Muley Ali, II. 319.
Lucas, Alcaid, punished, II. 286.
Lucos, river of, the Lixos of the Greeks, I. 23, 83, 84.
Ludaya, what, II. 191.
Lumthunes, II. 13.
Lunar years, I. 273.

M.

Magafin, what, I. 208.
Mahomet, Abdallah, and Abdulmomen, II. 21.

Mahomet, Ben Achmet, a Sharif, and his three sons, II. 54.
—————————— and his three sons, hypocrisy and ambition of, II. 54, Passim.
—————————— and his three sons, suspected by Muley Nasser, II. 57.
—————————— and his three sons, progress of, II. 58.
Mahomet, Ben Nasser, defeated, II. 34.
————————— death of, II. 35.
Mahometanism, by character despotic, II. 112.
Mamora, river of, I. 6, 7.
——— fort of, I. 26.
——— taken by Muley Ishmael, II. 199.
Mansooria, castle of, I. 34.—built by Almonsor, II. 29.
Manuscripts, Arabic, in Spain, I. 231.
Marabout put to death by Sidi Mahomet, II. 317.
————— sent by Mahomet, II. 160.
————— beheaded by Muley Abdallah, II. 243.
Marakesch, II. 15.
Mares, supposed error concerning, I. 168, 338.
——— and their colts housed in their tents, I. 169.
Markets, daily, I. 134.
——— buffoons, singers, dancers, barbers, and surgeons, at, *Ibid.*
Marriage ceremonies of the Moors, I. 130, 275.
————— licentious songs at, I. 277.
————— festivals, expensive, I. 278.
Matamores to preserve corn, I. 35, 285.
Mausoleum, in memory of Muley Mahomet, II. 218.
————— in memory of Muley Zidan, II. 223.
Mazagan, city of, I. 37.
————— magnificent cistern at, I. 38.
————— fanatic anecdote concerning, I. 39.
————— taken by Sidi Mahomet, II. 326.
Measures of Morocco, II. 388.
Mechanic arts, rude state of, I. 259.

Mediona,

Mediona, caſtle of, I. 87.
Melek Alcaid, cruel death of, II. 214.
Melilla, city of, I. 17.
―――― ſiege of, II. 328.
Mequinez, city of, I. 65.
―――――― Jews quarter at, I. 66.
―――――― Emperor's palace, I. 67.
―――――― inhabitants affable, I. 69.
―――――― women of, handſome, ſhew themſelves to Europeans, *Ibid.*
―――――― Spaniſh convent at, I. 70.
―――――― by whom founded, II. 8.
―――――― abandoned by Muley Mahomet, II. 89.
Meſhooar, what, I. 62, 209, 210.
Meſſiah, coming of the, anecdote concerning, I. 354.
Milood, a feſtival, I. 198.
Mines of iron, I. 106.
―――― of copper, *Ibid.*
Miſhboya, I. 119.
Mogodore, town of, I. 43,
―――――― begun in 1760, I. 44.
―――――― port of, I. 46.
―――――― built by Sidi Mahomet, II. 295.
Money buried, I. 251, 287.
Monopolies, remark concerning, II. 381.
Moors, indolent, I. 99, 349.
―――― ancient commerce of the, conjectures on, I. 102.
―――― plead by attorney, I. 216.
―――― ſeldom ſtrike, I. 219.
―――― diſpoſed to ſlavery, I. 248.
―――― naturally meager, I. 249.
―――― form and features of, *Ibid.*
―――― mournful looks of, *Ibid.*
―――― violence of their paſſions, I. 251.
―――― leſs ſenſible of pain than Europeans, I. 267, 269.
―――― little dainty, I. 270.

Moors chief meal after fun-fet, I. 270.
——— imagine themselves free, I. 280.
——— treat their slaves better than Europeans, *Ibid.*
——— avidity and meanness of the, I. 347.
——— jealousy of the, I. 356.
——— fanaticism of, II. 112.
——— resignation of the, II. 337.
Moors of the cities affirm themselves to be Arabs, I. 140.
——————— seldom have more than one wife, I. 143.
——————— have little variety of dress, I. 144.
Moors of the country, manners of, I. 121.
——————— form of their tents, *Ibid.*
——————— simplicity of the, in their camps, I. 122.
——————— hospitality of, I. 124.
——————— dress of, I. 126.
——————— wear no linen, *Ibid.*
——————— marriages of, I. 130.
——————— quarrelsome, *Ibid.*
——————— different tribes of, seldom intermarry, *Ibid.*
——————— antediluvian, I. 126, 136.
——————— anecdotes of the ignorance of, I. 136.
——————— have no glass, I. 137.
——————— receive no ideas from pictures, I. 138.
Morabethoon, or Morabites, II. 14.
——————— all put to death, II. 24.
Morbeya, river of, true name of, I. 37, 87.
——————— passage of, I. 89, 90.
Morocco, city of, I. 54.
——— founded by Abu Teffifin, I. 55.
——— pleasant plain of, I. 56.
——— quarter of the Jews, I. 59.
——— Emperor's palace, *Ibid.*
——— passed through a sieve, II. 23, 24.
——— stormed by Almonsor, II. 32.

Morocco,

Morocco, taken by Muley Mohamet, II. 72.
———— taken and plundered by the Negroes, **H.** 253.
Morocco, empire of, origin of the inhabitants of, I. 115.
———— women, how employed, I. 122, 125.
———— no inns in the provinces, I. 132.
———— not fortified, I. 304.
———— founded in blood, II. 114.
———— depopulation accounted for, II. 180.
———— state of, under Muley Abdallah, II. 293.
Mosque pulled down because defiled, I. 350.
Mosques, water in all, *Ibid.*
———— Jew or Christian must not enter the, I. 352.
Motard, Captain, bravery of, I. 317.
Mules, the breeding of, encouraged, I. 169.
———— used for travelling, I. 82.
———— trade of the English in, II. 356.
Muley, and Sidi, meaning of, I. 319.
Muley Abdallah, reign of, II. 93.
———————— cruelty of, II. 94.
———————— unsuccessful attack on Mazagan, II. 96.
———————— character of, II. 97.
Muley Abdallah, *vide* Abdallah.
Muley Abdelmeleck, death of, in the moment of victory, II. 99
Muley Achmet, brother of Abdelmeleck, reign of, II. 99.
Muley Achmet, nephew of Ishmael, partisans of, in the city of Morocco, II. 150.
——— ———— defeated by Muley Ishmael, II. 151.
———————— saved by the hospitality of a Shaik, II. 152.
———————— again defeated, II. 157.
———————— recovers the city of Morocco, II. 162.
———————— defeats Gerari, *Ibid.*
———————— treachery of a general of, II. 163.
———————— more beloved than Muley Ishmael, II. 164.
———————— surprized by Muley Ishmael, II. 166.
———————— defeated after victory, II. 167.
———————— besieged in Morocco, II. 168.

Muley

Muley Achmet, danger of, II. 170.
——————— flight of, from Morocco, II. 174.
——————— expedition of, into Sudan, II. 196.
——————— Tagaret, taken by, II. 197.
Muley Achmet, Sharif, reign of, II. 61.
——————— treachery of, II. 68, 71.
——————— taken by his brother, II. 70.
——————— misfortunes of, II. 72. Paffim.
——————— murdered in prifon, II. 93.
Muley Achmet Shaik, reign, character, and death of, II. 106.
Muley Ali, or Muley Sharif, reign of, piety and character, II. 115. Paffim.
Muley Ali, fon of Sidi Mahomet, loyalty of, II. 319.
——————— death and excellent character of, II. 340.
——————— brother of Muley Abdallah, elected emperor by the Negroes, II. 251.
——————— ferocity and avarice of, II. 252.
——————— money promifed to the Negroes by, II. 253.
——————— depofed, II. 254.
Muley Arſhid, rebellion of, II. 120.
——————— ingratitude of, to a faithful flave, II. 121.
——————— ſtratagems and cunning of, II. 121, 123, 124.
——————— abilities and diffimulation of, II. 122.
——————— enterprizes of, II. 123.
——————— acceffion of, II. 126.
——————— cruelty of, II. 121, 123, 124, 126, 129, 130, 133, 139, 142, 146.
——————— conquefts of, II. 122, 124, 126, 128, 129, 136.
——————— repulfed by the king of Sudan, II. 137.
——————— buildings of, II. 141.
——————— death of, II. 145.
Muley Daiby, fize and perſon of, I. 375.
——————— drunkenneſs of, *Ibid.*
——————— and a Jew, anecdote of, I. 376.

Muley,

Muley Daiby, and a monkey, anecdote of, I. 376.
———————— named succeſſor by Muley Iſhmael, II. 225.
———————— acceſſion of, II. 229.
———————— largeſs of, to the Negro troops, II. 230.
———————— ſubdues the inſurgents of Duquella, *Ibid.*
———————— avarice of, II. 231.
———————— drunkenneſs of, II. 233, 236.
———————— cruelty of, II. 233.
———————— teeth drawn by command of, I. 363.
———————— reſtoration of, II. 239.
———————— death of, II. 240.
Muley Dris, *vide* Dris.
Muley Haran, king of Tafilet, II. 149.
———————— reconciles his brother and nephew, II. 173.
———————— dethroned, II. 175.
Muley Iſhmael, *vide* Iſhmael.
Muley Mahomet, ſuperior qualities of, II. 207, 211.
———————— made governor of Suz, II. 209.
———————— rebellion of, II. 210.
———————— takes Morocco, II. 212.
———————— defeated by Muley Zidan, II. 214.
———————— taken priſoner, II. 215.
———————— puniſhment of, II. 216.
Muley Mahomet Ool Del Ariba made Emperor, II. 256.
———————— again proclaimed, II. 262.
———————— ineffectual expedition of, II. 263.
———————— depoſed, II. 264.
———————— amiable character of, *Ibid.*
Muley Meheris, rebellion of, II. 142.
Muley Mohamet, king of Tarudant, II. 63.
———————— defeats the king of Fez, II. 64.
———————— and his brother, enterprizes of, II. 66.
———————— kingdom of Tafilet ſeized by, *Ibid.*
———————— and his brother, quarrel between, II. 67.
———————— murders his nephews, II. 91.
———————— aſſaſſinated by a Turk, II. 93.

Muley Mohamet, the Negro, cruelty of, II. 90.
——————— dethroned, *Ibid.*
Muley Mohamet, son of Muley Sharif, reign of, II. 120.
——————— defeat and death of, II. 125.
Muley Muſtadi, elected by the Negroes, II. 266.
——————— retires to, and trades at Arzilla, II. 267.
——————— takes refuge in Sallee, II. 268.
——————— delivered from impriſonment, II. 269.
——————— again retires to Arzilla, II. 270.
——————— death of, II. 281.
Muley Shaik, firſt of the Merini, II. 51.
Muley Sidan, ſon of the ſecond Muley Achmet, II. 68, 70.
——————— reign of, II. 101.
Muley Yezid, *vide* Yezid.
Mulluvia, river of, I. 5, 17, 86, II. 181.
Muſic, I. 263.
——— Mooriſh, I. 342.
Muſkets, Mooriſh, I. 310.
——— diſcharged in the face of an ambaſſador, I. 342.

N.

Naſſer, Buſhentuf, aſſaſſinated, II. 60.
Negro women paint their cheeks, I. 284.
——— ſoldiers, eſtabliſhment of, I. 297.
——— ——— reduction of, I. 298, 299.
——— ſlave, fidelity and tragical death of, II. 121.
——— troops, how conſecrated, II. 190.
Negroes foreboded ſlavery at the ſight of Europeans, I. 110.
——— ſtate of, among the Moors, I. 279, 280, 282.
——— remarkably chearful and talkative, I. 282.
——— marriages of, *Ibid.*
——— houſehold furniture of, I. 283.
——— effect of the appearance of, on the Arabs, II. 4.
——— brought to Morocco by Muley Arſhid, II. 138.
——— increaſed and ſettled by Muley Iſhmael, II. 188.
——— ſtate of, II. 189.

Negroes

Negroes and Ludaya, the standing army of Morocco, II. 191.
────── effects of the introduction of the, II. 227.
────── power of the, II. 228.
────── oppose Abdelmeleck, II. 235.
────── hated by Muley Abdallah, II. 250.
────── take and plunder Morocco, II. 253.
────── refuse to deliver up their general, II. 256.
────── dissensions among, II. 257.
────── neutrality of, II. 261.
────── covetous avidity of, II. 254, 260, 261, 262, 264.
────── dissatisfied with Muley Abdallah, II. 265.
────── enfeebled by war, II. 270.
────── cut off by Abdallah, II. 271.
────── revolt of, under Sidi Mahomet, II. 318.
────── how disarmed by Sidi Mahomet, II. 323.
────── insolence and power of, I. 359.
Niger and Nile, I. 290.

O.

Oak, forests of, I. 104.
Oatas, Muley, accession of, II. 62.
────────── defeated by the Sharifs, II. 65.
────────── attacked by Muley Mohamet, II. 75.
────────── defeated and taken prisoner, II. 77.
────────── assassinated, II. 83.
Obeidallah, II. 11.
Officers, principal, the domestics of the Emperor, I. 209.
────── of Abdallah dragged at the tails of mules, II. 249.
Olive trees, I. 102.
Olon, M. de Saint, sent ambassador to Mequinez, II. 101.
Oppression, Moorish, I. 343.
Ornaments, marks of slavery, originally, I. 152.
Oxen plentiful, but small, I. 164, 343.

Pain,

P.

Pain, Moors less sensible of, than Europeans, I. 267, 269.
Paint and washes of the Moorish women, I. 127, 129, 153.
Painters sent to Morocco by Philip II.—II. 101.
Palace built by Muley Ishmael, I. 364. II. 178.
Palm tree, I. 104.
Partridges, insipid, I. 170.
Patriotism of a citizen of Rabat, II. 284.
Peas and beans sold by tale during the famine, II. 337.
Persian general, valour of, II. 78.
Physic, state of, I. 232.
Physicians, whom, *Ibid.*
Pigeons, large and excellent, I. 170.
——— stolen, anecdote of, II. 224.
Pilgrimage, veneration for those who have made a, I. 191, 193.
——— renders the beast of burthen holy, I. 192.
——— time of making, I. 193.
——— route of the caravan of, I. 194.
Pirates of Barbary, II. 351.
Plague in Morocco, dreadful, II. 180.
——— in 1752, II. 275.
——— foretold in Turkey, *Ibid.*
Population of Morocco, I. 303.
Portugal and Morocco, treaty between, II. 368.
Portuguese in Morocco, II. 53, 57, 67.
Poultry abundant, not good, I. 170.
Power, maritime, of Morocco, I. 312, 316, 319.
——— military, of Morocco, I. 295, 303, 306.
——— ——— ——— how established, I. 296.
Prayer, opinion of the Moors concerning, I. 345.
Prayers, Moorish, I. 350.
——— the Moors, how called to, *Ibid.*
Preachers put to death, II. 16.

Predestination, I. 200, 366. II. 114, 338.
Presents, or bribery, at court, I. 212.
Prickly pear, I. 161.
Progress, slow, of the Moors towards refinement, I. 366.
Prophecy, Moorish, I. 351.
Proverb, Moorish, I. 272, 278.
Provinces of Morocco, I. 1, 2.
Pudding, anecdote of, I. 347.
Punishments, chiefly pecuniary, I. 218.
Purchasing of men, barbarous custom of, I. 358.
Purse, story of a, I. 357.

Q.

Quintal of silver, what, II. 159.

R.

Rabat, town of, I. 28.
——— batteries of, rebuilt by an English renegado, I. 29.
——— walls of, and delightful gardens, I. 30.
——— built by Almonsor, II. 29.
Rabat and Sallee besieged by Sidi Mahomet, II. 281.
——— severe treatment of, II. 327.
——— how preserved from locusts, II. 334.
Rabits found only in the north of the empire, I. 170.
Ragusa, ship of, condemned, II. 371.
Rain, Moors sit naked in, I. 346.
——— how prayed for, I. 345.
Rains, regular and abundant, I. 94.
——— heavy, I. 344.
Rank, little distinction of, I. 260, 262.
——— instability of, *Ibid.*
Raquette, I. 101.
Rasalema, remarkable river of, I. 80.

Raw hides, plentiful, I. 164.
Religion of the Moors, I. 177.
——————————— which way, different in practice from that of the Turks, I. 178.
Ramna, province of, I. 12.
Renegado, anecdote of a, II. 142.
Renegadoes defpifed, I. 155.
——————— intermarry only with each other, *Ibid.*
——————— repent, and wifh to efcape, I. 156.
Reply of Muley Oatas to Muley Mohamet, II. 78.
Revenues of Morocco, I. 322.
Revolt of Muley Meffaoot, II. 64.
Rhyming not uncommon among the Moors, I. 229.
Rif, province of, I. 6.
Riperda, the Duke de, anecdotes of, II. 276.
Rio Salado, battle of, II. 44.
River of Negroes, battle of the, II. 65.
Roebuck, I. 170.
Rofaries played with like fans, I. 146.

S.

Sabbath, Moorifh, I. 273, 351.
——— derivation of, I. 273.
Sabo, what, I. 209.
Sabres, manufactur.d, I. 310.
Sacrifices, remark concerning, II. 183.
Saddles, form of, I. 337.
Saffi, town of, I. 41.
——— tombs and fanctuaries of, I. 42.
Said, Barrax, fhort reign and death of, II. 35.
Said, II. 41.
Said, brother of Abu-Said, valour of, II. 48.
Sailors, Moorifh, I. 320.
Saint, criminal, and emperor, ftory of, I. 181.
——— character and cunning of one, I. 186.

Saint,

Saint, carnal knowledge of one, with a woman, in the open street, I. 187, 356.

—— female, prostituted herself for the service of passengers, I. 188.

—— made humane by a bribe, I. 190.

—— a man made a, for being a rascal, I. 356.

Saints, or Santons, by trade, I. 180.

—— fools, madmen, and ideots, acknowledged to be, *Ibid*, *vide* Horses.

—— invoked by the women to make them fertile, I. 182.

—— eat scorpions, *Ibid*.

—— how venerated, I. 180, 183.

—— numerous, I. 184.

—— put to death by Muley Abdallah, II. 288.

Salah Reis, in league with Muley Buhafon, II. 85.

———— defeats Muley Abdallah, II. 86.

———— victory of, at the passage of the Seboo, II. 87.

———— discontented with Buhafon, II. 89.

Sallee, town of, I. 27.

—— river of, *Ibid*.

—— rovers, I. 313.

———— stones, their chief ammunition, I. 314.

Sallee and Rabat, government of, I. 315.

———— civil war between, II. 269.

———— municipal government of, II. 269, 281.

Salt pits, I. 104.

Salutation, manner of, I. 343.

Sanctaren, battle of, II. 27.

Sanctuaries, or hospitiums, where criminals are protected, I. 180, 188.

———— violated by Muley Abdallah, II. 259.

Sands of the desert, moving, I. 194. II. 197.

Santa Cruz, town of, I. 46.

———— by whom built, I. 47.

———— ruined by Sidi Mahomet, I. 11, 47.

———— taken by Muley Mohamet, II. 66.

Santa Cruz, deserted in terror, II. 219.
Scarifications, mode of making, I. 135.
Scavenger and murdered woman, I. 223.
Sebastian, king of Portugal, defeat of, II. 99.
Seboo, river of, I. 26.
—— passage of, disputed, II. 87.
Selim, Duquelli, hatred of Abdallah to, II. 255.
——————— killed by Abdallah, II. 258.
Seraglios of the Emperor and Grand Signior compared, II. 312.
Servility, Moorish, I. 348.
Setier of Paris, what, I. 328.
Shabanets, whom, II. 131
———— subjected by Muley Arshid, II. 135.
———— tortured by Muley Ishmael, II. 158.
Shad fishery, I. 27.
Shaik, generosity of a, II. 152.
——— treacherously murdered by Muley Ishmael, II. 172.
——— put to death by the forgery of Lela Zidana, II. 209.
Sharifs of the Mereni, II. 53.
———— massacred by Crom El Hadgy, II. 106.
Shaus, or Chaus, province of, I. 13, 86.
Shavoya, or Chavoya, province of, I. 13.
———— mountaineers of, massacred by Muley Ishmael, II. 158.
Sheep, hairy, and men woolly, I. 112.
——— and wool of Morocco, I. 163.
——— few black, I. 164.
Shella, a holy town, I. 34.
Shellu, less ferocious than the Brebes, I. 120.
Sherlof, general, brave conduct of, II. 329.
Sherma, or Cherma, province of, I. 12.
Shewmen and dancers, I. 264.
Ships of enemies allowed to trade with Morocco, II. 295, 383.
Shirts worn over the dress, I. 145.

Sidi

Sidi Mahomet, agitation of, at putting a governor to death, I. 211.
————— artillery of, I. 309.
————— knowledge of, how acquired, II. 279.
————— power of, while prince, II. 280, 286.
————— severity of, to Sallee and Rabat, II. 282, 283, 284, 326.
————— guilty of one act of cruelty, II. 285.
————— views of, on his succession, II. 293. Passim 303.
————— buildings of, II. 295, 296, 327.
————— a merchant, II. 298.
————— character and manners of, II. 307, 343.
————— domestics of, new clothed annually, II. 310.
————— prudence of the first wife of, II. 313.
————— children of, how provided for, *Ibid.*
————— ill education of the sons of, *Ibid.*
————— strange equivocation of, II. 329.
————— failure of, the attempt of, on Melilla, II. 330.
————— artifice of, to appease his subjects, II. 331.
————— declares war against Holland, II. 322.
————— great expences, and little wealth of, II. 345.
————— public declaration of peace by, II. 370.
Silver paid by weight, II. 159.
Slave trade, I. 111, 113, 281.
Slinging, ancient and modern practice of, I. 314.
Small-pox little mischievous, I. 233.
Snipes numerous, I. 170.
Soc, *vide* markets.
Soil of Morocco, I. 96.
————— light is ploughed with wooden plough-shares, I. 97.
Sorcerers, I. 288.
Southern Moors, bigotry and thievery of, I. 50.
————— make their ablutions with sand, I. 51.

Spain

Spain offended by Sidi Mahomet, II. 329, 332.
——— armament of, againſt Algiers, II. 331.
Spaniard and Engliſhman, I. 376.
Spaniard and Muley Iſhmael, I. 367.
Spaniſh convent at Mequinez for the relief of captives, I. 70.
——— fathers of, manners of phyſicking the Moors, *Ibid.*
Spaniſh Moors, family names of, preſerved in Morocco, I. 141.
Speech of Muley Mohamet to his brother, II. 74.
——————————— to his ſoldiers and chiefs, II. 69, 76.
Stone, diſeaſe of the, cut for by the Moors, I. 236.
Storks, ſinful to kill, I. 289.
——— emigration and food of, I. 290.
——— Arabs metamorphoſed into, I. 339.
Stratagem of Muley Mohamet, II. 77, 91.
Streets, dirtyneſs of, I. 364.
Succeſſion of Morocco precarious, II. 278, 348.
Sudan, generoſity of the king of, II. 138.
——— invaded by Muley Achmet, II. 196.
Suera, town of, I. 43.
Sugulmeſſa, city of, I. 15, 92.
——————— derivation of, I. 92.
Sun adored by the Negroes, II. 189.
Surgery, ſtate of, I. 135, 236, 269.
Sus, or Suz, province of, decayed by the deſtruction of Santa Cruz, I. 11.
Sweden, preſents ſent by, to Morocco, II. 362.
Swine held unclean, I. 350.

T.

Tafilet, or Sugulmeſſa, kingdom of, I. 15, 99.
——— dates of *Ibid.*
——— taken by ſtratagem, II. 91.
——— revolt of, II. 182.

Tafilet punished by Sidi Mahomet, II. 339.
Tagaret, capital of Sudan, taken, II. 197.
Tailors, *vide* Jews.
Talbes, what, I. 215, 227, 246, 289.
Tangiers, town of, I. 20.
——————— ceded to England in 1662, *Ibid.*
——————— bay of, favourable to piracy, I. 21.
——————— the English attacked in, II. 180.
——————— besieged by Muley Ishmael, II. 192.
——————— abandoned by the English, II. 202.
——————— taken by Muley Abdallah, II. 268.
——————— indulgence granted the Spaniards at, II. 366.
Tangiers and Tetuan, favourable situation of, I. 320.
Tanfif, river of, I. 9, 42, 63.
Tarudant, where, I. 48.
——————— city of, I. 54.
Taxation, state of, I. 330.
——————— of the Jews, I. 327, 331.
——————— excessive, I. 334.
——————— impolicy of, II. 297, 301.
Taxes allowed by the Koran, I. 322.
——— casual, what, I. 332.
Tea drank by the Moors, I. 271.
Tedla, province of, I. 13.
Teeth drawn as a punishment, I. 363.
Temperance of the Moors, I. 270, 347. II. 309.
Temsena, province of, I. 8.
——————— fertility and salubrity of, *Ibid.*
Tents of the Moors, I. 122.
Terraces on the tops of all houses, I. 143.
Tefa, castle and town of, I. 86.
Tetuan, city and port of, I. 18.
——— revolt of, under Muley Daiby, II. 233.
Theft, manner of preventing, I. 133.
Thieves, I. 254.
——————— anecdotes of, I. 254, 256, 258.

Thieves,

Thieves, how punished, I. 258, 268.
Tigers common, I. 170.
——— royal, unknown in Morocco, I. 171.
——— hunted by the Moors, *Ibid.*
——— tamed, I. 175.
Timoor, I. 119.
Tiles, coloured, I. 58, 69.
Titus, ruins of, I. 37.
Tombs, Moorish, not pompous, I. 291.
Toornadis, what, I. 156.
Torture of the iron ring, I. 362.
Tossing, punishing of, I. 362.
Towns of Morocco ill fortified, I. 17.
Trade, increase of, in Morocco, II. 297.
——— how injured by Sidi Mahomet, II. 298.
——— of the English to Morocco, II. 355.
——— between Holland and Morocco, II. 358.
——— between Spain and Morocco, casual, II. 366.
——— balance of, in favour of Morocco, II. 367.
——— of France, progress of, II. 373.
——— between France and Morocco, II. 378. Passim.
——— free, of Morocco, remarks on, II. 383.
Trades, no dishonour to Grandees, I. 262.
Tradesmen of Fez massacred by Muley Arshid, II. 133.
——— obliged to work gratis, II. 310.
Tradition, Mahometan, II. 11.
Travellers supposed safe, if a Saint be in company, I. 189.
Travelling, expeditious, between Fez and Mequinez, I. 82.
Treaties between Europe and Barbary, motives for the, II. 352.
——— of England and Morocco, II. 354.
——— between Denmark and Morocco, II. 360.
——— between Sweden and Morocco, II. 362.
——— between Venice and Morocco, II. 363.
——— between Spain and Morocco, II. 364, 365.
——— between Portugal and Morocco, II. 368.

Treaties

Treaties between Tuscany, Vienna, and Morocco, II. 369.
——— between the United States and Morocco, II. 372.
——— between France and Morocco, II. 377.
Treasury, impoverished state of, I. 335.
Tremecen taken by the sons of Muley Mohamet, II. 84.
——— recovered by the Algerines, II 85.
——— people of, demand assistance against the Algerines, II. 194.
Tythes in kind, I. 323, 330.
——— paid by tradesmen, II. 310.

U.

Umbrella, the distinctive mark of royalty, I. 210. II. 307.
United States of America, treaty of, with Sidi Mahomet, II. 372.

V.

Valedia, town of, I. 39.
Veles de Pegnon, or Gomera, fortress of, I. 18.
Venice and Morocco, peace between, II. 363.
——— tribute paid by, Ibid.
Virginity, proofs of, I. 277, 278.
Visits, manner of performing, I. 153.
Vizier, a, sewed up in an ox hide, II. 186.
——— remark concerning the title of, II. 187.
Vled, d'Elgerid, I. 15.
Vled, de Nun, I. 11.
——————— province of, I. 48.
——————— barbarous inhabitants of, I. 49.
Voltaire, error of, I. 141.
——— wrongly asserts the Turks inoculate, I. 235.
Vow of Abdulmomen, II. 23.

VOL. II. F f

W.

Wages not paid by the Emperor, II. 310.
Walking, anecdote concerning, I. 350.
Wall white wafhed, anecdote of, I. 144.
Walnuts, anecdote of, II. 146.
Wants of the Moors, few, I. 328.
Wars, civil, probable in Morocco hereafter, II. 347.
Watch dogs of the Douhars, I. 121.
Water melons, common, I. 100.
———— drank out of the ftomachs of dead camels, I. 195.
Wax candles, I. 272.
Wealth, ancient of Morocco, I. 324, 325.
———— left by Muley Ifhmael, II. 231.
Weaving, manner of, I. 125.
Weights of Morocco, II. 387.
Wild boar, common in Morocco, I. 175.
———————— how caught by the Lion, *Ibid.*
———————— fometimes conquers the Lion, *Ibid.*
Windus, Mr. the pocket of, picked, I. 348.
Wives and concubines of the Moors, I. 122, 128, 143, 274, 279.
———— of Muley Daiby, the revolt of, II. 237.
Woman murdered, ftory of, I. 221.
Women, ornaments of the, I. 126.
———————— mode of painting themfelves, I. 127, 129.
———————— treated as flaves by the country Moors, and yoked to the plough with mules, &c. I. 128.
———————— of the cities always veiled, I. 147.
———————— fhew their faces to foreigners, *Ibid.*
———————— foon old, I. 148.
———————— licentious, *Ibid.*
———————— of the fouth, handfomeft, I. 149.
———————— prefented for the ufe of travellers as an act of hofpitality, *Ibid.*

[427]

Women of the cities more addicted to dress than those of the country, I. 149.
────── dress of the, I. 150.
────── fattened like fowls, I. 151.
────── ornaments of, *Ibid.*
────── obliged to eat their own breasts, II. 224.
────── treatment of, by Sidi Mahomet, II. 311.
Woodcocks scarce, I. 170.
Wrestling, *vide* Spaniard and Englishman.

Y.

Yezid, revolt of, II. 3.
Yezid, Muley, revolt of, II. 319.
─────────── timidity of, II. 320.
─────────── sent on pilgrimage, II. 322.

Z.

Zaaron, a holy mountain, I. 83.
Zeneters massacred, II. 16.
────── rebellion of, II. 27.
Zidan, Muley, sent against Muley Mahomet, II. 215.
─────────── barbarous character of, II. 218.
─────────── suspected by his father, II. 219.
─────────── murdered by his wives, II. 222.
Zin, Muley, elected Emperor, II. 264.

ERRATUM.

Vol. I. page 269, line 5, for *tar*, read *pitch*.

www.ingramcontent.com/pod-product-compliance
Lightning Source LLC
Chambersburg PA
CBHW051739300426
44115CB00007B/623